100

ESSENTIAL
BOOKS FOR
JEWISH
READERS

100
ESSENTIAL
BOOKS FOR
JEWISH
READERS

RABBI DANIEL B. SYME
AND
CINDY FRENKEL KANTER

A Citadel Press Book
Published by Carol Publishing Group

A Citadel Press Book
Published by Carol Publishing Group
Citadel Press is a registered trademark of Carol Communications, Inc.

Editorial, sales and distribution, rights and permissions inquiries should be addressed
to Carol Publishing Group, 120 Enterprise Avenue, Secaucus, N.J. 07094.

In Canada: Canadian Manda Group, One Atlantic Avenue, Suite 105, Toronto, Ontario
M6K 3E7

Carol Publishing Group books may be purchased in bulk at special discounts for sales
promotion, fund-raising, or educational purposes. Special editions can be created to
specifications. For details, contact Special Sales Department, Carol Publishing Group,
120 Enterprise Avenue, Secaucus, N.J. 07094.

Manufactured in the United States of America

10 9 8 7 6 5 4 3 2 1

Library of Congress Cataloging-in-Publication Data

Syme, Daniel B.
    100 essential books for Jewish readers / Daniel B. Syme and Cindy
Frenkel Kanter.
        p. cm.
    "A Citadel Press Book."
    ISBN 0–8065–1906–1 (hc)
    1. Judaism—Abstracts. 2. Jews—History—Abstracts. 3. Jews—
Abstracts. 4. Best books. I. Kanter, Cindy Frenkel. II. Title.
BM40.S96 1997
016.296—dc21   97–34613
                                                                     CIP
                                                                     r97

To our parents,
Barbara and Marvin Frenkel
Sonia and Rabbi M. Robert Syme

Contents

PART III   Jewish Philosophy and Theology

PART IV   Jewish History and Anti-Semitism

PART V   Israel and the Holocaust

PART VI   Fiction and General Works on Jewish Themes

Preface

How do you pick *the* one hundred books that every Jew should read? You don't! It is an impossible task, since there are literally tens, if not hundreds, of thousands of books, plays, poems, and essays on Jewish themes or by Jewish authors. We have therefore selected one hundred books that we personally feel are valuable for an introduction to Jewish literature, values, customs, and accomplishments.

Each entry reviews the book's basic plot or contents, and is supplemented with information about the author, where appropriate. In certain instances, we also show the reader why the book had the impact it did at a particular time in history.

Please know in advance that some books which you believe should have been included will almost certainly be absent. We will leave those works for a second volume. If you are an author of one of those missing books, we extend our heartfelt apologies.

This volume could not have been completed without the help of many friends and family members. We express our profound gratitude to those talented individuals who contributed their time and writing skills to this undertaking. Rabbi Solomon Freehof, of blessed memory, who bequeathed a host of insights and written materials dedicated to this effort; Rabbi M. Robert Syme; Rabbi David Castiglione; Joyce Seglin; Harold Binder; Alan May; Jason Canvasser; Michael Simon; Nelson Lande; Ed Koral; Alice Phillips; and Ricki and Aaron Zitner. This book would not have been possible without the wonderful help of Daniel Kanter, who gave constant support and excellent suggestions, and Hannah Kanter, who patiently played alone so her mom could work.

We thank the staff of Temple Beth El in Bloomfield Hills,

Michigan, who typed and prepared the book for publication: Dawn Murrey, Jackie Haines, Patricia Ruda, and Betty Schare.

Finally, we thank David Hendin, who first suggested that we undertake this project, and our superb editor, Hillel Black, who took us the last mile.

D.B.S. and C.F.K.

PART I

Jewish Texts of Belief and Thought and Their Interpretation

1 The Hebrew Bible

The one book that must be read by every Jew—and any person seeking to understand Judaism—is the Hebrew Bible, referred to by Christians as the Old Testament. In the revolutionary 1965 document, *Nostra Aetate,* the Catholic Church made clear that one cannot be a good Christian without both knowing and respecting the teachings of the Hebrew Bible.

The thirty-nine books of the Hebrew Bible are grouped into three major sections: Torah, Prophets, and Writings. They are known collectively by the Hebrew acronym *tanach.* The Torah, or Five Books of Moses, is presumed by many to be the word of God, given directly to Moses at Mount Sinai and thereafter conveyed to the six hundred thousand Israelites who—according to the book of Exodus—witnessed the event.

Over the centuries, a school of biblical study emerged whose premise was that many human beings wrote the Five Books of Moses over the course of centuries and that it was ultimately edited into a single volume. To invest its laws and commandments with divine authority, its source was attributed to God.

The Torah has influenced human behavior, ethics, and values for over two millennia. The stories of the world's creation, of Adam and Eve in the Garden of Eden, of Cain and Abel, are taught in religious schools of virtually every faith, as a means of introducing young children to God, ethics, and values.

In Genesis we learn of Noah, Abraham and Sarah, Isaac and Rebecca, Jacob and Rachel and Leah. Joseph and his brothers become the twelve tribes of Israel, who are then enslaved by the Egyptians for over four hundred years. The book of Exodus has become a paradigm of deliverance from slavery, for Jews, African Americans, migrant farmworkers and the oppressed of all lands. Leviticus and Deuteronomy contain extensive legal material, while Numbers records the Israelites' wanderings through the

3

desert. No wonder, then, that the Five Books of Moses endure as one of Judaism's greatest gifts to humanity.

The second major section of the Hebrew Bible, Prophets, evokes the importance of social justice. The prophets were great religious activists, calling the most powerful rulers to account for inhumane and cruel acts and urging the people to be caring and kind. Jeremiah, Isaiah, Amos, and Micah are just a few of the prophets whose words have become part of the vocabulary of every nation that values justice and decency.

While the prophets were often ineffective in predicting events, they possessed a profound understanding of a natural law in which evil would be punished. Christians, in particular, place great credence in prophetic teachings, which they believe foreshadow the life of Jesus.

The third section of the Hebrew Bible claims no divine origin. This portion is comprised of inspiring, moving stories and poetry, such as the Song of Songs, possibly one of the greatest examples of erotic love poetry ever written. The Psalms promise comfort, peace, and hope. The book of Esther, in which the name of God is never mentioned, instructs Jews, and even non-Jews, to take responsibility for righting wrongs and combating evil. The book of Jonah demonstrates that one cannot escape a religious responsibility for speaking up against injustice and seeking and accepting genuine repentance.

By far the most widely studied book in the Writings is the book of Job. This story teaches that a divine plan exists but that we humans cannot know or understand God's purpose. Until the Holocaust, this position was oft quoted and generally accepted as a tenet of human existence.

The Hebrew Bible, then, is an indispensable volume for any Jewish library. It contains virtually every human situation encountered by modern men and women, along with lessons as timely today as they were thousands of years ago. A Hebrew Bible with a commentary is invaluable for Jews, Moslems, and Christians, who wish to know themselves and their origins.

2 The Book of Legends

Translated by William G. Braude

The Hebrew word *midrash* derives from a root meaning "to investigate." For the rabbis, that midrashic process involved taking a basic text, ritual, or natural phenomenon and asking, "Why is this so?" Out of this questioning often emerged a legend, a fanciful, but values-based, explanation. In retelling and remembering the legend, the value was also preserved. And thus emerged a body of literature called the midrash—thousands upon thousands of volumes and individual insights, which today often punctuate sermons and educational lesson plans.

Many of these midrashim are known and beloved by the average Jew. Until recently, however, the vast majority were inaccessible to Jews without significant Hebrew reading and comprehension skills.

The single most noted and quoted anthology of midrashim, entitled *Sefer Ha-Aggadah,* was initially published about 1910, arranged by the great Hebrew poet Hayim Nachman Bialik and the master editor Yehoshua Ravnitzky. These two brilliant writers selected hundreds of texts from the many thousands available to them and arranged by subject those texts deemed of greatest interest to their intended readership.

The resulting collection has provided generations of rabbis and scholars a virtual treasure trove of material for sermons, classroom instruction, and personal edification, dealing with biblical characters, Talmudic sages, parables, proverbs, and folklore.

Rabbi William Braude, a Reform rabbi from Providence, Rhode Island, opened *Sefer Ha-Aggadah* to the English-speaking public for the first time. In what was clearly his magnum opus, Braude completed this annotated translation just prior to his death in 1988. Sadly, he did not live to see the book's publication in 1992.

One set of midrashim relates that the sun and the moon were initially the same size. The moon, however, asked to be larger, whereupon God reduced it in magnitude to punish it for its arrogance. When the moon expressed its bitterness and disappointment, God gave it the stars to join it in the firmament. Thus did the Rabbis teach both the lessons of humility and the compassion of God.

In another midrash, the Rabbis explain that the first man was created singly to illustrate the value of each individual. Furthermore, they declare that if one saves a single life, that person is considered as having saved the entire world. By extension, no person is to say "my father was greater than your father," since we all derive from the same human being.

The Rabbis teach us how to effect reconciliation in a family by citing a verse in Gen. 32.4: "And Jacob sent emissaries ahead to Esau his brother." After having stolen Esau's birthright years before, and now finding Esau close at hand and ready to strike back, Jacob takes the first step in healing the relationship. Say the Rabbis, "When anyone seeks to conciliate...let him set before him this portion of Scripture, and he will learn from it the proper procedure in attempting reconciliation....

The Ten Plagues receive a great deal of attention, including the oddity that the Torah uses the singular form of the word *frog* for the second plague. This is no error, say the Rabbis. At first there was only one frog, but when he saw that the way was clear, he called for the others to come. We thus learn that evil unresisted inevitably multiplies in strength, hence our responsibility to stand up to hatred, bigotry, and oppression at the very first sign of its impending advance.

We derive from the story of the parting of the Red Sea a great moral regarding the power of faith. The legend holds that when the Israelites reached the Red Sea, they refused to follow the urgings of Moses to begin to cross. So great was their fear of drowning that they became immobilized—this in spite of the fact that the Egyptian chariots were in hot pursuit. Only after a single Jew, Nahson, the son of Amminadab, waded into the sea, performing an act infused with faith, did the waters divide to enable the Israelites to cross safely.

Jews are often referred to as "the Chosen People," specially selected by God to receive the Ten Commandments and the Torah. This designation has often been used by anti-Semites to denigrate Judaism as arrogant. Perhaps to counter bigotry, the rabbis affirm in one legend that the Israelites were coerced into accepting the Torah, that God lifted up Mount Sinai, held it above their heads, and declared: "If you accept the Torah, it is well; if not, your grave will be right here."

In close to nine hundred pages, Rabbi Braude opens the eyes of a modern generation of Jews to teachings derived from centuries of study and reflection. The insights to be gained, the wisdom to be wrested from seemingly obvious texts, spill forth in a fountain of scholarship. While the midrashic process continues unabated even in modern times, *The Book of Legends* remains a classic to be read and reread by all those seeking to enter the rabbinic mind.

3 New Reform Responsa

Solomon B. Freehof

4 Contemporary American Reform Responsa

Walter Jacob

Within Orthodox Judaism, Jewish law determines the guidelines for daily life. The Torah, Mishnah, Talmud, Shulchan Aruch, and other codified collections of legal rulings promulgated by authoritative Jewish scholars specify the correct means of observing laws relating to diet, marriage, divorce, real estate, business, and a host of other subjects.

No body of law, however, can anticipate every modern development, technological advance, or ethical dilemma. Hence, as American constitutional law permits interpretation based on existing precedents, so has Jewish jurisprudence grown and expanded by means of a sophisticated process known as the responsa literature.

For example, Orthodox Jews require that all males wear a *kipah* (skullcap), or other head covering at all times—or at least while at prayer in the synagogue. A man, rapidly balding, purchases a toupee which covers his head. He wonders whether, since his head is now covered, he is still required to wear a kipah in the synagogue. Unsure of the correct answer, he poses the question (*she-ay-la*) to a recognized Jewish scholar. The scholar reviews all the precedents and values that come to mind, then issues a written answer (*teshuva*) justified by those precedents. The question and answer taken together is called a responsum, and the larger corpus of such questions and answers becomes part of what is called the responsa literature.

The man is told that he must wear a head covering in spite of his toupee because of the Jewish value of *maarit ayin* (how it appears to others). The scholar rules that if the toupee is a very good one, no one will know that it is artificial, and the man will seem to be disrespectful of tradition.

Especially in recent years, modern liberal Jews have begun to study the responsa literature, not for legal guidance, but as a fascinating literature based on legal precedents, some drawn from thousands of years ago. Within Reform Judaism, the late Rabbi Solomon Freehof was considered the single greatest legal authority, and was respected by scholars of all denominations. Published in 1980, the *New Reform Responsa* is just one of the many collections he authored over the course of his lifetime.

New Reform Responsa, issued when Rabbi Freehof was well into his nineties, illustrates his brilliant legal mind and incisive thought processes, even as it demonstrates his capacity to apply Jewish law to situations characteristic of a rapidly changing world.

In one responsum, Rabbi Freehof responds to the question of a man requesting that his body be frozen after his death so that he and his wife might one day be buried at the same time. Rabbi Freehof finds justification in Jewish law for the practice of cryogenics but rules against the specific request based upon Jewish mourning practices, which specify that mourning cannot begin until the body is actually buried. He advises that if the man predeceases his wife, he be buried, then later exhumed and reburied in the family plot, a procedure in accordance with Jewish law.

Other questions posed and answered in this fascinating volume include the permissibility of artificial insemination and the permissibility of space travel by a Jewish astronaut on the Sabbath.

Rabbi Walter Jacob served as Rabbi Freehof's rabbinic associate for many years, then succeeded him in the pulpit and as a recognized authority on Jewish law. In *Contemporary American Reform Responsa,* Rabbi Jacob carries on the Freehof legacy in establishing the relevance of Jewish teaching to unique situations in American life.

Published in 1987, the book anticipated the cloning breakthrough of 1997. Jacob responds to the question of whether a person produced through genetic engineering rather than natural reproduction would have a soul. He begins by stating the mainstream Jewish legal position that ensoulment takes place at birth. He then follows with an explanation of the position of those rabbis who espoused the Neoplatonic, threefold division of ensoulment: one part at conception, a second at the point of embryonic development, and the third at birth. The great philosopher Maimonides believed that lower life forms had souls and divided their categories into animal, vegetative, and human, while Jewish mystical literature held that the soul had rational, moral, and vital elements.

Inasmuch as a clone might possibly begin as a fertilized ovum or genetic material, and since the resulting entity could possibly reproduce, Jacob concludes that so long as these factors hold constant, and that the potential for intellectual and moral development is maintained, a clone could be considered to have a soul.

In another responsum of importance to animal lovers, the question is raised as to whether or not one may say Kaddish, the prayer honoring the dead, in memory of a beloved pet. Jacob notes that pets were extremely rare in antiquity. Dogs were viewed as unclean scavengers, a perception that existed in some measure through Talmudic times. One Talmudic ruling states that if a woman spends her time primarily with lapdogs, her husband has grounds for divorce!

Domesticated cats are not even mentioned in the Bible, even though they were considered sacred animals in Egypt. By Talmudic times, their value for ridding homes of mice had been recognized. Nothing in Jewish law, however, addresses the profound affection felt for animals today. Rabbi Jacob, therefore, bases his decision primarily on the value of the dignity of those human beings who have lost parents or other loved ones.

"It would be absolutely wrong, and a mockery, to include the name of a pet in the weekly Kaddish list. Mourners would be shocked and angered to see their father and mother listed alongside a dog or cat. Whatever mourning for a pet which may occur should be conducted privately and outside of the purview of Judaism."

The responsa literature has something significant to say about virtually every situation in today's world. Whether one studies it for its authority or its values, responsa are a realm of inquiry worthy of serious attention.

5   Does God Have a Big Toe?
Stories About Stories
in the Bible

Marc Gellman

Marc Gellman, rabbi of Temple Beth Torah in Melville, New York, is a member of the faculty of the Hebrew Union College–Jewish Institute of Religion in New York. He holds a Ph.D. in philosophy from Northwestern University in Evanston, Illinois, and cohosts a weekly national cable television religious program with Msgr. Thomas Hartman called *The God Squad*. Gellman possesses a gift for storytelling, and the stories in this book reflect his love of people and his understanding of the child in all of us.

Does God Have a Big Toe? is a collection of twenty stories about events in the Bible. Rabbi Gellman's delightful sense of humor is reflected in all of the stories he has created. In just a few pages, each story teaches a lesson from the Bible. They are written in a style that everyone can enjoy and understand.

Rabbi Gellman has divided the book into two sections. The first section is composed primarily of stories derived from the biblical story of creation. Beginning with the creation of humans and their relationship to God, Gellman continues with the creation of animals and man's respect for each species of animal. In two to three pages, Rabbi Gellman teaches an ethical lesson and develops the concept of humans in relation to God's other creations. A third story is about time. The creation of a day was marked by the rising and setting of the sun, a week by this occurring seven times, and a month by four weeks of risings and settings. But Adam feared that after fifty-two weeks time would come to an end. When the sun rose the following day, Adam understood that God had created more than enough time.

Rabbi Gellman ends the creation section with a beautiful story about a tomato plant growing outside the garden. Its need for tending created the desire for Adam and Eve to leave the Garden of Eden to take care of the plant. Adam and Eve are happier living outside the garden where things need their help. This story accounts for the establishment of our partnership with God in caring for the world. Three stories about Noah and the animals follow, teaching about the flood, the rainbow, and God's need for Noah to be a partner in reminding the world of the way each of us needs to behave.

The second half of the book begins with the story "Does God Have a Big Toe?" from which the book derives its title. The story tells of the building of the Tower of Babel, but with a different slant than the original biblical story. This story begins with a child's question, "Does God have a big toe?"

The answer, according to the story, could only be found by building a tower to heaven in order to closely examine God's foot. God sees the people using all their supplies and time to build a tower and decides to stop this wasteful effort. God creates different languages so that the people cannot communicate. As they are unable to talk to one another, construction of the tower comes to an abrupt halt. The people coalesce into groups that speak the same language, thus creating the different nations of the world.

One parable explains how God chose Abraham to be the founder of a great nation. Another retells how Rebecca was selected to be Isaac's wife. Abraham's servant Eliezer and an angel disguised as a camel travel to look for the right woman for Isaac to marry. Rebecca is very kind and offers them water from her well. Due to her warmth and sensitivity, Eliezer asks her to return home with him to marry Isaac. The simplicity of this lovely story leads to a telling of how Jacob came to love Rachel and have her care deeply for him. In this story, Gellman makes clear that strong men have emotions and that it is permissible to cry.

"The Coat of Many Colors" is a story about the relationship of Joseph and his brothers. It begins with Joseph's dreams and the hatred his brothers feel toward him. It continues with his being sold into slavery, followed by his rise to power in Egypt. It then concludes with their reconciliation in Egypt during the famine.

The story emphasizes the strength of love and our capacity for forgiveness.

There are four stories about Moses. The first, simply called "Moses," shows why God selected Moses to lead the Israelites into freedom. The prerequisite was a Jew who understood freedom. The second story is about patience, the character trait that God felt was most important in selecting a leader. In debating the best way to test patience, the angels suggested several ideas, each of which God rejected in favor of choosing someone who will watch a burning bush. Moses is the only one who passes the test.

The third story is about the crossing of the Red Sea. It portrays the parting of the sea from the fishes' viewpoint and conveys the impact the parting of the waters must have had on the creatures of both land and sea.

A fourth tale illustrates miracles and who should be praised for them. In this story, the people constantly express gratitude to Moses for miracles. No matter what Moses says or does to attribute the miracles to God, the people are convinced that Moses should be thanked. Even the transition of leadership from Moses to Joshua and the occurrence of more wonders cannot convince the people that God was responsible. But finally, "Coming Home" relates how Joshua leads the people into the Promised Land, the Israelites thank God for bringing them home, and they at last realize the power of God.

The book concludes with "The Announcing Tool," a story about the selection of a way to announce the arrival of the New Year. After several methods are explored, a man named Enoch brings God a shofar, a ram's horn, as a possibility. God is pleased because the shofar is natural, loud, and if blown correctly, very beautiful in tone. The story relates the meaning of the New Year to the skill of blowing the shofar. As difficult as it is to play the shofar well, asking for forgiveness is even more difficult. Thus, decides God, the shofar is an ideal way to announce both the arrival and purpose of the New Year.

Stories have a certain power to teach both facts and values. In this volume, Rabbi Gellman masterfully does both.

6 Legends of the Bible

Louis Ginzberg

Legends are common to every culture. Building upon the facts of history, creative writers spun fanciful tales of heroes, heroines and great acts of courage, as well as values, ethics, and morals.

No book has engendered more legends than the Bible. And no single scholar contributed more to the literature of legend than Louis Ginzberg. Ginzberg, born in 1873, was descended from the famous Rabbi Elijah of Vilna. Ginzberg moved from his birthplace at Kovno in Lithuania, studied at the University of Strasbourg, then launched what was to be a lifelong quest to collect and publish the fullest possible corpus of Jewish legendary accounts.

Once Ginzberg entered the world of legend, he decided to reach beyond legends of the Bible alone. Ultimately, his collection outlined almost two thousand years of history. An earlier collection, intended for scholars, was published in seven volumes and in some forty languages. In this one-volume edition, Ginzberg writes for the average reader, culling the most comprehensible legends and presenting them in an easily readable format.

Legends borrow from folktales and folk belief. And gaps in the biblical text allow the questioning reader to provide fanciful answers to textual problems with no factual answers. For example, the Torah teaches that Cain killed his brother Abel. But *how* did he kill him? What was the murder weapon? One legend accepts that it was a stalk, another a hoe or sickle, a third a stone. One legend even suggests that Abel was bitten to death! The book is made up of such legends.

One legend imparted by Ginzberg holds that the world in which we live was not the first world created by God. Several worlds came into being before ours, but God destroyed each of them, unsatisfied with their level of perfection. Only after deciding that mercy and understanding were essential to the world was God able to leave our world intact in spite of all its imperfections.

A beautiful legend holds that when the time came to create the first human being, God gathered up dirt from all four corners of the earth and created Adam. In this manner, God assured that no person could ever claim superiority over another based upon one's place of birth. We all derive from Adam, a man whose essence contained the entire world.

According to legend, God personally officiated at the wedding of Adam and Eve. The angels served as witnesses, then danced and played musical instruments in each of ten bridal chambers which God had prepared for them.

One of the best known of biblical tales is the story of how Esau sold his birthright to Jacob for a bowl of lentils. But why was Jacob cooking lentils? And why was Esau so hungry? A fascinating legend relates that the day of this encounter was also the day on which Abraham died. On that very day, Esau was guilty of five crimes. He raped a betrothed woman, committed murder, doubted the resurrection of the dead, sold his birthright, and denied God. After he murdered a man named Nimrod, Esau raced home in an attempt to elude Nimrod's friends. That is why he was so tired!

Jacob was preparing lentils to serve his father, Isaac, for this was a traditional meal served to those who had lost a loved one, in this case, Abraham. Esau scoffs at this ritual act of kindness, and further shows his disdain for the power of a birthright by exchanging it for some of the lentils. He exults in the thought that he had obtained a sumptuous meal for something ephemeral and worthless. And thus, says the legend, the birthright passed to Jacob.

The biblical story of how Jacob and Esau reconciled is considered a model for the resolution of sibling rivalry. Jacob sends messengers to his brother, showers him with gifts, and asks that they set aside their bitter past. The Torah pictures the two as embracing, resolving their differences, and parting as friends.

But one legend tells the same story in a totally different way. In this version, Esau intended to kill Jacob and approached his camp with four hundred armed men. He rejected Jacob's gifts and pleas for reconciliation altogether. When Jacob approached, Esau was filled with fury, and decided that he would bite Jacob on the neck and suck his blood until he was dead. Jacob's neck turned as hard as ivory, and all Esau could do was gnash his teeth. Only then did Esau agree to accept Jacob's bribe, and received tribute for an entire year in return for sparing his brother's life.

How did Moses get his name? After all, it was a name of Egyptian origin, not known among the Israelites. According to legend, Moses actually had ten names but became known by his heathen name because it was given to him by Pharaoh's daughter, the woman who saved his life when he was an infant. This act of kindness by a non-Jewish woman resulted in Judaism's greatest hero receiving an Egyptian name, Moses, which means "drawn out of the water."

Another legend explains why the Torah was given on Mount Sinai. According to the tale, the mountains fought amongst themselves for this great honor. Mount Tabor claimed the right to the revelation on the grounds that it was the only mountain not covered with water during the great flood of Noah's time. Mount Hermon made its case on the basis of its central position during the crossing of the Red Sea. Mount Carmel, situated on the shore of the sea, remained silent, smug in its assumption that its geographic location made it a natural. But finally God chose Mount Sinai, owing to its humility and to the fact that no one had ever worshiped idols on its peak.

There is a magnificent legend regarding the death of Moses. On his last day on earth, he wrote thirteen Torah scrolls, one for each of the twelve tribes, and the last for the Holy Ark, never to be touched. He then asked the people to follow Joshua, whereupon God lifted Moses high enough to see the entire land of Israel. In addition, God revealed the future of Israel to Moses in great detail. Moses then climbed to the top of Mount Nebo to a secret place and died with no pain, after having ascended to heaven to speak with the Messiah. He died surrounded by angels, as God took his soul with a gentle kiss.

Ginzberg's *Legends of the Bible* is a poetic attempt by men of great insight to explain their world and the lives of their biblical ancestors.

7 Voices of Wisdom

Francine Klagsbrun

Countless collections of sayings, stories, and quotations fill Jewish bookstores and libraries. Rarely, however, does one find such a collection arranged by Jewish values, morals, and ethics. Francine Klagsbrun's *Voices of Wisdom* is just such a volume, and one of the first collections like it prepared by a female scholar.

The author has written or edited some twenty books for both adults and young readers, and has also contributed to national magazines such as *Family Circle, Ms.,* and *Seventeen.* Klagsbrun combines a journalist's skill and instincts with a rich Jewish background. She attended a Hebrew day school and eventually earned a bachelor of Hebrew letters degree from New York's Jewish Theological Seminary.

Oriented toward contemporary issues, Klagsbrun structures each section of the book so as to engage a modern issue from a Jewish perspective. She draws her teachings from a rich variety of sources: the Bible, midrash, Mishnah, Talmud, fables, folktales, mysticism, as well as the writings of contemporary Jewish thinkers.

The first major division of the book is entitled "You and Yourself," a natural chapter given the current preoccupation with self-help and self-realization. Klagsbrun wants the reader to understand that this tendency of self-involvement is not new in Judaism. Long before Leo Buscaglia, ancient Jewish teachers were addressing the same concerns. For example, Ben Sira teaches: "Trust your own judgment. A man's mind sometimes has a way of telling him more than seven watchmen posted high on a tower."

On being yourself we see the legendary Zusya: "In the world to come they will not ask me 'Why were you not Moses?' They will ask me, 'Why were you not Zusya?'"

17

Gossip and slander are certainly of concern to the general populace. Unfounded accusations about public figures—or ugly rumors about friends or ourselves—can destroy reputations in a moment. The Rabbis emphasized the danger of this ill-advised human characteristic:

"Rabbi Simeon ben Gamliel said to his servant Tabbai, 'Go to the market and buy me some good food.' The servant went and brought back a tongue. He then told him, 'Go out and bring me some bad food from the market.' The servant went and again brought back a tongue. The rabbi said to him, 'Why is it that when I said good food you brought me a tongue, and when I said bad food you also brought me a tongue. The servant replied, 'It is the source of good and evil. When it is good, there is nothing better; when it is evil, there is nothing worse.'"

If you are stressed out, like millions of other people, consider what the Talmud taught two thousand years ago: "Do not worry about tomorrow's trouble, for you do not know what the day may bring. Tomorrow may come and you will be no more, and so you will have worried about a world that is not yours."

A second chapter deals with our relationships with others, surely a topic much in the news today. Pick up any magazine and you will see the public's preoccupation with getting along with a boyfriend, girlfriend, spouse, sibling, or friend. Judaism has an enormous amount to say on these subjects. For example, the Rabbis praised differences among people as part of the wonder of creation: "A man strikes many coins from one die, and they are all alike. But God strikes every person from the die of the first man, yet not one resembles the other." In a like fashion, respect for others is a product of recognizing and valuing the uniqueness of every individual.

How do you know if your love is a powerful love? The midrash teaches: "If love depends on some selfish end, when the end fails, love fails. But if it does not depend on a selfish end, it will never fail."

A remarkable section from the wisdom of Ben Sira teaches us how to recognize a true friend: "When you make a friend, begin by testing him, and be in no hurry to trust him. Some friends are loyal when it suits them, but desert you in times of trouble. Some friends turn into enemies and shame you by making the quarrel public....A faithful friend is a secure shelter; whoever finds one has found a treasure."

We are cautioned against gossip: "It kills three people: the person who says it, the person about whom it is said, and the person who listens to it."

The chapter on "Love, Sex, and Marriage" will resonate with many moderns, young and old alike, for who among us has not yearned for a marriage or relationship rooted in true love? The Talmud glorifies the institution of marriage: "A man who does not have a wife lives without joy, without blessing, and without goodness."

By the same token, the Talmudic sages reflect an awareness of how hard people must work to make their marriage fresh and new: "When love is strong, a man and woman can make their bed on a sword's blade. When love grows weak, a bed of sixty cubits is not large enough."

Men are instructed to treat their wives with gentleness and tenderness: "A man should always be careful not to wrong his wife; for since she cries easily, she is quickly hurt.... A man must be careful about the respect with which he treats his wife, because blessings rest on his home only on account of her."

The great scholar Judah the Pious even gave advice on how to deal with one's in-laws: "If one's parents constantly argue with one's wife...and he knows that his wife is in the right, he should not rebuke his wife so as to please his parents."

And what does Judaism say about divorce, even though it is permitted? "If a man divorces his first wife, even the altar sheds tears, as it is written: 'You cover the altar of the Lord with tears, weeping and moaning.... Because the Lord is a witness between you and the wife of your youth with whom you have broken faith.'"

The author provides ancient sources on homosexuality, on the love between parent and child, and on adopted children. She quotes Jewish sources prohibiting drugs and alcohol. There is a chapter about keeping yourself healthy through the consumption of certain foods, maintaining a balanced diet, and regular exercise.

Francine Klagsbrun has created a treasure trove of Jewish sources, a sort of ultimate Jewish self-help book for the modern Jew. In reading it, you will become not only a more literate Jew but also, in following its precepts, a much healthier and happier person.

The Complete Dictionary of
English and Hebrew
First Names

Alfred J. Kolatch

The choice of Hebrew and English names for a newborn Jewish baby has long been a matter for animated family discussion and debate. One of the true heroes of those decisions has been Alfred Kolatch. His dictionary of Hebrew and English first names includes the original meaning of each name and its Hebrew equivalent. This has saved Jewish parents countless hours! This volume, originally published in 1984, contains more than eleven thousand entries, including biblical and Israeli names. Also included is a Hebrew name vocabulary, which enables the reader to find a Hebrew equivalent for virtually any English name.

Even more important, Kolatch enables the reader to focus on the importance of names in Judaism. From biblical times onward, names have expressed individuality, commemorated a great life event, paid tribute to the dead, or honored the living.

Naming began in the Torah when God named Adam, a name derived from the Hebrew word for "ground." Later, after the first woman was created, Adam called his wife Eve (in Hebrew, "Chavah," "life") because she was the mother of all living things. Eve named Cain from a Hebrew word meaning "possession" or "acquisition." And so it went, generation by generation, fathers and mothers naming their children on the basis of a variety of criteria.

Some people were named after birds and animals, like Jonah ("dove"). Others were named after plants and flowers, like Tamar ("palm"). The patriarch Isaac ("laughter") derived his name from the time when Sarah, his mother, laughed because God's messengers announced that she would bear a child at the age of ninety. Other names, like Korach ("bald") reflect a physical attribute, while still others actually contain the abbreviation for God's name within them: Yonatan ("gift from God"), Daniel ("God is my judge"), and Yoel ("God is willing"), to name just a few.

Kolatch takes us on a fascinating journey through world history, showing how biblical names ebbed and flowed in popularity. As Christianity arose, Torah-based names were supplanted in popularity by New Testament names and even by names associated with mythological figures. During the sixteenth century, biblical names again became popular as part of the Protestant Reformation. The Puritans were drawn to biblical names, as were the Quakers, and therefore a large number of early American immigrants bore names drawn from the Hebrew Bible.

Most Jews of Ashkenazic (Middle-European) ancestry name children in memory of a deceased relative. This custom began in the sixth century B.C.E., after the destruction of the First Temple in Jerusalem. The Ashkenazim never named children after the living, in the superstitious belief that to name a child after a living man or woman might shorten that person's life. On the other hand, Sephardic Jews, from Oriental communities, often named babies after the living, usually a grandparent or a parent. To the Sephardim, this custom was an expression of great honor and respect, and it continues to the present day.

Initially, names chosen were exactly the same as that of the relative. As time went on, however, modern equivalents were often substituted. Moses was an Egyptian name, Mordechai and Esther, Babylonian. The great Jewish philosopher Philo had a Greek name, while the name of the brilliant medieval Jewish scholar Saadia was Arabic.

Over time, Jews adopted two names: one secular for daily life, the other Hebrew for Jewish rituals and ceremonies. This practice enabled Jews to take more modern given names, often using only the first letter of the relative's first name. In addition, they began to name children after famous, non-Jewish historical figures who saved Jewish lives. Many Jewish boys, for example, were named for King Cyrus the Great and Alexander the Great.

With the creation of the State of Israel in 1948, the popularity of Hebrew names exploded once again. Hundreds of thousands of immigrant refugees poured into Israel, and they gradually took Hebrew names as part of their new Jewish identity. Especially following the Six-Day War of 1967, Jewish parents around the world, including the United States, began to look at Israeli Hebrew names with great interest and selected those Hebrew names as the given names for their children. That trend continues today.

As Kolatch illustrates, due in large measure to the influence of Israel, Jewish children are no longer named solely after biblical figures. Many children are named after biblical sites, such as Efrat, the place where the matriarch Rachel died and was buried. Jewish holidays, too, offer a rich source of potential names, such as Pesach ("Passover") and Menachem ("comfort," associated with Tisha b'Av). Names also derive from numbers, such as Rishona ("first"), and from the names of great Israeli figures such as Golda (after Israel's prime minister Golda Meir). With the increase in general Jewish literacy, formerly unfamiliar biblical names are being used as well: Asher, Hosea, Micah, Rena, and Yael, to name just a few.

Alfred Kolatch has made all these names—and thousands more—accessible to the average Jew. Skimming through this fine book is more than just a search for a name. It is in many ways an educational experience. Certain names jump off the page as powerful, beautiful, or gentle. The name Adina, for example, conveys a sense of gentle loveliness, while the name Ariella literally means "lioness of God." One boy's name, Lior, means "light is mine," while the feminine name Liba means "love" or "heart."

This volume contains a history of Jewish naming practices, ceremonies for naming both boys and girls, and special provisions for naming adopted children and those who have come to Judaism through conversion. There is even guidance as to appropriate naming procedures when a child is born out of wedlock and the father's name is either unknown or not to be used.

This book belongs in every Jewish home, for there will always be occasions when a new child in the family, a grandchild, or the child or grandchild of a friend will require a Hebrew name. When that time comes, all one need to do is share this work with the happy parents or grandparents. The rest will take care of itself!

9 The Book of Miracles

Lawrence J. Kushner

The story is told of a little boy who returned home from religious school after a lesson on how the Jews crossed the Red Sea. When asked by his parents to repeat the story, he related how the Jews came out of Egypt in tanks and troop carriers, pursued by Pharaoh and the Egyptians in jet fighters. The Israelites, he continued, boarded a waiting fleet of battleships and crossed the Red Sea, while destroying the entire Egyptian air force with an artillery barrage.

The parents, stunned, demanded an explanation. "But, Josh," they said, "that's not how it happened at all. What a ridiculous story!" Undaunted, the little boy replied, "It sure makes a whole lot more sense than what they really told us!"

The notion of miracles—moments in which the laws of nature are suspended, seemingly by a supernatural power—is exciting to little children. They react with awe, for example, to the biblical Red Sea story, to the dramatic description of Moses receiving the Ten Commandments, and to the account of manna falling from heaven to feed the Israelites as they wandered in the wilderness.

As these same children grow up, they often decide that they have been taught fairy tales as if they were fact. This awareness often brings with it a sense of betrayal, and thus cynicism about Judaism in general.

In recent years, many rabbis and Jewish teachers have begun to eliminate the word "miracle" from these stories altogether, speaking instead of "legends." This, too, has its price, for if children read the Torah simply as a series of fictitious bedtime stories, chances are they will never experience the sense of the spiritual, of awe and wonder, that these ancient traditions can evoke.

Rabbi Lawrence Kushner, in *The Book of Miracles*, sets his mind to achieving an almost impossible task. He aims at telling the story to children, presenting it as legend, yet somehow preserving a sense that God was present and played a role. Kushner, who has written numerous books for adults on spirituality, now presents children with a gift to be embraced and cherished.

He speaks of the biblical story of the patriarch Jacob. According to the Torah, Jacob dreamt of a ladder on which angels were going up and coming down. In the story, God appears and speaks to Jacob. When Jacob awakes the next morning, he exclaims, in Kushner's adaptation: "Wow! God was in this very place all along…and I didn't even know it!"

Kushner continues to talk to children in language they can understand, taking the biblical "miracle" and making it live for them: "To be a Jew means to wake up and keep your eyes open to the many beautiful, mysterious, and holy things that happen all around us every day. Many of them are like little miracles: When we wake up and see the morning light…when we help those around us and feel good. All these and more are there for us every day, but we must open our eyes to see them."

Suddenly, a formerly old and distant story becomes a clear and present lesson for today. The message is that miracles are all around us. We just need to be open to them.

Kushner's treatment of the story of Moses and the burning bush in the desert is masterful. The Bible relates that before Moses became a great leader, he was a shepherd. One day, while taking care of the flock, he saw a burning bush that was not consumed. According to the story, God used the burning bush to attract Moses' attention and then spoke to Moses from the bush.

The author asks an obvious question, once you think about it. If God wanted to get Moses' attention, why did God use a little bush? God could have divided an ocean, made the sun stand still, or done something else equally miraculous.

Kushner suggests that maybe this wasn't a miracle at all, but just a test. All of us see burning wood at one point or another in our lives, at campfires or at home in our fireplaces. One of the most important things we have to do is to watch the wood and the flames long enough to make sure that the wood is actually burning. Otherwise, the fire just goes out! In other words, we have to pay attention.

Kushner says that the real purpose of the burning bush was to see if Moses could pay attention. Only then was he entrusted with the leadership of the Israelites. By the same token, each of us earns rewards by learning to pay attention. If we pay attention in school, we get better grades. If we pay attention to what our parents tell us to do, we stay out of trouble. What could have been presented as a supernatural miracle becomes instead for the child a miracle of the will.

Kushner even makes the creation story contained in Genesis understandable to children. He begins by talking about the need for a blueprint if you wish to erect a building. You need a plan, a clear depiction of where each wall, each pipe, each electrical outlet, will be placed, lest the building wind up in shambles. The same is true of music. You have to write the notes down exactly as you want them to be played. Otherwise the musicians will play a jumble of notes with no melody, rhythm, or harmony.

As we look at the creation story, the author suggests that it was the fulfillment of a blueprint, a plan developed by God for a new world. Each piece in turn was created and put in its proper place. Only after the blueprint was followed exactly and the project finished did God rest. By implication, Kushner teaches, each of us needs a blueprint for our personal lives. We need to have a sense of where we are moving in terms of career, family, and the realization of our dreams. In life, nothing is certain. But if we have that mental blueprint, we have a much better chance of attaining our goals.

In succeeding examples, Kushner takes other miracles of the supernatural and transforms them into miracles that can take place in our time. If our sense of the spiritual invests us with the ability to see and appreciate the many miracles that surround us, then we and God can join together spiritually in the modern world.

10 Honey From the Rock

Lawrence J. Kushner

The Jewish mystical tradition is in many ways the most neglected area of Jewish study. Part of the reason is superstition. We are taught by our rabbinic sages that one may not delve into the classics of Jewish mystical thought until the age of forty, and then only with a trained teacher present—else we will go mad!

The inaccessibility of the Jewish mystical literature has led many Jews to assume that they must look elsewhere if they are inclined in this direction. Thus, thousands of Jews are well informed about esoteric Eastern religions, but uninformed about their own heritage.

Recently, a renewed interest in mysticism and the spiritual world has emerged. A cadre of talented interpreters of original mystical sources has appeared in Jewish communities throughout the world, Gershom Scholem being the most revered and respected. Rabbi Lawrence Kushner represents the best of American Jewish filtering of mysticism through the prism of the mind of a master teacher, making profound insights available to students of all ages.

Honey From the Rock, initially published in 1977, represents an early step in Kushner's spiritual evolution. Blending mysticism with exquisite psychological insights, Kushner opens a window to understanding the presence of God in our lives and how that presence is made manifest in the world.

The author relates a moving story about a conversation with religious schoolchildren in his temple. He asked them how many of them believed in God, and found to his dismay that not a single child raised a hand. When, however, he asked how many of them had ever been close to God, every hand shot up. Adults may have "God concepts." The children had God!

26

Slowly, gently, we are drawn into a mystical mode of experience, based on examples every person can easily understand. For example: "You are watching television. Then you turn the sound down like you used to do when you were a kid during the commercials and laugh at the funny lady whose lips moved without making any sounds. Then you turn the contrast knob so that the speaker seems barely visible through some dark foggy mist. Then you turn the brightness all the way down so that the screen is completely black. You see nothing. You hear nothing. But you continue staring at the black soundless glass rectangle. For something is there. Someone is speaking and looking. Only you can't see them. From within a darkened space a message issues, a reality that will not be seen or heard or understood. Just as the eye will never see itself. But nevertheless there is something going on there." With this simple illustration, Kushner illustrates the mystery of God, as well as his absolute faith that God is omnipresent. He acknowledges the difficulty of finding God but never doubts that God awaits our human discovery.

Kushner speaks of entrances, pathways to holiness, through nature, through the smiles of children, through music and art, and, of course, through solitude and prayer. Once we sense our spiritual rootedness, we may even be ready to understand that each of us is potentially a messenger of God, a vehicle for the realization of God's will.

The author reminds us that one of the most important people in the Torah is called only "Ish"—somebody. This nameless person directs our ancestor Joseph to his brothers. Had Joseph not found his brothers, Kushner teaches, he would never have been sold into slavery or brought his family down to Egypt. As a result, the Jewish people would never have become slaves, left Egypt, received the Torah, and become a great nation and a holy people. This anonymous man, then, changed the course of history as a messenger of God.

Each of us, too, is only "Ish," someone. We, too, may be God's messengers of goodness and kindness. Our task is to open our eyes to that potential sacred mission.

With illustrations such as these, Kushner creates a structure within which each person might take a tentative first step into the world of the transcendent. *Honey From the Rock* will not acquaint the reader with the great thinkers of Jewish mysticism. Instead, as the title suggests, we are treated to a taste of honey, a bit of the sweetness of new awareness that derives from the spiritual quest.

Honey From the Rock whets the reader's appetite for more. Fortunately, the available literature on mysticism, whether from Rabbi Kushner or his colleagues and disciples, continues to grow with each passing year.

11 Voices Within the Ark: The Modern Jewish Poets

Howard Schwartz and Anthony Rudolf, Editors

As the people of the Psalms, Jews hold poetry especially dear. In reading poetry, one can experience the magic of language in brief passages over and over again. Poets see the world through a special set of lenses and give us a new perspective on life.

In *Voices Within the Ark*, Howard Schwartz and Anthony Rudolf include works by more than 350 contemporary Jewish poets. The poems published in this volume were originally written in nineteen different languages. It is unusual to find so many poets from so many different cultures gathered in one volume.

The variety of Jewish poets represented include Joseph Brodsky and Osip Mandelstam from Russia, Nelly Sachs from Germany, Edmond Jabès from France, Oscar Levertin from Switzerland, Michael Hamburger from Britain, and Yehuda Amichai from Israel.

There are poems about Israel and about the Holocaust. Primo Levi's "Shema" and Paul Célan's "Death Fugue" are among the most moving Holocaust poetry written; both men were survivors who later took their own lives.

The poems of Miklós Radnóti were retrieved from the mass grave in which the Nazis buried him. While Radnóti's poems do not mention Judaism, they are about being a victim in war.

Of the American poets, Allen Ginsberg's now classic "Kaddish" is included. So is Delmore Schwartz's "Sarah." The editors describe Muriel Rukeyser's work as "something of an undiscovered continent to the reader" because she did not belong to a particular group of poets, as did Schwartz and Ginsberg. Her epic poem "Akiba" is included. Marvin Bell, Linda Pastan, David

Ignatow, and Philip Levine are also significant poets whose work is represented.

Canadian poets, such as Irving Layton and A. M. Klein are included, as are younger poets such as Joseph Sherman. The editors explain that the need to assimilate in Canada was not as strong as in the United States. Thus Canada remains "one of the last bastions of Yiddish, so that even today it is not unusual to find young Canadians who speak Yiddish."

Voices Within the Ark includes renowned as well as obscure poets. The editors provide brief introductions to each poet and pay particular attention to new voices. Readers are given the opportunity to encounter poems they do not know. It is unlikely in a gathering of poets whose sole common thread is their religion that the writing will be consistently of high quality; what one looks for, instead, is the voice of the Jewish people.

On discussing their requirements for determining whether a writer was Jewish, the editors admit they did not "relish the position of having to operate like a *Bet Din,* a rabbinic court of justice, in order to make such a determination." What about poets born as Jews who left Judaism? The decision was based on the individual's self-identity. For example, Brodsky was born Jewish, but converted to Christianity. However, he identified himself with his ancestry, as seen in "A Jewish Cemetery Near Leningrad." Boris Pasternak, also a Christian convert, is omitted because Jewish themes are not part of his work.

Yehuda Amichai's beautiful poem, "I Am Sitting Here," reflects Jewish connectedness to each other and the world. It reads, in part:

> I am sitting here now with my father's eyes,
> and with my mother's graying hair on my head,
> in a house that belonged to an Arab
> who bought it from an Englishman
> who took it from a German
> who hewed it from the stones
> of Jerusalem, my city.
> I look upon God's world of others
> who received it from others.
> I am composed of many things.
> I have been collected many times.

PART II

Jewish Observance
and Jewish Values

12 The New Jewish Wedding

Anita Diamant

Published in 1986, this wonderful book about planning a Jewish wedding lovingly explains Jewish traditions and customs while addressing contemporary issues. Anita Diamant wrote it to fill the void she discovered when looking for a book to help her and her fiancé plan their own wedding. They were searching for "a book that would not only supply us with the theological and historical background we needed to understand traditional Jewish wedding practices, but would also invite our explanation of and participation in the traditional." She also wanted some practical advice about the details of planning the wedding and the reception.

Written during the first year of her marriage, while she was still a bride (one tradition holds that the woman and the man "remain a bride and groom for a full year after the wedding"), Diamant's wedding was fresh in her mind. Her preface is a casual letter to the reader that sets a personal tone, making the book feel more like informed advice from a friend rather than the ultimate authority on what to do.

In the letter, she shares that this was her second wedding, her husband's first, and that he is a "Jew by choice." She realized that she wanted a traditional Jewish wedding when her rabbi told her about the ancient custom of *yichud*, the ten to fifteen minutes the couple spend alone together in seclusion just after being married, savoring their new status, and breaking the fast that tradition prescribes on the wedding day. Describing yichud at her wedding, she writes: "A magical relief, a moment of truth, an island of peace in a gloriously hectic day."

After the letter, the book is divided into four sections: "Making the Tradition Your Own," "Ways and Means," "Celebrations and

Rituals," and "Husbands and Wives." Marriage is a "holy obligation—a mitzvah—required of every Jew," she tells us, and in the
next four sections she continually shows ways in which the
wedding day and the events leading up to it can be enriched and
made more personal. Her suggestions can help alleviate problems
along the way.

The first section "lays the foundation for the many choices—
some big and some little—you are about to make. It puts your
wedding in context, which includes not only Jewish history,
theology, and generations-old customs but also the concerns of
modern life." Some of the subheadings in this section include
"Modern Options," "How Jewish a Wedding Do You Want?,"
"Anticipating Conflict," and "When Jews Marry Non-Jews."

The second section helps transform concepts into realities.
Diamant also explains why certain customs were practiced historically, and some of the history is surprising. There are no
restrictions on where a wedding may be held; in the Middle Ages,
weddings sometimes took place in cemeteries because such a life-
affirming celebration was believed to ward off plagues.

Under this heading, there are numerous suggestions for ways to
adapt or incorporate customs into a contemporary wedding. One
such example is under the subheading "The Huppah." We learn
that the huppah (wedding canopy) symbolizes the home: we learn
its history and ways to create a contemporary one. It can be made
at a prewedding party where guests write blessings onto the fabric
using watercolor pens, or friends can create individual squares
which can be sewn together. One way to include non-Jewish
friends in the ceremony is to have them hold up the posts of the
huppah. Later, such a personal huppah can become a family
heirloom, perhaps used as a wall hanging in the couple's bedroom.

Although there are many ideas for creating a harmonious
balance between old and new, the book is also full of ways to
involve not only the couple, but the community of family and
friends which supports them. "Planning the Party" (in the second
section) encompasses a wide array of suggestions for working out
all the details of the wedding, from finding a rabbi to hiring a
caterer. The author's thoroughness is seen in each stage of
planning. Copies of sample wedding invitations illustrate different design options, as well as both Hebrew and English texts.
Examples of ketubahs (marriage contracts) are also shown, and
prayers, poems, and songs are included.

Every important subject is covered, from appropriate clothing for both the bride and groom to the actual exchange of rings. The author explains customs and their origins. She offers suggestions for the music (she explains the history of klezmer music in Europe as well as its absence here until recently). The photographs can include traditional portraits balanced by candid, more casual shots which will evoke more intimate memories.

"Celebrations and Rituals," the third section, "describes the full round of parties and practices that constitute a Jewish wedding. There are customs to mark every stage of the making of a marriage—before, during and after the 'main event' under the huppah." However, the book emphasizes ceremony over festivities, guiding couples through Jewish ways of enriching the ceremony as well as involving both bride and groom as much as possible.

One such example is "Tenaim: Celebrating Engagement." The tenaim are "the conditions of the marriage"—a kind of joyful prenuptial agreement made during the engagement. Diamant reports on the history of the tenaim, and illustrates ways in which various modern couples have chosen to write theirs: a family tenaim, an engagement-party tenaim, and a tenaim written following the havdalah ceremony that concludes the Sabbath.

In the third section, the author also discusses "Celebrating Community" as well as "Spiritual Preparation," which deal more with the privacy, seriousness and holiness of marriage. Traditional and new ways to participate in the mikvah (ritual bath) are included.

In the fourth section, Diamant discusses "living as a bride and groom," "A Jewish Home," Tay-Sachs disease, and divorce. In the appendixes, there are many wedding poems, as well as a "Traditional Tenaim Text." She lists a directory of artists and offers interesting biographies on the poets. Only one line of poet Muriel Rukeyser's is quoted in the book, so her biography is not included. Still, the line seems to sum up all the amazing options offered in *The New Jewish Wedding*. Rukeyser wrote, "To be a Jew in the twentieth century is to be offered a gift."

13 On Women and Judaism

Blu Greenberg

Orthodox Judaism demands faith and devotion equally from both sexes while deliberately excluding women from full participation in the religion—not even allowing them to study the Talmud. This important book, published in 1983 and written by an Orthodox mother of five, Blu Greenberg, addresses women's role in Judaism and provides a scholarly analysis of Orthodox practice. Most important, she offers suggestions for change, all the while using halachoh (Jewish religious law) as her model.

For less observant Jews, Greenberg's writings offer fascinating insight into Orthodox life. With great love and respect for the religion, and a steadfast devotion to family life, Greenberg's discussions are thoughtful and brave, whether the topic is divorce or the mikvah.

An entire section is devoted to the laws of the mikvah and *niddah*: "Niddah...has several meanings, depending on the context: the laws pertaining to niddah; the state of being sexually unavailable; that time of month that includes menstrual flow and after-period; a woman in a state of niddah."

Ever acknowledging her love and respect for Judaism, Greenberg views halachoh as "the divine way to perfection," and offers suggestions for change that are clearly against the mainstream of Orthodox practice—although not necessarily against halakhic thinking.

Her concerns might well represent the voice of an entire generation: women who have raised children and now reflect upon how they want Judaism to be for their daughters. Greenberg shows how Judaism limits women's potential and denies both sexes benefits that would enrich society as a whole. She rejects fears that equality in religion would hurt the family.

Keenly aware of differences between the sexes, she addresses women's causes with a gentle reflective urging for change, with family life being of primary interest. What is particularly admirable about her writing is its honesty: "Taking the risk at its very worst, if giving religious equality to women should turn out to be a dreadful mistake for ritual life, there ought to be that recognition and assurance that halakhic Judaism will outlast the folly of any single generation."

For years she accepted Judaism's "second-class status" for women, and even admits it *still* feels comfortable because of its familiarity. However, she also experienced inequity firsthand: girls weren't allowed to study Talmud, even though it was a fundamental goal for boys. One day she dropped in early at her children's skating lessons and found her son off the rink, silently saying his afternoon prayer. She felt pride in her son and also realized that Judaism is truly remarkable: "What power it has to compel a fourteen-year-old boy to rise to the moment or simply to touch base. Would that this power be extended to girls, to mature women."

It wasn't until 1973, however, when asked to give the opening address for the First National Jewish Women's Conference, in New York, that she had to articulate her feelings. She discovered that her ideals didn't fit into one category; Judaism didn't incorporate the equality she believed in; "feminism fell short in some basic human values." Her talk addressed both issues.

The conference was a pivotal point in her life. Amazed at the initiative of inexperienced volunteers, who nevertheless organized the conference for five hundred people, she found that the women there weren't hostile to Judaism, but shared a great love for the religion. Many came to Judaism through feminism, looking at gender issues first, then their religious identities. Only a fraction were angry and outspoken, yet in a "bloodless revolution" focus on them could discredit everyone.

There, during a women's minyan, she was surprised to hear how beautifully a woman read the Torah. She stood in the back, not wanting to partake. However, she was invited to have the honor of *hagba'ah* ("the raising up of the Torah before it is returned to the ark"). She resisted, but the leaders were gently persistent; when she raised up the Torah, she found it "an exhilarating moment." She writes, "It was the first time I had ever held a Torah scroll."

After the conference she still wasn't ready for other ideas: a woman wearing a kipah or a female Orthodox rabbi. Transforming her views has taken many years; she has been influenced by the writings of other women, including Cynthia Ozick and Rachel Adler. One admires Greenberg's thinking, which stems from her belief about God: "My belief in the perfect God does not allow me to believe that God favors one sex over the other in constituting a holy congregation."

Greenberg shows how halakhic law has evolved throughout history. Women have been treated fairly well, although the Talmud seemed to perpetuate ideas of "passivity and dependency." Traditional Jewish exclusions, such as being left out of a minyan, do not serve a positive purpose today. Communal prayer is cathartic, and should not be reserved for men alone. Also, a women's minyan allows women to learn skills that traditionally only men have been able to develop: "leading prayer, reading the Torah, even acquiring a familiarity with the order of *tefilot* that men routinely develop."

Judaism's inability to fully include women in synagogue life is highlighted in the examples of Ruth and Dan, both of whom recently lost their spouses. Ruth and her husband were active in the synagogue for years; after her husband died, Ruth found no place there for herself. Dan, however, became more active: he joined a daily minyan, and being part of the group anchored his life. Synagogues clearly need to find a place for all women—including the single, divorced, and widowed.

What about women who wish to say Kaddish? Women should "be included in the obligation of time-bound mitzvot (as they are in many instances) yet be allowed an exemption during child-raising years, when the immediate, open-ended claims of child upon parents cannot be put off." They would become exempt because of the halakhic model—"one who is busy doing one mitzvah is exempt from another." The exemption could end when the youngest child reaches a certain age; thirteen, for example, would be meaningful for males, twelve for females.

By making this part of Jewish law, women would adhere to its requirements. Very few people would follow such strict rules of conduct in religious life if they were not mandated by law; their very requirement is what enables ordinary people to adhere to the laws, which in turn elevates their lives. Making an exemption based on gender becomes a positive rather than a negative, recognizing the religious importance of raising a family. The goal would be "exemption by function for either sex."

Greenberg also addresses the changing roles in parenting, based on what is best for individual families rather than societal expectations; she envisions a future when employees would offer paternity leave readily.

Responding to feminists who have challenged the idea of mikvah, she sees mikvah as "an attempt to attach some measure of holiness to a primal urge." She welcomes her visits, knowing that she is doing exactly what Jewish women have been doing for centuries. Such rituals allow her to define herself as a Jew.

Her views on abortion are progressive; personally opposed to it, she nonetheless supports legalized abortion while acknowledging her ambivalence. Just when she feels certain about her views, she learns something new and her opinions change. *On Women and Judaism* is precisely about that: slow change, thoughtful and deliberate, to improve and include.

14 Forty Things You Can Do to Save the Jewish People

Joel Lurie Grishaver

After Israel's Six-Day War in 1967, an explosion of interest in Jewish roots captured the minds of American Jewish teenagers and adults. Tourism to Israel increased geometrically, with an accompanying demand for conversational Hebrew classes, Israeli melodies, and more exposure to Jewish culture "back home."

After a summer away, a whole generation of Jewish campers returned to their temples to teach their peers these new Jewish "treasures." The more talented among them began to compose an entirely new genre of American-Jewish songs, creative liturgy, and ritual. And gradually the young people grew to adulthood and assumed leadership of U.S. Jewry, determined to take mainstream Jewish education and transform it in radical ways.

One of the most creative Young Turks of that early era was a talented writer and artist, Joel Lurie Grishaver. Beginning with his wildly popular illustrated text *Shema Is for Real*, the name Grishaver became synonymous with innovative, if offbeat, materials, which many old-line teachers didn't understand, but which students loved.

Published in 1993, *Forty Things You Can Do to Save the Jewish People* is one of Grishaver's best works to date. Though devoid of the cartoonlike artwork that characterizes virtually all of his texts for young people, this volume appeals to more mature readers without sacrificing accessible style, a clear message, and unpretentious language.

Recognizing that fear of assimilation is a paramount concern of many Jewish parents, the author offers a host of ways in which to strengthen and reinforce Jewish identity in children. For exam-

40

ple, he urges parents to start a "Jewish Expectations Photo Album." He urges that even before children begin their Jewish education, parents should label the pages of a photo album with the pictures they hope to take of their child's Jewish experiences over the next fifteen years. Then, he says, make those experiences happen so that you can take the pictures and put them right where you envisioned them. Join a synagogue and enroll your kids in Jewish day care, nursery school, and religious school. Insert the pictures of your child on the first day of Jewish school, at consecration, reciting the Four Questions at a seder for the first time, at a Jewish camp, at bar or bat mitzvah, and confirmation, and on through adulthood. Dream the dream and make it happen.

Another of Grishaver's suggestions is to remember the Sabbath even if you don't observe it fully. If you go on vacation, take a traveling set of Shabbat candlesticks with you. Light the candles in your hotel room. Try to have some wine and bread at dinner and recite the blessings quietly as a family, even at Disney World. Build visits to Jewish places into your vacation time whenever possible: the Lower East Side in New York, the Holocaust Museum in Washington, D.C., the old synagogues on the Caribbean islands. Show your children that you know you are a Jew.

Furthermore, says Grishaver, rather than try to force your kids to attend services when you are at home, find a temple where both you and they look forward to going to services. Perhaps the music will be the draw, or a great rabbi, or friends with whom you and your children can sit, or the Oneg Shabbat after services with tasty cookies and punch.

Another way the author urges us to proceed is to fill our homes with Jewish aromas. In an era of microwave ovens and take-out food, we need to take a bit more time to make at least a few Jewish dishes whose smells will remain among our children's earliest memories.

The Jewish holidays also offer extraordinary opportunities for Jewish memory making: wearing Purim costumes at least as elaborate as those donned on Halloween, and sending Purim *shelach manot* baskets to family members and friends; parading with flags on Simchat Torah and assuring that your temple not only encourages children to march but gives them candy apples or caramel apples at the end of services. You can give your children one gift for *each* of the eight nights of Chanukah, and make certain your home is festooned with Chanukah decorations. Having the biggest and best Passover seder you can create, letting your kids help to make the foods, is another way. You can turn the hunt for the afikomen into a big deal and invest the custom of opening the door for Elijah with great mystery. Build a sukkah in your backyard, and sleep outside in it at least once in your life.

Grishaver offers many ways in which to make children feel Jewish and allow them to live joyful Jewish experiences, seeing parents as role models for Jewish values such as tzedakah and social justice, and joining as a family in these experiences. He urges parents to fill their homes with Jewish objects, ranging from Jewish ritual objects to a collection of sports cards of Jewish athletes to Jewish books, games, and computer software. And he stresses the importance of a family trip to Israel.

Last, but not least, writes the author, "Collect, tell, and retell the stories of Jewish innovation and survival, passing them on to your children in the names of your teachers, for that is the surest path to the brightest possible future."

15 Talking About Death

Earl A. Grollman

16 A Candle for Grandpa

David Techner and Judith Hirt-Manheimer

17 Bubby, Me, and Memories

Barbara Pomerantz

Conventional wisdom once held that death should not be discussed with young children, except in the most general of terms. Children, the thinking went, are not capable of dealing with the harsh reality and finality of death, of going to the funeral home, of seeing the body of a loved one in a casket, of attending the funeral, going to the cemetery, watching the casket being lowered into the ground, or observing the mitzvah of placing a small bit of earth on the open grave.

In more recent times, however, the realization has grown that depriving children of the opportunity to know the truth, to participate in the service, and to grieve in their own way may be far more traumatic than shielding them from the pain which adults feel is harmful.

Each of these three books proceeds on the assumption that children are far more sophisticated than adults may think, that they may even be better able than their parents and family to

43

accept and understand death, if it is presented to them carefully and sensitively.

Rabbi Earl Grollman is widely respected as one pioneer in talking about death with children. *Talking About Death* (1970), a volume intended for parents, faces head-on the major issues for parents in this realm, urging an end to denial and a recognition of the child's need to express profound feelings in an age-appropriate manner.

Grollman begins by advising adults to be honest with children, gently, sensitively, allowing them to articulate their fantasies, anger, protest, and grief. He cautions against fairy tales and half-truths, and instead advocates language that may seem harsh to a grieving adult who is reaching out to a child in pain.

Rabbi Grollman provides a story which he suggests be read to young children after the death of a loved one. It enables parents to say simply and directly that the loved one has indeed died, that death is permanent, and that the loved one will not come back: "The body does not move. It does not breathe. The heart does not beat. The body is still...quiet and peaceful. There is no hurt, no pain, no life." The story encourages the asking of questions, the sharing of memories, the expression of emotions, and a constant emphasis on the fact that our loved ones will always remain in our hearts. A detailed discussion guide follows the story, enabling the adult to respond to children's reactions to the story, line by line.

David Techner is one of America's most widely known and respected funeral directors. He has appeared on countless network television talk shows, and he lectures across North America. His unique skill in speaking about death to children has earned him the confidence of clergy and parents alike. In a program that would have been unthinkable a generation ago, he brings classes of students on visits to the Ira Kaufman Memorial Chapel in the Detroit area, showing children every aspect of the chapel and answering each and every question posed by searching young minds.

In *A Candle for Grandpa* (1993), Techner and Judith Hirt-Manheimer lead young readers through the process of a Jewish funeral in a story, told by a young boy, of his grandfather's death. Children learn about the shomer, or guard, who remains with the body until it is prepared for burial by the *chevrah kadishah* (burial society), in a ceremony of ritual purification called taharah. The story explains the presence of the bag of earth from Israel commonly placed in the casket, the custom of keriah—cutting a black ribbon to be worn for seven days—and the service at the funeral home and at graveside. The authors follow this sensitive account with solid straightforward answers to the questions most often asked by parents and by children: Should my child be allowed to attend the funeral? View the body? Go to the cemetery? Why did my loved one die? Will I die, too? What happens to a body in the ground?

Bubby, Me, and Memories (1983), by Barbara Pomerantz, won a National Jewish Book Award for its loving portrayal of the relationship between a young girl and her grandmother. In a volume reminiscent of a family photo album, the author speaks in the voice of the granddaughter, sharing precious memories of personal, private moments with her Bubby: of walks in the parks and hugs, of reading time and gifts on Chanukah, of baking challah and listening to Bubby sing lullabies.

Then Bubby dies, and the young girl is devastated. But she comes to realize that death is a part of life. Bubby is not just asleep. Bubby did not go on a trip. Bubby is dead and is never coming back. The little girl comes to feel the pain of loss but also learns that it will ease with the passing of time. Above all, she comes to appreciate the times she and her Bubby shared, the love that bound them together, and the memories she will carry with her all her life.

Each of these three books possesses healing power. Each deserves a place in the library of every Jewish home.

18 Holy Days

Lis Harris

When Lis Harris, a staff writer for the *New Yorker,* came upon a box of family photographs that included one of an old man in a thick coat and fur hat, who looked Hasidic, her curiosity about her Jewish identity was piqued. Asking her mother who the man was, she heard, "Nobody in our family." The author's completely secular upbringing did not expose her to her own religious heritage. Suddenly she wanted to know more about her religion and its past. This desire to learn about her roots set the tone for *Holy Days,* published in 1995, in which Harris writes about the family of Moshe and Sheina Konigsberg and the large, strong Lubavitcher community of Crown Heights in Brooklyn, New York.

Sheina, a divorced, secular woman who previously lived a life of affluence in the Midwest, felt an intense spiritual emptiness in her life before she became more observant. Her transition to her new life is explored in a general way, but what Harris does most fully is take us into the Lubavitcher world of the twentieth century, with the roaming, curious eye of a secular Jew. Her superb reporting skills allow the reader to comprehend some of the mind-set behind Hasidic life.

In uncovering different facets of Orthodox life, many stereotypes or preconceived notions are dispelled. Among the fifteen chapters in *Holy Days* are "The Neighborhood and the Family," "A Brief Social and Religious History of Hasidism," "The Mikvah (Ritual Bath)," "Scenes from Days of Awe," and "A Wedding." The discussion of the mikvah is particularly interesting; Ms. Harris eventually immerses herself in one. Her description of a spa with all the amenities of the twentieth century takes both her and the reader by surprise. The mikvah exudes a womblike, soothing feeling, and she understands the reason women feel drawn to the experience there. Leaving the building which houses the mikvah, Harris describes reentry into the secular world as she gets into a cab.: "The driver is a garrulous, handsome Haitian. Loud monotonous music blasts out of the radio. Hanging over his mirror is an air deodorizer, which fills the car with an overpowering sickly-sweet smell. Competing with the air deodorizer is the sharp scent of his aftershave, which he keeps in a kit on the front seat. At a long red light, he splashes extra on. My ablutions have made me feel tender, almost porous, and the harsh smells are overwhelming. Is this how Moshe and Sheina feel when they traffic with the outside world?"

Harris speaks about the division between the secular and the religious world, noting that most of the concerns of the secular world are completely out of place in the world of the Hasidim. Everyday cultural influences and concerns have nothing to do with the religious life. Witnessing this deliberately planned lifestyle she admits, too, that she wishes life could have such definitive answers. She admires the Hasidim for their certainty of belief, even if it is one she can't fully accept as truth. To Harris, her own life is like a puzzle which will never be completed; their life, absent of individual egos, feels answered and full.

Although Harris also covers the historical and political world of the Hasidim, including the Satmarers and the Lubavitchers, and the importance of their rebbe in their daily lives, what's more compelling are the workings of their daily lives. Seeing the Konigsberg family at home on Shabbat, for example, is fascinating. The importance of their strict observance is explained by both Moshe and Sheina.

Sheina tells her: "'I feel like I'm getting a break,' she said, as she placed a heavy water pitcher on the table. 'Once you get some of the more complicated things out of the way, like cooking the food in advance...it feels more like a holiday. What if you were flown to a quiet tropical island every week? Wouldn't you be pleased if you were permitted, even obliged, to just put aside your everyday burdens and everyday chores? I don't really know what other people's lives are like, but I doubt that most families get the chance we do to just sit around and talk to one another every weekend.'"

Over a dinner "so copious that it would not have been a calamity if one or two courses had slipped away unnoticed,"

Harris asked Moshe "why it was, apart from emulating the actions of the Creator, that ceasing to work on the Sabbath honored God."

He replied: " 'What happens when we stop working and controlling nature?' he asked, peering at me over the top of his glasses. 'When we don't operate machines, or pick flowers, or pluck fish from the sea, or change darkness to light, or turn wood into furniture? When we cease interfering with the world we are acknowledging that it is God's world.' "

A visiting rabbi from South Africa expanded on Moshe's answer: " 'Once the Jews left Egypt they were no longer enslaved. But of course the ordinary workaday world always involves a kind of servitude, and for any people, especially poor people, work can be awfully grinding. But no one is the master of any Jew on the Sabbath. Every body and every soul is free on that day. Tyrannical countries have always tried to force Jews to work on Saturdays, to mock this gesture of independence. East European Jews fought anti-Sabbath edicts and statutes for centuries.' "

What Harris is compelled to report, though, isn't about learning to be pious or dutiful. "But in real life what was amazing about the Konigsbergs and those around them was the passion with which they strove to submerge themselves, with all their quirks and weaknesses, to better serve what mystical author Gershom Scholem calls 'the everlasting unity' and to see in the world, with all its quirks and weaknesses, 'the presence of transcendence.' "

19 Jewish Music

Abraham Idelsohn

Jews who go to the synagogue on a regular basis come to know the melodies and rhythms of its liturgical music. The melodies often enable the worshiper to master the Hebrew of the prayers and thus to participate fully in the service. But where did these melodies arise? Why do they have that certain tone and cadence that marks them as Jewish? In short, what is Jewish music?

Abraham Idelsohn, known as "the father of Jewish music research," was born in Lithuania in 1882. He attended a number of Jewish academies, sang in synagogue choirs, studied cantorial music privately, and general musicology in Berlin and Leipzig. An ardent Zionist, Idelsohn moved to Palestine in 1906, where he researched the melodies of some three hundred synagogues. In 1921, after serving in the Turkish army during World War I, he accepted a professorship at the Hebrew Union College in Cincinnati, where he taught liturgy and Jewish music almost up until his death in 1938. His version of the song "Hava Nagila" lives on as the most popular rendition of that melody.

While Idelsohn's *Jewish Music* is scholarly rather than popular in style, it remains a definitive volume on the history of the genre. Idelsohn begins by examining what we can reasonably infer about the music in the Temple in Jerusalem. Undoubtedly influenced by the music of surrounding cultures, the ancient Israelites utilized a large and small harp, a shofar (ram's horn), a form of trumpet, a small pipe or flute, a large pipe called a halil, and a double flute. Temple musicians also played cymbals and little bells, creating an orchestra of sound that filled the Temple with melody, sung by a minimum of twelve adult choir members.

After the destruction of the Temple in Jerusalem, instrumental music was eliminated, but vocal music was retained and transplanted into the synagogue. Drawing from folk melodies, composers recast the prayers of worship into liturgical form. In some instances, the leader would sing a line, echoed by the congregation. In other instances, the leader and congregation would sing alternate lines. This antiphonal singing was clearly the forerunner of the English responsive reading.

Secular music in Temple and post-Temple days borrowed heavily from other Middle Eastern cultures, then from Greek influences. Here instruments continued to be used, but unfortunately the music was never committed to writing, and therefore was most likely lost. It remained an oral tradition.

Idelsohn examines what is known or assumed about many different manifestations of Jewish music. Oriental Jewish music, for example, derived from folk melodies, had no harmony and was often improvisational. Only when chanting the Torah and other books of the Bible became an integral part of the worship service was a whole set of cantillation marks introduced which guaranteed a measure of uniformity to the singing of the words.

As the Jews went into exile and the synagogue replaced the temple in Jerusalem as the venue of prayer, music was composed that entered the liturgy for each of the major service elements. Each individual community created its own melodies, many in a minor key, reflecting supplication to God and somber reflection. Babylonia, Italy, Germany, Persia, Poland, and Russia were among the earliest Jewish communities to enrich the liturgical repertoire. The Jews resisted heathen music, as did the Christian church, determined to invest worship with a unique religious cast.

Over time, certain members of the community who had a talent for leading prayer were honored by being asked to perform that function for the congregation, along with chanting from the Torah. The skills required for that task were so formidable that the once-volunteer position became a profession, that of the chazan, or cantor.

The word *chazan* derives from a Hebrew word meaning "to oversee." The cantor saw to it that the service ran smoothly and efficiently, under the supervision of the rabbi.

Even as many temples utilize creative music today, the synagogues of old encouraged spontaneous expression of prayer through song by its members. Occasionally, an original prayer in song would so capture the soul of the congregation that it was preserved as a regular element in the worship service. In time, the chazan would introduce rhythmical music into prayer, bringing new hymns composed specifically for the synagogue. The great Jewish poet Yehuda Halevi and the mystical leader Isaac Luria were two men whose poetry and music entered the liturgy. Arabic melodic influence was felt quite strongly, and the congregants began to know and sing familiar melodies.

In about the tenth century, Jewish musical influences were manifested in Germany and other western European countries. Idelsohn tells us that leaders of the church, fearing that the sophisticated melodies might entice their members to the synagogue, banned them from any church service. Indeed, when Jews were confronted with the choice of conversion or death during the Crusades, they often sang the Alenu prayer evoking awe and fear among their executioners.

Wherever possible, Idelsohn provides the names of the composers of melodies with which most modern Jews are familiar. The Kol Nidre melody for Yom Kippur, for example, was improvised until the sixteenth century, when it was finally formalized by the chazanim (cantors) of that era in Germany. He gives a nicely detailed history of the great Italian composer Solomon Rossi, and his introduction of harmony and polyphony into Italian synagogue music. We learn how Leon Singer, a British choir member in a London synagogue, became a famous opera singer after writing the melody to the Yigdal prayer.

Idelsohn spends a great deal of the book illustrating how Reform Judaism influenced Jewish music, with the composers Solomon Sulzer and Louis Lewandowski being in the vanguard of that musical revolution. He concludes the book with sections on nonsynagogal Jewish folk music, Hasidic song, klezmer music, along with addenda on great musical arrangers and the place of the Jew in American music in general.

Though Idelsohn's book is largely encyclopedic in its approach, it deservedly stands as one of the classics of scholarly Jewish musical literature.

20 My Generations

Arthur Kurzweil

Jewish history as we know it is about three thousand years old. A generation is approximately thirty years. Therefore, only one hundred generations separate each of us from the beginnings of the Jewish people. Almost all of us know or knew our parents and our grandparents. If we were fortunate, we knew our great grandparents as well. That is three generations right there! Therefore, only ninety-seven people separate us from Abraham, the first Jew. If we could just reconstruct our personal family history going back through those ninety-seven people, who knows what ancestors we might discover?

Musings such as these have led increasing numbers of modern Jews to an interest in genealogy and family trees, and no author explains that process better than writer and editor Arthur Kurzweil in his fine volume *My Generations* (1983). Though initially written for young people, the book has become a staple in many parts of the Jewish and non-Jewish communities for reestablishing family memories once considered lost in the dim past.

Kurzweil follows the classic educational mode of starting with the known and moving to the unknown, awakening glimpses of our personal history in the process that will lead us back in time. He starts by asking those beginning their odyssey to create a map of their neighborhood, with pages reserved for photographs of their home, synagogue, school and other places of happy memories. The next step is the creation of a family telephone directory, a listing of family members' addresses and phone numbers in North America and abroad, followed by a listing of all the places they personally have lived until the present.

Pushing on, Kurzweil then asks the budding genealogist to

create as much of a record as possible of family members who immigrated to America: their names, countries of origin, mode of transportation, year of arrival, age upon arrival, place of settlement, as well as information about those who made the journey with them. Photographs of those relatives should be included, wherever possible. Obviously, this step necessitates contacting other family members throughout the world, who may add to the database and enrich the collection of photos. Returning to the primary researcher, the author now calls for some personal mementos: a birth certificate, *brit milah,* or baby-naming certificate, followed by a reconstruction of the life histories of parents, aunts, uncles, and cousins. All of the previous research enables the creation of a basic family tree, with all possible photographs, dating back to great grandparents.

Kurzweil leaves plenty of room for interesting family details. He asks for the researcher's photo and that of the family member the researcher most resembles. He includes space for the listing of all languages spoken by living family members. Seemingly small questions such as these then serve as a launchpad for thrusting deeper into the past.

The author opens up the fascinating subject of names. What is your English name? Your Hebrew name? For whom were you named? How about your siblings? Your parents? Your grandparents? What was the original family name? Was it changed? If so, why? And thus, via this method of inquiry, the family moves back in time, perhaps another one or two generations.

Kurzweil does not overwhelm the reader with research. He pushes, then pulls back, mixing assignments requiring a great deal of effort with those as simple as securing autographs from living family members, listing personal favorite holiday foods, securing favorite family recipes passed down from one generation to the next, or finding Jewish family heirlooms and determining their history. He takes the reader on a tour of the family library, on a search for its oldest books, their origins, and the manner in which they came to be part of their collection today. He sends the reader to search for old family documents: passports, telegrams, handwritten letters, or school papers.

Every family has its favorite sayings, funny stories and jokes, and space is made for them, as well as for names of pets.

The reader records personal life cycle events, such as bar or bat mitzvah, the speech recited on that occasion, the names of favorite teachers, and photos. There is also room for a record of each family member's secular and Jewish educational experiences, their occupations, and organizational affiliations.

Gently, Kurzweil urges the reader to visit the graves of family members, to record the dates of their yahrzeits, and to prepare a list of family members who perished in the Holocaust and whose burial places are unknown.

If the reader follows the book's instructions and activities from beginning to end, the result will be a mass of information invaluable to succeeding generations of the family, but also a means to a detailed family history, a family photo album, and sufficient clues to enable others within the family to take the project one or two steps further. The reader will not get all the way back to Abraham. He will, however, open the door to a past of which he was never fully aware, a past that helped to make him who he is today, a past that can only enhance a sense of self, a debt to those now gone, and an obligation to generations yet to come.

21 The Jewish Way in Death and Mourning

Maurice Lamm

Jews have historically defined ritual and culture in relation to those around us, either by rejecting the practices and values of other peoples or by integrating them and making them our own. In twentieth-century America, certainly with respect to Jewish custom and the observances surrounding death, we have tended to mirror American practices, while moving away from many of traditional Judaism's prescriptions.

No longer are most Jewish families intimately involved with every aspect of attending the dead—from assembling the casket to filling in the grave—and all the various customs, rituals, and observances originally promulgated to guide and comfort us. For example, Orthodox law requires that at the time of death the eyes and mouth of the deceased must be closed by his children, other relatives, or friends. This practice is rarely observed today. Jewish law also requires a literal tearing of one's clothing by child, parent, sibling, or spouse as a visible manifestation of grief. This practice has given way in many instances to the cutting of a black ribbon, affixed to the clothing, which is worn for seven days—the shivah period—following the burial.

The rise of the death and dying movement, the increased use of hospice care, the implementation of living wills, and a nation-wide return to spiritual roots have evoked a Jewish reinvestment in death ritual. *The Jewish Way in Death and Mourning*, written by Rabbi Maurice Lamm, a noted author within the field of death and dying, serves as an invaluable guide to Orthodox Jewish customs in relation to the care of deceased loved ones and their surviving family members.

First published in 1969, *The Jewish Way in Death and Mourning* takes the modern reader on a journey through Jewish legal requirements and traditions as they relate to death. While the book does not consider issues such as physician-assisted suicide, home versus institutional care, or the use of heroic versus palliative measures, it does present a how-to practicum in what to do, how to comfort, and how to seek solace within Jewish tradition.

The book describes in detail requirements and observances from the moment of death to burial, and even beliefs in an afterlife.

The book's seven divisions include: "From the Moment of Death to the Funeral Service," "The Funeral Service and Interment," "Mourning Observances of Shiva and Sheloshim," "Year-Long Mourning Observances," "Post-Mourning Practices and Procedures," "Special Situations," "The World Beyond the Grave," and an appendix including a guide for a chevrah kadishah (Jewish burial society) and considerations for infant deaths. A sample listing from the heading "From the Moment of Death to the Funeral Service" includes: initial care of the deceased, autopsies, embalming, caskets, flowers, timing, and viewing.

Special considerations for suicides, mourning by Kohanim (descendants of Aaron, the high priest), and instances of delayed notification, are covered under "Special Situations." For example, a Kohen may not enter a funeral chapel even if the deceased is a close relative. He may, however, stand outside the chapel to hear the service. In the case of an intentional suicide, the body is to be buried at least six feet from surrounding graves, and no eulogy is to be delivered.

Unlike most halakhic resources, *The Jewish Way in Death and Mourning* is written for the lay individual. Although thoroughly researched and complete, its purpose is not to present a catalogue of source material and historical rabbinic argument. The author presents what he considers the authoritative position regarding the topics covered, with a decidedly traditional bent. For more liberal Jews, Lamm's vehement opposition to cremation, embalming, viewing the body, the use of flowers—most things associated with secular twentieth-century American death customs—may be a bit disconcerting. This more traditional grounding will equip the modern reader returning to the roots of Jewish tradition and law with better understanding and deeper knowledge. Readers should not necessarily feel bound by Lamm's guidelines. Instead, they should utilize the information as a point of reference, one source enabling informed decisionmaking.

Obviously, no one written guide can take the place of community resources and rabbinic counsel. But, as a reference tool and guide, *The Jewish Way in Death and Mourning* is superb. Drawing from the author's own observation, that the way in which a society regards death profoundly reflects the way in which it regards life, those seeking to invest their lives more richly and fully from the well of Jewish tradition will want to have Maurice Lamm's work as a guide.

22 A Bintel Brief

Isaac Metzker, Editor
Diana Shalet Levy, Translator

This wonderful book contains sixty years of letters from residents of the Lower East Side to the Yiddish newspaper the *Jewish Daily Forward*. The voices, direct and compelling, bring the past alive, whether the issue is a woman's right to vote or unfair labor practices. That such a rich array of letters is assembled in one collection attests to the popularity of the *Forward* itself. When guidance was sought—and answers seriously awaited—the editor was put in the position of a mentor. As one reader wrote, the *Forward* reminded him of the old country where people would go to the rebbe for advice.

The *Forward* was considered a workingman's paper, and its editor, Abe Cahan, not only saw the need for reporting news in the traditional sense, but realized that his readers, immigrants themselves, needed answers to personal questions about their lives. In 1906, the daily feature "A Bintel Brief" first appeared. The subjects were as diverse as the concerns in people's lives; there are letters about personal politics (particularly socialism), World War I, unions, freethinking, Judaism, matchmakers, and, of course, love. These letters were written not only by survivors of pogroms but of the Holocaust as well.

There are letters from people directly affected by the famous fire at the Triangle factory, including a fourteen-year-old boy whose sister supported the family by working at the factory and was killed in the fire, and a woman who survived because of her bridegroom's bravery, while he lost his life trying to save others.

The *Forward* became one of the largest and most significant Yiddish newspapers in the United States. "A Bintel Brief" earned a unique kind of trust. It allowed people to write their woes to the paper and know they would receive sage counsel. Many of them looked to the editor as the last word. Cahan's advice was given with integrity and genuine care; it was wise, insightful, and sometimes humorous, without being condescending. Immigrants felt more at home in their new land because of the quality of the people working at the *Forward*. The paper's Yiddish comforted them, bringing them back to their origins.

Today's readers have the privilege of hearing first-generation immigrants speak in their own voices. The book's introduction, written by its editor, Isaac Metzker, provides a historic overview of Jewish immigration to America at the turn of the century. "From 1881 to 1925...2,650,000 Jewish immigrants managed to come to America from Eastern European countries alone. At that time this total amounted to a third of the Jewish population of all of Eastern Europe." Talking about the difficulties of adapting to the new country, Metzker tells how hard it was to live without the Jewish calendar as a primary guide; in the old country, Jewish lives revolved around their holidays, and the Sabbath was always observed. In America, daily Jewish life was so different that even keeping kosher wasn't always possible. When they experienced the unique problems of being greenhorns (new immigrants), they knew they could turn to the *Forward* as their friend.

In America, many of these Jewish families lived in tenements on New York's Lower East Side, in squalid conditions, peddling, often working in the needle trade. (The ready-made clothing industry was created by such Jewish immigrants.) Life was harsh and lonely; working conditions were terrible, and the new country was much more of a struggle than people had ever anticipated. Still, America, with its promise of equal opportunity, gave Jews enormous hope.

Journalist Harry Golden wrote the book's foreword. The letters themselves have sometimes been edited, and the responses shortened. It is truly a lesson for young American Jews to read of the struggles that many of their people endured. Often the letters are deeply touching because of their authenticity and the seriousness of their problems. One such letter comes from a father who can't keep himself from kissing his little girl even though he knows he should not; he has consumption, or tuberculosis, which was prevalent among those working in sweatshops on the Lower East Side.

The letters also reveal profiles of remarkably resilient and kind people. A girl with four siblings writes to the editor, feeling as though she must contribute monetarily to her family (children often worked in factories). Her mother is pregnant, has three boarders, and takes care of all the children. Her father is frail and working to support the whole family. They want her to stay in school; she looks to the editor to guide her. His advice is to obey her parents by continuing her education from which they will derive more satisfaction than if she contributed financially.

Golden writes: "The hunger for education was very great among the East Side Jews from Eastern Europe. Immigrant mothers who couldn't speak English went to the library and held up the fingers of their hand to indicate the number of children they had. They then would get a card, give it to each of their children, and say, 'Go, learn, read.'.... I graduated from P.S. 20 with George Gershwin, Edward G. Robinson, Paul Muni and Senator Jacob Javits, all sons of immigrants."

Some of the letters are about more superficial topics. One man has a sweetheart with a dimple on her chin; he wants to marry her, but he has heard that people with dimpled chins lose their first spouse. The editor writes back: "The tragedy is not that the girl has a dimple in her chin, but that some people have a screw loose in their heads!" A twenty-two-year-old man doesn't like his red hair, which people tease him about. Echoes of Martin Luther King's "I Have a Dream" are heard in 1909 in the editor's response: "A person is not valued by the hair on his head but by what is in his head."

This column not only aided readers by giving advice but enabled mothers to find lost children and locate fathers who had abandoned their families. So many men left their families that the *Forward,* with the aid of the National Desertion Bureau, traced them through a special column with pictures of the men, entitled "The Gallery of Missing Husbands." The paper also gave readers names and addresses of places to go to help implement social change.

The letters in this volume begin in 1906 and end in 1967. The column ended in the mid-seventies because there was no longer a need for it. One of the loveliest letters, written in 1956, asks, "Were the old days really that good?" This writer recalls the specifics of life in Russia: houses lit by kerosene lamps, mud in the town streets, fear of gentiles, and extreme poverty. The writer recalls New York as a new immigrant, climbing many steps to the small dark, airless rooms without bathrooms, a bathtub in the kitchen, and the fourteen- to sixteen-hour workdays, six days a week. It puts the earlier letters into perspective. They span several generations and focus on the concerns of Jews everywhere, addressing all kinds of issues and receiving all types of advice.

A Bintel Brief provides a glimpse into American history and into the lives of ordinary Jews whose extraordinary struggles made it possible for us to live so well today.

23 Number Our Days

Barbara Myerhoff

Respect and honor for the aged are fundamental Jewish values. The Ten Commandments, for example, never ordains *love* for parents, but declares you should "*Honor* thy father and thy mother." Furthermore, honoring parents is one of only two commandments in the entire Torah for which extended life is promised. Jewish worship services contain numerous references to reverence for the elderly, and the High Holiday liturgy contains a plea to God: "Do not cast me out in my old age."

One of the greatest fears of older people is being forgotten and alone during the autumn years of life. For those who have not been blessed with wealth, whose children live far away, whose bodies are crippled with illness, the only option is often residing in a home for the aged or in an apartment building designed for the elderly. To their credit, many Jewish communities maintain such facilities. In some measure, then, even if their families cannot be with them on a regular basis, these precious souls have a decent environment in which to live out their remaining days. There are friends to be made, activities in which to participate, tasks to fill the hours of each week.

But what really happens in these centers? What is the quality of life there? In *Number Our Days,* author Barbara Myerhoff takes us inside one such center in California, evoking the fears and anxieties, the hopes and dreams, of a group of elderly Jews.

The tone of this sensitive and moving book is far different from that of newspaper or television nursing home exposés or the bulletins issued by the homes themselves. That uniqueness is attributable to the special qualities of the author. Barbara Myerhoff, then chairperson of the University of Southern California's anthropology department, had already gained a national reputation in her profession for her study of the Huichol Indians of Mexico, which was nominated for a National Book Award.

Then, receiving a grant to study the process of aging, she decided that, as a Jew, she would study her own people rather than deal with another exotic group. Establishing a relationship with a small Jewish community center near her home, she spent the next two years interviewing elderly Jews and becoming a part of their lives. This book is the warm and tender result of that research. A documentary film based on the book won the Academy Award for Best Short Documentary in 1977.

Myerhoff recalls the day in 1973 when she first entered the Aliyah Senior Center. Following the crowd of some 150 elderly Jews into the center for a state-funded kosher hot lunch costing only sixty-five cents, she glimpsed the environment and the programs it offered. Bulletin boards listed classes on history, holidays, and gerontology, as well as upcoming films. Pictures and posters filled the walls, portraying Yiddish writers, scholars, Zionists, Jerusalem, Golda Meir, and Moshe Dayan. Arts and crafts projects by the seniors were also prominently displayed: scenes from their past, Jewish ritual objects, and biblical and rabbinic teachings portrayed in calligraphy.

Myerhoff, a stranger in this place, was soon approached by a woman named Basha. Basha, not quite five feet tall, came to America from Eastern Europe. Like most of the members of the center, she was a survivor, struggling to maintain her dignity, pay her bills, and fill her days with meaning. It was Basha who, having established Myerhoff's credentials, began to introduce her to others: her friend Faegl and the center's director, Abe. Ultimately accepted as a good Jewish girl with a Ph.D., Myerhoff began her work.

Myerhoff's insights into the psyche of these Jewish elderly are quite remarkable. For example, she shows us how they have constructed their own world, with standards far different from those of younger Americans. The usual indicators of success—wealth, power, physical beauty, youth, mobility, security, social status—mean nothing to them. Since they have access to none of these things, they create a culture of their own, redefining the criteria that would make them feel fulfilled. Ceremony, symbol, ritual, companionship, discussion, perspective—these are the things that give meaning to their lives.

The book reflects the substance of the "Living History" course led by the author, where center members were encouraged to share and reminisce about their lives. From the twenty or so members who regularly attended the class, Myerhoff focuses on a handful, and one in particular, who spoke to her as both a social critic and a Jew.

Shmuel Goldman, a tailor, was one of the brightest and most philosophical members of the center. For him, the fact that every Jew there had a coat was a sure sign that the Jews had made it in America. Shmuel was a socialist, ritually nonobservant, yet still sang songs from the liturgy in his home. He and his wife Rebekah told stories of the Russian pogroms, of Cossacks who killed Jews in the streets.

Shmuel, a deeply sensitive man, did not show that softer side to those at the center. Many of the members avoided him because of his socialist views. Some even attacked him as a communist. Yet, when Shmuel died, the center was crowded with people paying tribute to his memory. He, after all, was one of them, and his loss diminished the community.

Subsequent chapters of the book reveal the deepest feelings of this group of Jewish elderly. A large segment of membership consisted of Holocaust survivors, many of whom lived with constant guilt at having survived while their entire families died. Others, from the perspective of old age, now questioned the whole purpose of religion. What benefit has it brought to the world?

One of the most charming aspects of the book is the progressive revelation of self that grows with the trust between Myerhoff and her subjects. Historical facts evolve into stories of dances, broken hearts, suffering, pain, and joy that touched the members' lives. That same comfort level also frees the members to confront one another in arguments in the author's presence, conflicts often filled with personal insults. But as one member says: "We fight to keep warm."

With love and great affection Barbara Myerhoff took these elderly Jews into her heart and told their stories with the respect and dignity they deserved. She demonstrated profound respect for the aged. Her tragic death shortly after winning the Academy Award robbed the university community of a superb anthropologist and the Jewish community of a beautiful soul who truly cared about her people.

24 Good People

Danny Siegel

During the summer of 1963, the international Jewish community convened a World Jewish Youth Conference in Jerusalem. Thousands of high school and college students from all over the world gathered to be addressed and inspired by Israel's top elected officials, to tour the pre-1967 borders, and then to return home to share their experiences with adults and peers alike. Among the participants in that conference was a Conservative Jewish teenager named Danny Siegel, whose Jewish literacy was so superb that he was able to address the large audience in fluent Hebrew.

A few years later, the same Danny Siegel became an adult professional in the United Synagogue Youth Movement, leading summer trips to Israel for teens. Friends, knowing of his journeys to Israel, began to give him small amounts of money for charity—five dollars here, ten dollars there—asking Siegel to find people and causes whose work might be unknown by the larger Jewish charities, yet who need and deserve support.

Over the course of more than two decades, the annual reports issued by Siegel to his donors created a confidence in his judgment and caring, so much so that the ZIV Tzedakah Fund grew into a recognized national Jewish charity itself. By 1995 it was distributing over $200,000 a year to worthy causes inside and outside Israel, under both Jewish and non-Jewish sponsorship.

Good People is a compendium of ideas, resources, and names of people who are making a difference in the world, mostly with ZIV Tzedakah Fund Support, and championed by Siegel, who is now known throughout North America as a passionate advocate of tzedakah, of righteous Jewish charity. A recipient of the coveted Covenant Award, Siegel now speaks at conferences and conventions throughout North America and abroad. Accompanied by some of his "Mitzvah Heroes," he urges young people and adults alike to take a personal role in *tikkun olam,* the mystical concept of healing the world.

For example, Siegel relates the moving tale of Shoshana Weinstock, the Annie Sullivan of Israel, who has made breakthroughs in teaching blind and deaf children in the Jewish state.

Another chapter contains a listing of what Siegel calls mitzvah phone numbers, those of people who have created specific tzedakah projects that serve specific groups of people. You can find a person (rather than an organization) who is ready to help you or your group participate in projects such as bone-marrow testing, gathering cribs for needy children, starting a Jewish battered woman's shelter or a community food bank, donating leftover foods from community events to the hungry, making synagogues accessible to the disabled, and using pets to visit hospital patients.

Among Siegel's more ambitious projects was the purchase of three horses which he then shipped to Israel! The mitzvah horses, costing twenty-one thousand in donated dollars, were trained for use in Israel's Therapeutic Riding Club, and helped those with severe physical disabilities to learn to be proficient in a sport that gave them a sense of accomplishment.

A most striking program is exemplified in Siegel's advocacy of the Eden Alternative, an approach to care of the elderly in nursing homes that utilizes birds, dogs, cats, and plants. Research shows that the aged in this environment have a fifteen percent lower mortality rate than residents of other institutions and require 50 percent less medication than those in comparable institutions.

Ranya Kelly, "The Shoe Lady of Denver," once found five hundred pairs of brand-new shoes in a Dumpster, discarded by a store instead of being given to charity. Angry at the waste, Ranya began haunting mall Dumpsters at night and eventually collected more than 165,000 pairs of shoes which she has distributed to people in need. On an annual budget of only $15,000, Ranya's Redistribution Center now collects and distributes over $1.5 million in merchandise annually. After an appearance on "60 Minutes" and after being honored by President Bill Clinton, Ranya pursues her passion with gentle zeal, drawing others to her in the process.

A delightful section of the book serves an empowering function by illustrating specific human problems that required creative solutions, the response achieved, and the individual who thought of it. For example, people in wheelchairs wanted to use a local beach but the wheels of the chairs kept sinking into the sand. One creative individual designed huge wheels for standard wheelchairs that allowed the owner to move on the sand with ease.

Siegel challenges his readers to identify a human problem that requires a solution, think about it, and solve it, a process that has often yielded remarkable results in his workshops.

To be sure, Danny Siegel is sui generis, one of a kind. Yet his message is simple. Get involved. Stick your neck out. Help the poor and needy, not as a nice thing to do, but as a command from God. Above all, Siegel reminds his readers, we—each of us—have the potential to change the world.

25 Putting God on the Guest List: How to Reclaim the Spiritual Meaning of Your Child's Bar or Bat Mitzvah

Jeffrey K. Salkin

Putting God on the Guest List was written as one rabbi's response to the modern observance of the bar or bat mitzvah (son or daughter of the commandments) ceremony. Rabbi Salkin felt that the true spiritual meaning of this rite of passage was getting lost in the arrangements being made for the celebration. Although most youngsters do in fact have a meaningful religious experience at the time of the bar or bat mitzvah, Rabbi Salkin felt that this experience could and should be enhanced. This book covers the philosophical and historical elements of the ceremony.

While analyzing the roots of the ceremony, Salkin displays a great deal of sensitivity to today's transitional Jewish family. He focuses on mitzvot, Jewish laws, and their meaning in our lives. The goal that this religious ceremony should encompass, beyond the actual day, is presented as a spiritual journey for the entire family. While acknowledging the fragmentation of family life in our culture, Rabbi Salkin defines ways in which a family can use the process of preparation to create a unifying experience, while at the same time growing together religiously.

Beginning with the experience of the thirteen-year-old, and expanding that experience to parents and grandparents, Rabbi Salkin suggests ways in which more meaning can be put back into our lives through the bar or bat mitzvah.

In today's world, the bar or bat mitzvah rite has grown

significantly in importance. What was traditionally an automatic rite of passage has become an all-encompassing family event. The emphasis has shifted from a young person becoming a part of the Jewish community to a more personal and individual ceremony designed to meet the needs and desires of each individual family. Like much in the value systems of today, the bar or bat mitzvah is directed toward self. The chain of tradition, however, is still significant, and from this sense of commitment to continuing the family tradition, the book develops an approach to enhance every aspect of study and family involvement.

The feelings that encompass this moment may find their roots in Torah and God, but an understanding of why this is so is needed to make those feelings more than a moment in time. The meaning of Torah and why it is read is discussed. The fact that Torah contains all that Jews hold sacred provides a basis for real spiritual growth and study. Torah study is an excellent opportunity for putting religious obligation back into the bar and bat mitzvah.

With the performing of mitzvot—divine obligations commanded in Torah—God can become active in our lives. Each time a bar or bat mitzvah selects a mitzvah or mitzvah project, he or she is making a connection to the Jewish people and a Jewish way of life. Rabbi Salkin proposes the performance of mitzvot as a way to create "living Torah" in our lives and bring Jewish values to our daily existence. Whether a child chooses *gemilut chasadim*—acts of loving kindness, a nonfinancial way of giving—or tzedakah—the act of giving money for a sacred purpose—*choosing* to perform these mitzvot at all is the closest way people can imitate God. Each type of mitzvah is explained, and specific projects are suggested. The study of Torah, honoring the Sabbath, self-repair, improvement of our treatment of animals, our relationship to Israel, or remembering our history—in all these our sense of self-esteem and connection to God are enhanced.

One chapter of the book addresses the celebration. The Jewish roots of "the party" actually derive from the Shulchan Aruch (Code of Jewish Law). "It is the religious obligation of the father to tender a festive meal in honor of his son's becoming a bar mitzvah, just as he might do when the boy marries." Scholars point out that references to a celebration go back even further. The planning of the party today, however, no longer has any connection to its historical beginnings. The party has become an event in and of itself, an outgrowth of general celebration in America. Although every family will choose to celebrate in its own way, plans should ensure that what is being celebrated is not forgotten.

The feelings of the parents and the reasons for the decision to have a youngster become a bar or bat mitzvah are not always clear, even while they are going through the process. The various struggles with religion are present. For many, a lack of faith or a sense that they are not really religious tops the list, while the notion that religion is divisive is foremost in the minds of others. Rabbi Salkin not only responds to these doubts, but also asserts that most people are more religious than they think they are.

One section of the book outlines the Sabbath morning service, explaining each prayer and its reason for inclusion in the service. In a concise format, Rabbi Salkin zeroes in on the Jewishness of the prayer and its meaning for the congregation of today. Whether someone is preparing for a family bar or bat mitzvah or simply seeking to be more familiar with the worship service, this section elucidates the topic and provides an excellent introduction to a better understanding of Jewish worship.

The changing Jewish family presents special concerns, each requiring sensitivity in planning. Divorce has become more common and tends to create added tension at a highly emotional time in the life of the family. If these tensions are discussed and dealt with appropriately, they should in no way impact on the real meaning of the day or the preparation surrounding it. In the same manner, a non-Jewish parent or grandparents will require assistance in finding a comfortable way of being involved. If all the issues are dealt with openly and honestly, the spiritual meaning of this ceremony will prevail, and the total experience will be holy.

The bar or bat mitzvah is a gateway, a first step in the direction of a Jewish education. Having acquired the skills requisite to participating as an active member of the congregation, a teenager is finally ready to approach a deeper investigation of Judaism. If the bar or bat mitzvah is looked at as a beginning, there is a great promise for a meaningful Jewish life.

26 The First Jewish Catalog

Richard Siegel, Michael Strassfeld, and Sharon Strassfeld

27 The Second Jewish Catalog

Richard Siegel, Michael Strassfeld, and Sharon Strassfeld

28 The Third Jewish Catalog

Michael Strassfeld and Sharon Strassfeld

The Jewish Catalogs are three of the preeminent self-help, how-to books of Jewish practice. When the authors set out to write the *First Jewish Catalog,* they probably could not have imagined the revolution in Jewish education they would inspire. They soon realized they had only begun to evoke the Jewish experience and within three years published the *Second Jewish Catalog* (1976), and the third four years later.

Over the course of seven years, these volumes would provide a hands-on, do-it-yourself guide to Jewish living. Although no previous formal Jewish education is required, the editors encourage readers to use supplementary sources in making their way through the material: a bible, siddur, the Jewish Encyclopedia, a Jewish friend, a rabbi, a teacher. "Much ritual," the editors concede, "simply cannot be translated, like a recipe, from reading to action; rather, you should be modeled for, guided, responded to personally."

The Jewish Catalogs were born out of the counterculture revolution of the late 1960s—and more specifically, the parallel Jewish response most expressed through the Chavurah movement, of which the editors were leaders. The Chavurah movement consciously broke with existing modes of Jewish education, worship, and daily expression and encouraged its adherents to embark seriously upon a journey of personal Jewish rediscovery—learning and living Jewish tradition. To help facilitate the process, the original catalog and its subsequent volumes were conceived as guides and models, catalogs of useful resources that in the process of being compiled became resources in and of themselves.

In the Talmudic tradition, the Jewish Catalogs are a compendium of information covering the vast scope of Jewish living. The reader can learn how to hang a mezuzah, put on tefillin, bake challah, as well as to recite the blessings associated with each. (The *New York Times* referred to them as "…a cross between the *Whole Earth Catalog* and the Babylonian Talmud.")

Topics are covered in articles written by a variety of experts in their own right. No attempt is made to edit out an author's particular religious bent. Even when covering issues such as intermarriage, the editors maintain neutrality, choosing instead to provide opposing views from respected authorities. A curious aside does note, however, the inclusion of intermarriage under the general heading of *Exile,* along with "Surviving the Army" and "Jews in Prison."

In general, the editors assume that tradition, ritual, prayer, mitzvah, and community belong to every Jew. They also enthusiastically defend and encourage all Jews to discover, create, and travel their own journey. They never presume to preach one level of observance over another, only to educate and enable. Thus, as a general rule, the various denominational threads of *Klal Yisrael*—the body of Judaism—are woven together, emulating a rather messianic ideal.

No single work, and certainly not one limited to three volumes, can encapsulate all there is to know and learn about Jewish life. Nevertheless, the Jewish Catalogs present a comprehensive array of topics, teaching the material with integrity and depth, occasionally injecting whimsy.

The *First Jewish Catalog* covers an eclectic spectrum of Jewish life. Included are lessons in making a tallit, and even a shofar.

Introducing readers to the workings of the Jewish calendar, it also instructs how to establish and maintain a kosher kitchen. It guides the reader through Shabbat, the festivals, the Jewish wedding, the background and use of a mikvah, and the rituals associated with mourning and attending to the dead. The catalog also considers the scribal arts, the realms of Jewish music and film, how to bring the Messiah, how to learn as a Jew, and the Jewish value of hospitality, and provides a how-to for creating a Jewish library—bibliography included. Wherever Hebrew blessings are included, they are accompanied by transliteration and translation.

The second and third volumes attempted to fill in the gaps of the first book and extend its scope. The hands-on enabling approach, as well as characteristic humor, are continued. In the *Second Jewish Catalog,* subtitled *Sources and Resources,* the editors focus on life cycle events, including adoption and Jewish genetic diseases. It also addresses sex and sexuality, the art of Jewish dating, and divorce. Reaching out to incorporate all members of the Jewish community, the *Second Jewish Catalog* also treats the deaf and blind communities, including information on signing and Hebrew braille.

The volume broadens the discussion on Jewish education, including a lesson on preparing a sermon, and arts and crafts tips for crafting Jewish educational games. It outlines the layout of synagogue geography, choreography, and etiquette, discusses prayer, prayer books, and rabbis, and adds to the information on Jewish arts. It ends with a sixty-four-page Jewish yellow pages, with two hundred headings and thousands of listings, including Jewish publishers, artists, musicians, and camps.

The third catalog, departing slightly from the previous two, is decidedly less hands on. The editors discuss community-centered values such as tzedakah, social action, Israel, synagogue life, and *mentslichkite.* (This volume includes a cumulative index to all three books.)

There is no escaping the influence of the times during which the catalogs were written. Note in particular the *Second Jewish Catalog*'s treatment of pre-AIDS sexuality. While presenting the standards and mores of traditional Jewish law, there is no mistaking a counterculture orientation. A significant portion of the *Third Jewish Catalog* champions cold war Soviet Jewry. It ends with the hopeful sentiment: "May the time come soon when this chapter is irrelevant."

The fact that this chapter and other dated material remain is no drawback to the catalogs' overall value. Jewish learning does not exist in the vacuum of any one generation, and thus each successive generation can visit the fount of Jewish wisdom as long as the moment and inspiration demands. In this regard, the Jewish Catalogs are classic additions to the vast wealth of Jewish literature and instruction.

29 Basic Judaism

Milton Steinberg

Rabbi Milton Steinberg was one of the most insightful Jewish thinkers of the twentieth century, particularly the post-Holocaust era. His premature death in 1950 at the age of forty-seven deprived the American Jewish community of a great scholar.

Basic Judaism, written over fifty years ago, is one of the classic legacies Steinberg bequeathed to literature. Indeed, five decades after its initial publication, it still ranks as a revered point of entry into Judaism for Jews and non-Jews alike.

In a slim 172 pages, Steinberg surveys Jewish law, theology, ethics, Zionism, ritual, and institutions in an accessible, easy-to-read style that has passed the test of time. Though many authors have tried to match Steinberg's terse, concise style, his work remains a staple of Jewish adult education and introductory Judaism courses throughout North America.

Steinberg states that his major purpose is to craft "a book on Judaism, written from within Judaism and hence sympathetic to it, concerned with it for its own sake...unencumbered with details and as free as possible from doctrinal and ritualistic dissensions. For only from such a book can the undecided Jew and the inquiring non-Jew come to see Judaism as believing Jews see it, to comprehend why it has elicited from them such intense and sustained loyalty...." And indeed he achieves his goal.

Steinberg begins by dealing with the nature of Judaism, primarily as a religion, laying out the seven major strands of Judaism which he intends to explore: doctrine, morality, ritual, law, literature, institutions, and Israel. He notes the more than four thousand years of Jewish history that encompass his interest—from the Semites prior to Abraham through the patriarchs, Moses, the prophets, the psalmists and sages, the commentators, poets and philosophers, the mystics, historians to modernists, and Zionists.

Interestingly, Steinberg begins, not with history, but with the Torah. Inasmuch as Jews are "the people of the book," he initiates the exploration of Judaism with *the* book that underlies all of Jewish history. We learn how a Torah scroll is made, its legal and ethical components, its concept of a Jewish people, and the manner in which it has been and is perceived, ranging from God-given, to God-inspired to humanly crafted. There is the Torah and the Torah tradition, which ranges far beyond the original text to all relevant literature.

Inevitably, then, we come to the concept of God, the debate regarding dogma, and the vast spectrum of God concepts espoused by philosophers throughout the ages. Without referencing esoteric philosophic texts, Steinberg simply lists the notions of God most often held by contemporary Jews: creator, spirit, lawgiver, guide of history, helper, liberator, savior, and mystical presence. For the beginner, these sections provide a summary and point of entry into Jewish theology. At the same time, they potentially spark interest in a particular approach that may lead to further study.

One of Steinberg's greatest contributions to the post-Holocaust Jewish literature was a rather dispassionate examination of the question of theodicy: If God is good, why do the good suffer and the evil prosper? At a time when others were declaring God to be dead, Steinberg rehearsed ancient and modern responses for his readers: that evil is the result of individual or communal wrong-doing, that evil is required if we are to know the meaning of goodness, that evil is merely the absence of good, that evil is a label we attach to those things that harm us, and of course the view that the world and its pain are far beyond human understanding.

Not once does Steinberg question God's existence, maintaining a stance of faith even in the face of Nazi genocide.

Steinberg also offers a superb overview of the Jewish ethical and moral concept of life. We see that Judaism views life and living life to the fullest as good and that we as human beings have free will, with no intermediaries between ourselves and God. As free beings, we also are accountable for our decisions, whose nobility is measured by performing mitzvot, the Torah's commandments, according to traditional Judaism. Love of God requires caring, respect, and sensitivity to our fellow human beings and, especially, acts that embody those values.

A particularly intriguing section of the book deals with the notions of peoplehood, Israel, and Zionism. Inasmuch as *Basic Judaism* was published one year prior to the establishment of the Jewish state, Steinberg speaks of Palestine rather than Israel as the focus of Jewish aspirations, and of the Hebrew language as "somehow related" to Jewish destiny.

Steinberg affirms Jewish universalism, declaring that all individuals and faiths are equally precious in the eyes of God, and that Judaism does not seek to wean others away from their faith. He clearly delineates the Jewish view of Jesus as a great teacher, but not as a deity.

The concluding sections of *Basic Judaism* briefly describe the Jewish holidays and life cycle events, the roles of the rabbi and the synagogue, the insistence upon the centrality of community in Judaism, and even a glimpse of Judaism's view of the world to come.

Even though dated in some respects, *Basic Judaism* remains an important building block of any Jewish library.

30 The Jewish Home: A Guide for Jewish Living

Daniel B. Syme

When a Jew and a Christian engage in discussion of their religious traditions, each will often say, "I'm not really religious." The words are exactly the same, but the meaning of those words is radically different.

When a Christian disclaims a religious lifestyle, it almost always means that he or she does not attend church. Indeed, the religious life of most Christians revolves exclusively around the church. Try to name a single Christian religious ceremony that takes place in the home. Apart from saying grace, there does not appear to be one.

On the other hand, when a Jew says, "I am not religious," it may indicate sporadic attendance at religious services, but far more commonly it indicates an absence of observance in the home.

Judaism is a home-centered religion. Virtually all of its major holidays and life cycle events have a home component that dwarfs the significance of the temple service. A fascination with the home as a focus of ritual observance draws most Christians to a study of Judaism.

Many Jews, on the other hand, take their rituals and symbols for granted. They rarely ask why things are the way they are, but sometimes wonder about the origins and meaning of rituals performed almost by rote.

The Jewish Home by Rabbi Daniel B. Syme offers a simple, easy-to-read explanation of Judaism's holidays and life cycle events in a question-and-answer format. This slim volume raises questions that few Jews and Christians ask openly, perhaps because they consider them so elementary that they will be considered "dumb." The beauty of *The Jewish Home* is that it puts into print questions that are rarely articulated and lets the reader see that he's not the only one who wants to know.

For example, the Passover seder is by far the most popular Jewish holiday home observance, especially for children. The youngsters avidly search for the afikomen, looking forward to the prize awarded for its discovery. But who ever asks how the afikomen really got its name?

The Jewish Home tells us that *afikomen* is a Greek word meaning "dessert." During the Middle Ages, mystical powers were ascribed to this small piece of matzoh. Some Jews took it with them on long ocean voyages to prevent violent storms. Others hung it in their homes to ward off demons.

How about the holiday of Chanukah? Jews routinely use small, colored candles in the menorah, but why?

From *The Jewish Home* we learn that when candles replaced oil in the menorah, some Jews were concerned that their Chanukah lights might be confused with white Christian prayer candles. Hence, the use of small, colored candles in most Jewish homes.

Not surprisingly, many questions come from both Jews and non-Jews regarding appropriate actions at the time of a death and funeral. *The Jewish Home* explains customs relating to death and mourning in great detail, along with their origins.

We learn, for example, that Jewish funerals are to take place as soon as possible after death. We are taught that instrumental music and flowers are generally not permitted during the funeral, and that, instead, a contribution to a charity in memory of the departed is preferred, in order to make the tragedy a blessing to the living.

The reader learns how to conduct oneself in the house of mourning, waiting until a member of the family welcomes them, then following the lead of the family in terms of discussion. The chapters on death and mourning succinctly and clearly explain practices unfamiliar to most. The covering of mirrors, sitting on low stools, eating specific foods such as lentils and eggs—all these have deep and profound significance and a values orientation that makes them vehicles for teaching as well as observance.

The Jewish Home, therefore, is a most accessible volume for the adult reader, Jewish or not, who wishes to understand and appreciate Jewish holidays and life cycle events.

PART III

Jewish Philosophy and Theology

31 I and Thou

Martin Buber

Since its publication in German in 1923, *I and Thou* has become one of the seminal works of contemporary theology. It has not only pushed Judaic philosophy beyond its traditional bounds, it has had an even stronger influence on Christian theology, where Buber's "I-Thou" concepts have been adopted by such contemporary Protestant theologians as Paul Tillich.

Professor Buber's philosophy starts with the relationship between man and the world. He postulates two basic forms of relationships. "To man the world is twofold in accordance with his twofold attitude." These attitudes are identified by the terms "I-It" and "I-Thou." To Buber It and Thou are not two different things but two different kinds of relations between one subject— "I"—and the same object.

The I-It relationship is one in which I recognizes It as an object, especially of experience and use, while the I-Thou is when I responds with its whole being to Thou.

The I-It is the realm of objectivity, the realm of experience which Buber interprets as perceiving, thinking, and feeling. It includes all those activities of the I in which there is an object or thing. It is only through the I-It relation that objective knowledge is acquired and technical advances are made. This I-It relation is unilateral, the I initiates the relationship for its own purposes.

The I-Thou relationship, on the other hand, is characterized by mutuality, openness, directness, and presentness. It is a true dialogue in which both partners speak to one another as equals. In an I-Thou relationship, the focus is so open and intense that it fills the consciousness. Everything is incorporated into the Thou; Buber says, "All else lives in His light."

Buber's two sets of relationships correspond roughly to the

physical world and the spiritual world. He includes thinking and feeling in the physical world. His focus is on the individual's relation with the world. In Buber's system, the physical world and the spiritual world are not two different worlds but two different aspects of the world we all live in. The difference is in man's relation to all the items in this world. Buber claims that all the elements in the world, including the physical, have a spiritual aspect. His thesis is that this spiritual aspect is activated when man approaches it with complete openness and total focus. Like some of the romantic poets, he sees the whole world in a flower or in a grain of sand.

Buber moves from societal concerns into metaphysical areas. He begins by seeing love as the unique quality of the I-Thou relation. Love is the responsibility of an I for a Thou. Buber, who enjoyed a long, happy marriage, says that marriage is consummated by a couple's mutual revealing of the Thou to each other; only thereby do they participate in the Thou, which is the unifying ground in which mutual relations in all realms are possible.

He also claims that the I-Thou relation is the basic source of all art. A piece of music, for example, can be analyzed in terms of its notes, verses, bars, and on that level it is an I-It relation. If the same music is encountered in a living relation in which all the components are integrated and experienced as an inseparable unity, it becomes an I-Thou relation.

Each encountered Thou reveals the inner nature of all reality, and everything can be a Thou. Throughout life the I-Thou encounters continue, but they are not ordered; they are only a sign of the world order. All of the Thous encountered have a living center, and the extended lines of these relations meet in the eternal Thou. Man cannot be satisfied with a temporary I-Thou relation. His inborn Thou can only be consummated in a direct relationship with the Thou which cannot become an It, his term for God, the ultimate Thou.

Buber states that "in the relation with God unconditional exclusiveness and unconditional inclusiveness are one." This means neither giving up the world nor giving up the I but simply giving up a self-asserting instinct by regarding all in the love relation of the Thou. A life affirming this relation is characterized by action filled with meaning and joy.

Buber claims that this I-Thou love relation, lived and experienced in the present, is the real source of knowledge about God, rather than some theoretical codified dogma. Buber's book is actually a sharp attack on all talk about God and all pretensions to knowledge about God; he tries to save the religious dimension of life from the theologians. He says that the pervasive sin of religion is substituting the object for the relation, making the Temple of God into a God of the Temple, or making the scripture of God into a God of the scripture. He sees the God-man relation as one of a polarity, of being totally dependent on God and yet totally free. This leads him to conclude that we need God in order to exist, while God needs us for the very meaning of life.

Buber was strongly influenced by European philosophy, particularly by Søren Kierkegaard's thinking on absolute commitment, on truth as existential or lived truth, and on the centrality of the individual. He was also strongly influenced by his lifelong study of Hasidism, with its emphasis on joyous life in the real world, making everyday practical activities an act of worship, and on the warmth of community as a response to the loneliness and anxiety of the individual. In *I and Thou*, he combines the epistemology of the contemporary German philosophers with the metaphysical spirituality and pantheism of the Hasidim.

The Greeks visualized their gods and represented them in marble and in beautiful vase paintings. The Hebrews expressly forbade attempts to make God an object, either visual or concrete. Our God was not to be seen; He was to be heard. He was not an It but an I or a You.

The only God worth keeping is a God that cannot be kept. The only God worth talking about is a God that cannot be talked about. God is no object of discourse, knowledge, or even experience. He cannot be spoken of but he can be spoken to; he cannot be seen, but he can be listened to. The only possible relationship with God is to address Him and to be addressed by Him here and now, or, as Buber puts it, "in the present." For him the Hebrew name of God, YHVH, means "he is here" (*er ist da*). When "I" confront you, when I encounter "You," I encounter Him.

Some critics feel that Buber is an existentialist or a mystic and find little Jewish content in his writings. Others, however, see in his insistence on a direct relation to God and encountering God in everything in the real world a return to the clarity and directness of the Old Testament.

Buber's I-Thou concept is a romantic, ecstatic, mystical experience that opens one to understanding the sacred nature of the secular world. His most significant idea may well be that the sacred is here and now. It is a concept that has captured people's imagination and become a familiar part of the religious and philosophical dialogue. *I and Thou* is a book that is probably more talked about than read.

32 Man's Search for Meaning

Viktor E. Frankl

In the first part of Dr. Viktor E. Frankl's extraordinary book, *Man's Search for Meaning,* the author recounts his years at Auschwitz. His perspective is not only as a prisoner but also as a psychiatrist. Thus his story is told with both a compelling intimacy and a professional distance.

In the book's second part, Frankl explains logotherapy (*logos* denotes "meaning" in Greek), a form of therapy which involves choice and personal responsibility, which he developed out of his concentration camp experience. Because Frankl found meaning even in the intense suffering of a concentration camp, he believed that anyone, particularly those prone to despair during ordinary times, can discover meaning in their lives. Every individual will hopefully find personal meaning in life. We, individually, must ask what life demands of us, rather than what we want from life, and then answer by acting responsibly.

When Frankl wrote this book in nine straight days in 1945, he wanted to publish it anonymously, using only his number: 119,104. Friends persuaded him to allow his name to appear on the title page, and that is how it originally was printed. Written with intense honesty, the book struck a chord among people everywhere and became a bestseller. Recounting his firsthand experience in the camps with great intimacy, he showed us how he found meaning through tragedy.

Pain, which comes to everyone in life, is not without value. If we allow it, it can be a call for growth and transformation. This, then, is ultimately a book about hope, resounding with an optimism that even during ordinary, peaceful times is uplifting.

A familiar aspect of Holocaust literature emerges from Frankl's book. He recounts hellish experiences of Auschwitz, but also relates how he sought and found pleasure, not merely in spite of his surroundings, but precisely because of them.

To speak of happiness, no matter how minute, as an Auschwitz prisoner, is stunning. Frankl knew that regardless of any physical pain and degradation he was forced to endure, no one could rob him of his self-respect. Only he had the power to choose where to focus his thoughts. He drew strength through countering his physical pain by focusing on images which nourished his inner life.

The grotesque existence of Frankl's life at Auschwitz is overwhelming. He writes about how to ward off a Kapo's blow: when excrement splashed up into a prisoner's face while cleaning the latrines and sewage, he should appear indifferent, never expressing revulsion or attempting to wipe it off.

Another anecdote reflects on the horror while revealing Frankl's empathy. Sleep, no matter how brief, was a reprieve. One night he watched a fellow prisoner writhe in the midst of a nightmare. About to wake him, he realized it would be better for him to dream: no nightmare could be as frightening as the reality this man experienced when awake.

Meanwhile, amid the shock, the detached curiosity, the apathy, there was also grim humor. Prisoners, hairless and naked in the showers, tried to have fun—because, after all, they were actually washing with *water!* One feels the desperation that precedes such laughter and the release that it brings.

The harder external conditions became, the more one needed to look within. Thus one's spiritual life could be enriched in the camps. Prisoners who had a satisfying intellectual life beforehand were often able to survive better than those in robust health who lacked a stronger inner life. One feels this unequivocally about Frankl, who chose to hold on to hope because he understood that it was a prerequisite for the will to live. He saw men lose it, then die. He decided to be mentally strong. His first night at Auschwitz he promised himself he wouldn't commit suicide by running into the electrically charged barbed wire.

Later, he forced himself to get outside of his physical self by seeing how he could benefit from what he was enduring. He imagined the war over and that he was now speaking on a podium to an audience about his experience in the camps. In this image, he felt restored to dignity and validation.

Finding something positive to sustain him emotionally was

imperative. By blocking out certain images and focusing on positive ones, he was able to know pleasure in solitude, even for five minutes: sitting on a shaft leading to water pipes, staring at the blue hills of Bavaria, rather than the lice-ridden corpses nearby. One of his fondest memories is of nights when he roasted pilfered potatoes alone in front of a fire made with stolen charcoal.

The most poignant passages of the book have to do with Frankl's loving recall of his wife. Amid the constant pain, he pictured her and thus willed himself to live. "The salvation of man is through love and in love." He discovered that "love goes very far beyond the physical person of the beloved. It finds its deepest meaning in his spiritual being, his inner self. Whether or not he is still alive at all, ceases somehow to be of importance." Even a man with "nothing left in this world still may know bliss, be it only for a brief moment in the contemplation of his beloved."

Thinking he might die soon, Frankl forced a tearful friend to memorize his will. One wonders what a man who is without possessions has to leave, and discovers how rich a man he really was. "Listen, Otto, if I don't get back home to my wife, and if you should see her again, then tell her that I talked of her daily, hourly. You remember. Secondly, I have loved her more than anyone. Thirdly, the short time I have been married to her outweighs everything, even all we have gone through here."

In another section, Frankl explains that one can find kindness in any group of people. He tells of a prison guard who was so compassionate that he chose to spend his own money on medicine for sick prisoners. After the war, prisoners hid the guard in the Bavarian woods, telling an American commander that they would not disclose his whereabouts until the American swore that no harm would come to this SS commander. The promise was kept, and the SS commander wound up supervising a clothing collection from nearby villages for the newly freed prisoners.

Frankl has truly given the gift of himself to his readers.

33 When Living Hurts

Sol Gordon

The late 1960s and 1970s were turbulent times in America. The Vietnam War, Kennedy and King assassinations, drugs, and acid rock left the country divided, angry, confused and despairing. For the first time, an American president, Richard Nixon, resigned in disgrace. Conscientious objectors fled to Canada or went to jail rather than fight in what they considered to be an immoral war. Young soldiers whose love of country had led them to enlist for duty in Vietnam found themselves, upon their return, shunned as pariahs by many Americans. The world had turned upside down.

No group within our society was affected more drastically by the tenor of the 1960s and 1970s than teenagers and college students. Nothing was predictable. The events that shocked the general public traumatized and devastated young people. Imitating their older role models, they, too, turned to alcohol, drugs, and a nihilistic lifestyle that bespoke a sense of despair and hopelessness. And slowly, steadily, a one-time minor tragedy in America began to grow into a major societal crisis.

There was a time when the words *youth* and *suicide* were hardly ever mentioned in the same breath. In those instances when a young person took his or her life, it most often became a family secret, attributed to an accident and thereafter never discussed inside or outside the family.

By the late 1970s and 1980s however, America's dirty little secret exploded in the media. Young people were committing suicide in unprecedented numbers. The rate of youth suicide tripled in just three decades. Suicide became the second leading cause of death among those between fifteen and twenty-four years of age, and the toll was climbing.

America reacted in stunned disbelief. Radio, television, and film produced features dealing with youth suicide. But while the sensationalists had a field day with the event of suicide, a few serious psychiatrists and psychologists began to wrestle with the far more important question of how to identify potential victims, get them help, and save their lives.

Medical journals provided a forum through which practitioners might gain knowledge of suicide's pathology and treatment, but precious little material accessible to the average parent or teen appeared in bookstores or magazines.

Then, in 1985, a brief paperback volume entitled *When Living Hurts* was published by the Union of American Hebrew Congregations. Scarcely noticed because of its small publishing house, the book was destined to save hundreds, if not thousands, of lives.

Author Sol Gordon, a professor of psychology at Syracuse University, had spent decades reaching out to young people in pain. His highly successful volume *You* became a must read among teens during the 1960s. Now Dr. Gordon turned his attention to the issue of depression and suicide, in a book that has become a classic of the self-help genre.

Writing directly to young people and utilizing extensive Jewish sources, Gordon pulls no punches as he speaks in their language with a critical message. Between 600,000 and 800,000 young people attempt suicide each year, with between 6,000 and 8,000 completing the act. In *When Living Hurts,* however, Gordon urges activism and optimism. In lieu of adopting a morbid tone, Gordon instructs young people and adults on how to save lives.

He begins with the assertion that everyone, sometimes, feels depressed, sad, and lonely. Then Dr. Gordon teaches young people the warning signs of impending suicide attempts or actual suicide. Clearly, succinctly, he instructs his readers on what to do or not to do, how to get help, and how to see that those providing assistance follow through.

Knowing that the vast majority of those contemplating suicide do not want to die, Gordon lets the teen reader know that he may be the only person told of a friend's intention. Dr. Gordon gives teens permission to break vows of silence when life is at stake, understanding that a confidence betrayed in life-or-death circumstances may be the only lifeline for a peer.

This is a positive, upbeat, and hopeful book. It emphasizes

life, not death. The fact that there are now over one hundred thousand copies in print testifies to its immediacy as one answer to a major American problem.

Every Jewish parent, and every Jewish child age ten through adult, should read *When Living Hurts*. Frequently, a life will be saved as a direct result.

34 God in Search of Man

Abraham Joshua Heschel

God in Search of Man is a twentieth-century philosophy of man's relationship to God, a covenant of word, deed, and faith. Heschel approaches his philosophy as a Jewish theologian and mystic. This work is a continuation of, as well as a more practical approach to, Heschel's earlier work, *Man Is Not Alone*. While well entrenched in tradition and history, Heschel applies historical teachings to present-day existence and the daily demands it places upon us.

The author divides this work into three major sections, "God," "Revelation," and "Response," corresponding to the three pillars of Jewish tradition—God, Torah, and Israel. In the first section, through a biblical prism, Heschel defines how we may find God in our lives. He applies our relationship with God to modern occurrences. Heschel focuses on why we experience God, not the hows of our experiences. In order to understand Heschel's premise, we must first assume, as did the biblical prophets, that God is in our lives. Heschel then clearly defines our relationship with God as a two-way phenomenon: God is in search of man, and our faith in God is our response to God. Faith is the outcome of awe.

For Heschel, questions come from God, and we supply answers through our faith. Our faith yields powerful religious truths through moments of insight. Once we realize that what is meaningful for one must become meaningful for all, and what is good for one must become good for all, we grasp the oneness of God. For Heschel, religious trust and oneness constitute transcendence and our capacity to reach beyond ourselves. However, it is important to understand that our faith must involve more than our beliefs and sense of awe. It must then be made manifest in what we do with this feeling—how we live our lives.

Heschel affirms that a sense of wonder or "radical amazement" is basic to being a religious person. Although both science and history may provide explanations for most occurrences, it is with wonder that a religious person must evaluate personal existence. The realization that all that is has an order and purpose leads us in turn to an awareness that God as a creator must be the reason. Heschel attaches a great deal of significance to maintaining our sense of wonder but fears that our sense of wonder may become lost as technology proliferates and logic predominates our thought. According to the author, Jewish worship and prayer are two means of keeping our sense of wonder alive.

In the section "Revelation," Heschel maintains that God never addresses the community. Rather, God seeks out single souls that display a constant quest for God as vehicles for expression of the divine will. The prophets were such sensitive souls, voices of God reaching out to humanity. Judaism is a partnership of Torah and God, a written instrument of God's revelation. The Bible articulates in detail what God demands of us, but we must make choices. There is an impulse in each of us for evil as well as good. Through our love for, and awe of, God, we receive the assistance that we need to overcome our evil inclination. In his view, the prophets were men who understood this, who could embrace man and God at the same time. Their message shows us that whatever we do to people, we are also doing to God.

Heschel applies the message of the prophets to all of history, and believes that their message is still valid today, as an example of how we should live. Accordingly, we must be involved in social justice and show compassion for all people. We are created in God's image, and, as such, we are a constant reminder of the presence of God, for good or for ill. Our essential holiness imposes a critical burden upon each of us, and thereby a responsibility to bring new meaning and understanding of God to every generation as descendants of the prophets and vehicles of revelatory insights.

The third section, "Response," outlines specific actions that we must take in our lives. It is through our deeds that we can give meaning to our existence and our faith. As partners with God, we perform these deeds—God's mitzvot—and thus confirm that we are not alone. In building our lives, we must do so as if they are works of art, worthy of concentration—*kavvanah*. To live with kavvanah implies an awareness of and an attentiveness to what we do. We approach the mitzvot with kavvanah, but we must also approach God with kavvanah. As we act, we begin to feel a sense of the transcendent, rooted in religion, a structure within, from which we can create the sacred.

We are free to choose our own life path. If we develop our sense of awe and wonder, if we embody prophetic ideals in our daily lives, if we act as if we are partners with God, intent upon becoming models of God's will for humanity, we Jews then succeed in answering God, the God who is constantly in search of us.

35 To Life!

Harold S. Kushner

Harold Kushner's *To Life! A Celebration of Jewish Being and Thinking,* published in 1993, is a wonderful informative book for any person wishing to learn more about Judaism. Rabbi Kushner writes about the Jewish people and the religion's laws and traditions in an easy, understandable way, punctuating his text with occasional jokes.

Covering the spectrum of Judaism, he includes chapters on "What We Believe About God," "Why We Love Israel," and "Why Some People Hate Us." He also explains how Judaism differs from other religions and why being Jewish is important, taking readers through the Jewish holiday and life cycle events from births to funerals. Our religion emphasizes the importance of celebrating life's events more than other religions "perhaps because we invest more of our belief in this world and rely less on a World to Come."

In a chapter entitled "The Stories We Tell About Ourselves" he explains what it means to be the chosen people: how God instructed Moses to give the Israelites the Torah at Mt. Sinai, the "forming of a Covenant" (a contract) where "God and Man have obligations to each other. We owe God something, the obligation to discern and choose the good, in exchange for God giving us life, health, food to eat, and people to love us." He also writes, "What does God get out of the agreement? He gets the one thing He cannot do for the world Himself, the phenomenon of people freely choosing to be good."

God promised us that if we obey His laws we would feel His presence in our lives, and we would be given a land of our own. That's why it's important, as Jews, that we live up to God's expectations. We need to perform mitzvot because "you are supposed to do it as a Jew."

Kushner defines a good Jew "as someone who is constantly striving to become a better Jew." In the chapter entitled "The Sacred Deed—Making the Ordinary Extraordinary," the reader is shown how being a Jew means experiencing life in the fullest sense by turning every event, no matter how ordinary, into something holy, a time when we can feel the presence of God in our lives. "You can be religious in the way you treat food, money, sex, not only the way you treat the Bible."

He encourages non-religious Jews to lead a more meaningful Jewish life by following Jewish traditions meant to elevate the ordinary into the holy. Jews can begin by starting each day with prayer, observing Shabbat, and avoiding gossip. Every time we acknowledge the sanctity of our daily lives, we are affirming God.

Jews also need to become members of a synagogue and a community because "holiness is found in joining with other people, not in fleeing your imperfect neighbors to be alone with God." Reading Jewish literature and looking for Jewish role models in biographies are important as well.

Although Judaism means being part of a people, a whole community, it is a community in which individuals can disagree about the interpretation of what one prayer means (such as the mourner's prayer, the Kaddish), but still say the prayer together.

And because Judaism is about life, Judaism sees death as a tragedy. It is a tremendous loss to have someone we love taken from us. If the deceased was a kind person, then that person enriched the world in a godly way, so a little bit of God has left the world.

We don't know what happens after we die (since no one has come back to report it), but we do know about the here and now. Judaism acknowledges the need to experience grief, and has supplied us with a way for getting through it. That is why we say Kaddish with other mourners (so as not to feel alone), and why we do nothing but focus on our grief after a loved one has died. This is why, too, the bereaved are served food when sitting shivah; their souls are empty, and the community needs to nourish them.

Immortality is achieved through our living on in the hearts of others, by our words and deeds, and in the ways our actions have enriched the world. Thus Judaism believes in the power of the individual and the ripple effect and is more concerned about doing than feeling. It's all right to have negative feelings; it's not acceptable to act on them.

When we have chosen a life based on goodness, which is what God wants for us, we will have improved the world. As Jews, "we teach the world lessons about the value of education, the importance of family and community, the obligation of tzedakah, the nobility and resilience of the survivor of persecution, and the potential holiness of the most ordinary of moments."

Kushner writes of Jewish optimism, our ability to endure and thrive despite our drastic history of oppression. He also puts that oppression into context: for most of Jewish history Jews have been free, and our experience with slavery has helped us become an empathetic people who seek justice. Judaism is not about living in the past, but about the here and now, while acknowledging history and respecting its lessons.

36 When Bad Things Happen to Good People

Harold S. Kushner

Why do the good suffer? Why do the evil prosper? This classic dilemma captures the question of theodicy, of God's justice. From the beginning of time, men and women have sought an answer to this question. If God is all-powerful, goes the logic, how is it conceivable that decent, blameless people live in poverty, die of terrible illnesses, and endure persecution and oppression?

By the same token, how could an all-powerful God who "cares about people" allow vicious, evil tyrants to rule countries, accumulate untold wealth, execute enemies, and live to a ripe old age?

Rabbi Harold Kushner's book *When Bad Things Happen to Good People,* published in 1983, seeks a response to the question of theodicy. That, however, was not the intent of Rabbi Kushner's fine work.

The author never claims knowledge of *why* bad things happen to good people. His sole goal, rather, is to guide us in extending love and care to men and women who have suffered cruel disappointment and tragedy in life.

Kushner explains that the motivation for the book was the tragic death of his fourteen-year-old son Aaron. At the age of eight months, Aaron was diagnosed with a rare disease called progeria, "rapid aging." Rabbi Kushner and his wife, therefore, lived with the inevitability of the early loss of a child for over a decade. In a very real sense, then, the book is not an intellectualized treatment of theodicy, but a profoundly personal attempt to come to terms with the sometimes brutal and tragic events of life.

Kushner begins with an overview of ways in which Jewish tradition has dealt with misfortune.

The Hebrew Bible is in large measure given to linking personal tragedy with some imputed sin or misconduct. If we suffer, then we must have violated the commandments. Try telling that to grieving parents who have lost a week-old child or to families of survivors of the Holocaust.

Equally difficult is the notion that unmerited suffering is part of "God's greater purpose," which we endure for some ostensibly enabling reason. How hollow that must sound to a terminal cancer patient or a quadriplegic patient confined to a wheelchair for life.

Rabbi Kushner proceeds with a detailed examination of the biblical book of Job, whose essential message is that we humans cannot possibly fathom the tragedies of life. We did not create the universe. We did not fashion the world. The author affirms that only God the Creator knows why things happen as they do. Therefore, any challenge to God's justice is presumptuous, even arrogant.

The fact is that those in pain will feel anger, hurt, and resentment, regardless of any rationale. The question of why bad things happen to good people, then, is unanswerable.

Kushner assumes that in the face of tragedy, our response to it takes on paramount importance. Perhaps, implies Kushner, Hitler could have been stopped if the citizens of Germany had rejected him and his followers at the ballot box and in the streets. We often lose sight of the fact that every act of Hitler was instituted within the electoral mandate extended to him by German voters.

A second notion offered by Kushner is that we must not hurt ourselves a second time after having been battered and bruised by life. Turning anger and guilt inward often compounds the impact of tragedy. A mother blames herself for her child's suicide. A son blames himself for a father's death after an argument between them. Grief is normal, natural, understandable. Overwhelming guilt serves no purpose.

Rabbi Kushner suggests that prayer is one possible productive response to tragedy. Even though it may not change or reverse reality, it can serve to give us the strength we need to carry on with the tasks of life.

Above all, Rabbi Kushner urges us to reach out and embrace others who need us in their time of travail. There can be few more comforting words to a cancer patient than those articulated by a cancer survivor. The wordless embrace of a parent who has already lost a child often means more to parents whose loss is more recent than the well wishes of caring friends.

When bad things happen to good people, each of us is a potential healer, a representative of the best in the divine image that none of us can fully comprehend. In spite of our inability to explain the why of suffering, we can ease it, and thus help to heal the gaping wounds of loss that, without our sensitivity, might destroy those who endure its pain.

37 Peace of Mind

Joshua Loth Liebman

One of the most famous stories in all of Scripture describes a wrestling match between the patriarch Jacob and an angel. They struggle all night until dawn, with Jacob releasing this messenger of God after he, Jacob, is given a new name—Israel—and a blessing.

This beautiful tale expresses a rather profound idea. There is constant struggle going on in human experience, a struggle between that which is earthbound, mortal, emotional, and that which is super-mortal, ascending into the spiritual and intellectual realm. The conflict between emotion and intellect was never more evident than in the historical struggle between traditional faith and philosophy. In the Greek world, the philosophers were the first to doubt the existence of the traditional gods. Religion confronted philosophy in disputation through the Middle Ages. Then the Jewish, Christian, and Muslim scholastics finally achieved peace between the two constructs by laying the groundwork for a philosophy of religion, namely, theology.

In a similar manner, religion and astronomical science wrestled, and debated their assumptions to the present day. Religion and physics attempted each in its own way to explain the origin of the universe. Religion and biology fought over the origin of life, whether it was the product of creationism or evolution. And during the last generation, religion was challenged again, this time by the sciences of psychology and psychiatry.

In the midst of the initial skirmishes, in 1946, Rabbi Joshua Loth Liebman wrote *Peace of Mind,* a book portraying the struggle between psychiatry and religion. The fact that a rabbi possessed the requisite knowledge to write a book such as this is remarkable in and of itself, but also reflects a reality in Jewish life during that era. Through the 1940s and even into the 1950s, the rabbi was often the most highly educated person in the congregation, possessed of significant general knowledge, and frequently held a doctoral degree. Therefore, the rabbi could speak on many subjects: literature, political science, or psychology, with authority. Today, all that has changed. A rabbi speaking on any secular subject will almost certainly do so in the presence of an expert in that field. Thus, rabbis today speak less and less about these realms than they did in days past.

Joshua Loth Liebman was a rare combination of a rabbi, an expert in philosophy, and a gifted public speaker. He could easily have written an esoteric volume, accessible only to scholars. Instead, he crafted a bestseller for the average reader and won their hearts in the process.

Liebman begins by justifying a book on psychiatry. At the time, many considered the field irrelevant. After all, millions were starving and trying to recover from the war's devastation. How could a book on inner peace help them? Liebman responds that inner turmoil is common to every society regardless of its ideology or affluence. He states what was then a revolutionary idea, but what for us is a truism: a healthier world will be built by emotionally healthier people.

Peace of Mind was clearly written for an American readership, a secure postwar United States where food and shelter were almost universally available, a society which had the luxury of neuroses. With his clear and almost poetic style, Rabbi Liebman urges the reader to "be yourself" and "like the person you are." Had he published this book today, he would have been a smash hit on the television talk-show circuit, selling videotapes and audio books by the hundreds of thousands. Sadly, Liebman eventually was himself plagued by the psychological demons he sought to defuse for others and suffered severe depression.

Will this book give the reader peace of mind? No person can give another inner peace. The Israeli Nobel Laureate in literature, S. Y. Agnon, wrote a story which makes this point.

In the story, a totally righteous man is visited by a group of angels at the behest of God. They tell him that God has decided that his goodness must be rewarded, and that he may have anything he requests. The man thinks long and hard, pondering all the material treasures that are his for the asking. Finally, however, he tells the angels that, while he is honored by God's offer, there is nothing he truly needs or wants.

The angels are aghast, and look at one another in amazement. No one has ever refused to accept such a gift from God. They tell the man as much, and demand that he ask for something, anything, from the Creator. Thus admonished, the man again ponders the opportunity, then finally responds: "There is nothing of a material nature that I need to want. But please tell God that I would very much appreciate a little peace of mind."

The angels, relieved, depart to convey the righteous man's answer to God. After what seems only a few moments, a voice thunders in the stillness. It is the voice of God. "In six days I created the heavens and the earth. And on the seventh day I rested. But I did not create peace of mind!"

As the righteous man stands in silence before the presence of God, he realizes the import of the message. Since God did not create peace of mind, it is not God's to give. Even God cannot give us inner peace. That is a gift which each of us must find for ourselves.

The legacy of Rabbi Joshua Loth Liebman lives on today. The myriad of self-help experts who proclaim that they have the answer to serenity still echo the insights raised by this brilliant teacher half a century ago. In spite of their best efforts, none have exceeded the profundity of Liebman's simple message: "Be yourself." "Like yourself." Those two goals, combined with faith in God, are still our best chance to attain true peace of mind.

38 J.B.

Archibald MacLeish

The Bible has engendered the creation of a vast body of literature. That is one of its greatest qualities. Hundreds of thousands of books, maybe half of the books in the Western world, were written under the inspiration of the thoughts originally expressed in Scripture. At times when the mood of humanity was striving toward ethical idealism, it was the prophets who inspired. In days of human tragedy and despair, it was the great philosophic book of Job, in the Bible, which often inspired new writings, plays and novels.

Archibald MacLeish based the play *J.B.* on the book of Job. The biblical book of Job has a narrative prologue, the bulk of it philosophic debate, and an epilogue that is also narrative. The narrative prologue takes place on earth and in heaven. On earth there is the righteous Job, a good man—happy, healthy, righteous, confident of his nearness to God.

In heaven there is a debate between God and Satan. Satan says: "I have just been walking through the earth." God says, "Did you see my servant, Job? How righteous and how good he is." To which Satan sneers, "Yes, he is good. He is good because you have made him happy. Take away his happiness and you will see on what a shaky foundation his faith in you is based." So God says, "Very well, test him."

Satan comes down to earth and orchestrates undeserved misfortunes which heap themselves on Job. His children are killed; his wealth is taken away. He and his wife quarrel. She tells him to curse God and die, but he will not, and thus ends the narrative prologue.

Then Job's three friends come and argue with him. His friends are concerned with preserving the doctrine that God is just. If

God is just, why did Job, who is a righteous man, suffer? That is the heart of the philosophic center of the book, the debate between the three friends and Job. They insist that since God is just, Job must be a sinner, whether he knows it or not, or else God would not punish him. Job says: "I do not know why God punishes me, and I do not claim that I am all-righteous, but I am not aware of any sin in me, and in order to justify God, I will not belie my own character. But I trust in Him. Yea, though He slay me, yet will I trust Him. But I will speak my word in His presence." Then God appears from the whirlwind, and eventually Job is restored to happiness.

This is the theme upon which MacLeish bases his remarkable play. Instead of heaven and earth, he has a huge old circus tent. It is empty. The people have all gone. Only two old, broken-down vendors are left, one a balloon vendor, the other a popcorn vendor. Both were once famous actors, but now this is the way they earn their living. At the end of this huge tent, there is a high platform, a stage. The two old actors, carrying their wares, stumble toward the ladder and climb up on the stage, and they say, "Let us do some acting; nobody is here to see us." When the actor called Zuss and the other actor called Nickles debate what they should play, one says: "Let us play the old drama of Job." The other one says, "Job suffers undeservedly; millions who happen to be in the wrong city at the wrong time, or happen to belong to the wrong people, or who happen to have the wrong colored skin. They are playing Job, the man who suffers unjustly." And they finally say, "Oh well, it is a universal subject. Let us debate it."

So Zuss puts on his mask, Nickles puts on his mask, and they start talking, the voice of God through Zuss, and the voice of Satan through Nickles, and we understand the names now. Zuss is reminiscent of the Greek word for God, and Nickles is old Nick, Satan.

In the main body of the tent there appears the life of J.B. (meaning Job, of course), an American businessman on Thanksgiving Day, with a happy family of sons and daughters, a loving wife, and prosperity. Then the children are killed in various brutal ways, and finally the atomic bomb (it is not clearly stated) comes, and the world is devastated. J.B. says, "Maybe we did something wrong," and his wife says, "I will not have you slander yourself and your children. Whatever reasons God has puzzles me, but do not say that you are not innocent." She leaves him in anger.

Three friends come to console him, and they are all in tatters. One represents the old church, a second represents psychoanalysis, while the third represents communism, three movements in the modern world. The old churchman says, "Of course you sinned. You have in you the sin of Adam, the old original sin of Man. Every human being deserves punishment." The psychoanalyst says, "Sin is foolish to talk about. It is simply your subconscious. Your subconscious leaves you through the old complexus to do whatever you do." The communist says to him, "It is all the history of society and you have come to the stage in the history of society where you have to suffer."

These sorry comforters leave him. At the end of the play, his wife comes back to him from the midst of the ruins. She holds in her hand a flowering sprig of forsythia, the first to bloom in the spring, and she says, "Look, J.B., out of a dead world nature is trying to be reborn," and he says, "Yes, somehow life will come again out of the ashes; so let us stay together, blow thou on the ashes of my heart, and in the glow of that we will live."

MacLeish's ultimate message is that in the tragedy of the modern world love still exists. The world is full of families, husbands, wives, children, and the great reservoir of human love that exists in the world consoles us for its sorrows and keeps us from absolute despair. That may not be the meaning of the biblical book of Job, but that is the meaning of MacLeish's play, and what he means to say on the basis of the book of Job to the modern heart.

MacLeish has combined the book of Job with the end of the Song of Songs. The Song of Songs concludes with these words: "Many waters cannot quench love." MacLeish teaches that the many sorrows of the world will not destroy the reservoir of human love that keeps us from desperation. That is the theme of *J.B.*

39 The Nine Questions People Ask About Judaism

Dennis Prager and Joseph Telushkin

In 1975, *Eight Questions People Ask About Judaism* was published and became an overnight bestseller in the Jewish community. The authors were two young men, once high school friends, then just twenty-seven years of age, who worked together on this, their first literary endeavor. Joseph Telushkin, a rabbi, went on to write a number of books on Jewish literacy and other scholarly topics. Dennis Prager, known as an incisive thinker, world traveler, and expert in five languages, became a radio talk-show host and then a television celebrity, taking on the major issues of the day in every area of society: politics, ethics, and religion, to name just a few. Though both authors have gone their separate ways professionally, the staying power of this collaborative effort was so compelling that an expanded version was issued in 1981, with an additional question and enriched content.

The book's preface explains how the book came into being, with each author offering personal perspectives on their Jewish rootedness. Prager affirms that he traveled the world, seeking a way of life—religious or secular—which had the capacity "to unlock whatever goodness lies in human beings." He was obsessed by issues of good and evil, aghast at the cruelty so apparent among people and nations. In a sense, he left his Judaism, and only after a search through some sixty countries, returned to Judaism, convinced that his quest was concluded. Joseph Telushkin, on the other hand, never strayed from Judaism. Beginning at the age of six, he was steeped in Jewish observance and scholarship, ultimately attending Yeshiva University. While he shared many of his friend's concerns, he always sought the answers within Judaism.

The nine questions posed by the authors have the ring of external queries. These are issues that Jews have debated for centuries. Therefore, the questions are the same, but the responses reflect the twentieth-century perspective of two young intellectuals.

The first question, "Can One Doubt God's Existence and Still Be a Good Jew?" receives extensive and sensitive treatment. The authors state that the question of whether or not God exists is life's most crucial question.

But there is no way, infallibly, to prove or disprove God's existence. Our Jewish ancestors wisely understood this fact, and therefore never made belief in God a criterion for being considered a good Jew. Judaism has always stressed action more than faith. Those who lived in accordance with Jewish law were considered good even if they doubted God's existence. The assumption was that faith would develop as observance increased. The authors conclude that the most productive course in life is to live as if God did exist.

Another intriguing chapter asks "How Does Judaism Differ from Christianity, Marxism, and Humanism?" Each of these three movements, the authors point out, was founded by a Jew. Each is derivative of Judaism. How shall we understand the fundamental break that each made with Judaism that renders it incompatible with a Jewish perspective?

One example will suffice. Christianity, for example, essentially did away with the fundamental Jewish emphasis on action as opposed to faith. Indeed, it reversed their primacy altogether. Furthermore, three major dogmas of Christianity are totally antithetical to Judaism. Judaism does not accept the Christian notion of original sin, a taint with which every person is supposedly born. Judaism holds that each of us is born unblemished, with free will, and with both a good and an evil inclination. Both inclinations are essential in life. The goal is to keep them in balance. Nor does Judaism accept the Christian concept of a Second Coming. Jews never considered Jesus the Messiah, and thus a Second Coming is an untenable concept.

Finally, Judaism rejects the Christian principle that Jesus died for our sins. This is totally foreign to Judaism, inasmuch as Jews have ample opportunity to atone for sins personally without any intermediary. For these and a host of other reasons treated by the authors, the differences between Judaism and Christianity are irreconcilable. They are two distinct religions.

Prager and Telushkin devote an entire chapter to answering the question: "Why Shouldn't I Intermarry—Doesn't Judaism Believe in Universal Brotherhood?" The authors recognize that their response to this question must address both the reader's emotion and intellect, but they confront the issue head-on. In good Jewish fashion, they first answer the question with another question: "Do you care if the Jewish people and its distinctive values survive?" If the reader's answer is yes, then it follows that the person he or she wishes to marry will share those same values. If the person is Jewish, wonderful. If the person is not Jewish, say the authors, he or she should convert. They then go on to urge that neither a Jew nor a non-Jew who does not share a commitment to the Jewish future should be the spouse of one who does hold these feelings dear.

What if you are an uncommitted Jew? Then, the authors urge, begin to study and live Judaism now. Do not marry someone out of the faith just because you do not currently cherish Jewish tradition. Just to cite one example: Theodore Herzl was an assimilated Jew whose experience with anti-Semitism led him to become the founder of Zionism! Change is possible. Act accordingly.

This chapter has obviously evoked a great deal of discussion among those who are more tolerant of intermarriage. There is a great value, however, in studying this treatment of the issue, since it does not partake of the extremist rhetoric of some segments of the Jewish community.

The last section of the book suggests a number of ways in which an individual seeking to reclaim Judaism or to begin a Jewish life might do so. Observing Shabbat, involvement with Israel, adopting certain rituals, practicing tzedakah, and refraining from gossip and slander are all mentioned as points of entry to Jewish living, ethics, and values. After urging readers to send children to a Jewish day school, they append a basic bibliography for study of Judaism by adults.

40 What Happens After I Die?

Rifat Sonsino and Daniel B. Syme

A writer once observed that our fear of death is the greatest tribute we pay to life. Death is the great unknown. Indeed, Sartre's existentialist philosophy is predicated upon the inescapable reality of death. As human beings we strive to be immortal, yet are confronted by our mortality. The anguish caused by that unavoidable clash of will and reality leads to great pain, which Sartre called the existential dilemma.

What Happens After I Die? presents a spectrum of ways in which great Jewish thinkers, ancient and modern, have spoken of what lies beyond. Beginning with the Torah and concluding with the personal statements of the authors, the reader engages virtually every notion of life after death that has gained currency over thousands of years of Jewish history.

An interesting aspect of the book consists of a clear demonstration that a belief in life after death emerges far earlier in Judaism than commonly assumed.

The book begins with an examination of the biblical notion, which has elements of a negation of belief in life after death, reflecting sentiments echoed in the mythology of surrounding cultures. The Gilgamesh epic in particular is contrasted with the Eden story. In both instances a serpent plays a key role in robbing humanity of an afterlife.

But there is no denying the human impulse to immortality, and the Torah reflects the striving for the infinite, again echoing similar development in proximate cultures. As we know, the Egyptians practiced mummification, believing that after death life went on, including eating and drinking with loved ones. The Babylonians, on the other hand, believed in a realm of the dead, ruled by its own king and queen.

111

The Israelites spoke of a place called Sheol, a place of quiet and silence, to which all people descended after death. This was not a heaven or hell, but rather a neutral place of repose. No one knows what the word *Sheol* means, but it is clear that it was initially conceptualized as a place beneath the earth, from which the dead did not emerge.

As Sonsino and Syme point out, the evolution of the notion of an afterlife continued, with stories of Enoch and Elijah being taken by God in mysterious ways, and with legends of the prophet Elisha actually reviving the dead. The Torah prohibits necromancy, the consulting of the dead to foretell the future, which means that the practice must have been widespread.

How do you consult with the dead if they remain in Sheol? The story of King Saul and the witch of Endor demonstrates the shattering of former absolutes, as the prophet Samuel actually emerges from Sheol to speak to the king as he goes into battle.

From this moment on, we see the slow, but steady and inevitable progression toward a belief in physical resurrection. After all, if human beings could raise the dead, surely God could do so as well. Thus begins an examination of texts suggesting or proclaiming an afterlife in the books of Ezekiel and Daniel, long before the rise of Christianity, which borrowed these notions from Judaism.

In succeeding chapters in *What Happens After I Die?* the reader is exposed to the full blossoming of belief in physical resurrection as a Jewish dogma within the society of that era. The text explains the vision of a world to come and the concept of a messiah, portrayed as a flesh-and-blood descendant of King David, who would reign over a restored monarchy.

The authors emphasize that Judaism envisions no hell, but rather speaks of a netherworld where souls are purified for a period of up to twelve months before returning to God.

Among the other classic thinkers whose views of life after death are treated are Maimonides, Baruch Spinoza, Moses Mendelssohn, and Mordecai Kaplan.

In a startling chapter on Jewish mysticism, the authors demonstrate that Judaism contains a profound commitment to the possibility of reincarnation, about which few Jews are even partially aware.

The balance of this important treatment of a difficult subject concludes with a series of first-person reflections on the afterlife by modern Jewish thinkers, including Rabbi Alexander Schindler, Blu Greenberg, Rabbi Harold Schulweis, Dr. Eugene Borowitz, Arlene Agus, and Dr. Alvin Reines. Each of these scholars offers a personal sense of what life after death might entail. Drawn from Orthodox, Conservative, and Reform perspectives, these chapters depict every aspect of Jewish spirituality. But the search for the answer to our mortality continues.

41 9½ Mystics

Herbert Weiner

The search for mystical experience has become quite popular in modern times. In the past, those seeking the transcendent, out-of-body experiences, or an ascent to a higher plane, were often dismissed as antisocial or unbalanced. All that has changed. It was, perhaps, the Vietnam War that triggered the flight from the real world that characterizes a mystical era. Drugs were one manifestation of that rush to escape, as was the acid-rock music of nihilism.

Others, however, chose the path of mystical study and practice. The Beatles became disciples of the Maharishi, whose followers then brought transcendental meditation to America. Countless groups arose, some genuine manifestations of religion, others destructive cults, almost inevitably centered on a guru whose wisdom and otherworldly insight could show them "the way."

Many Jews joined ashrams and communes, chanted and meditated, totally oblivious to the rich mystical literature within their own Jewish tradition. This ignorance was not really their fault, for the kabbalah, the mystical literature of Judaism, remained essentially hidden from them. Those few who did write about it did so in esoteric language, far removed from the understanding of the average Jew.

In 1969, however, Herbert Weiner, a Reform rabbi and author, wrote *9½ Mystics*, a clear and concise introduction to the life and teachings of mystical Jewish masters. Confessing that he had deliberately moved away from pure scholarship to a more popular style, Weiner shattered a barrier that had long separated Jews from their mystical heritage.

In a lengthy introduction, Weiner defines kabbalah, the great body of Jewish mystical writings, as "that which is received";

profound insight; an awareness of mystery and legacy from past generations of teachers. He warns the reader that to enter the realm of kabbalah is to surrender all expectation of logic and rational discourse. The student of mysticism is destined to confront chaos, disorientation, and fundamental challenges to cherished beliefs. Perhaps that is why Jewish tradition holds that one must not study the kabbalah until the age of forty, and then only with a trained teacher present, lest he risk total madness.

Weiner begins his journey by introducing the reader to a seventy-five-year-old mystic named "Mr. Setzer," who lived in lower Manhattan. Setzer became his teacher, acquainting him first with the ten spheres—*sefirot*—of the universe, and then with increasingly complex ideas of the kabbalah. The two became close, but the old Setzer, who believed that he should be world-famous, slowly saw his health deteriorate, and journeyed to Israel shortly before his death.

Weiner next writes of the great mystical scholar Gershom Scholem, the spiritual father of most contemporary teachers of Jewish mysticism. Weiner briefly reviews some of Scholem's writings: his speculation as to the author of the Zohar, the central book of Jewish mysticism, as well as his systematic analysis of the intricate philosophical system of the sixteenth-century Isaac Luria.

Like Scholem, Weiner also seems fascinated with the story of the false Messiah, Shabbetai Tzvi. Born in Ismir, Turkey, he studied the kabbalah as a young man. Afflicted with manic depression, he came to what is now Israel to seek help from a man known as Nathan of Gaza. Nathan convinced him that he was indeed the Messiah destined to save the world. Astonishingly, as the rumor of Shabbetai Tzvi's exalted status spread, normally sensible people around the world began to sell their possessions and prepare to travel to Jerusalem for the momentous event.

But not everyone was pleased with this fantastic tale, especially the Sultan of Turkey. Summoning Shabbetai Tzvi, he presented him with an ultimatum: convert to Islam on the spot or lose his head. Tzvi converted, then was imprisoned for fifteen years. In spite of this bizarre act, Shabbetai Tzvi's reputation as the Messiah was preserved by Nathan of Gaza and his followers. Some Jews even converted to Islam to emulate his example. By the early eighteenth century, a power-mad genius named Jacob Frank built on the Shabbetai Tzvi legend, to convince followers to

convert to Catholicism, violate the laws of the Torah, and engage
in sexual orgies. Needless to say, Shabbetai Tzvi did not prove to
be the Messiah, and Jacob Frank and his movement faded into
obscurity.

After moving through a number of Gershom Scholem's teachings, Weiner continues the tale of his personal odyssey by
introducing several mystical teachers, a few of whom attained
international prominence some twenty-five years after the book's
publication: Zalman Schachter, an Orthodox rabbi who published a how-to volume for constructing an interior life based
upon mystical techniques, drawing heavily on Indian mysticism;
and Rabbi Adin Steinsaltz, then a twenty-six-year-old scholar,
already recognized as a genius by his teachers and peers, who
today is in the midst of translating the entire Talmud with his
personal commentary.

In another chapter, Weiner delves into Hasidism, a movement
founded by the Baal Shem Tov, which today has in many ways
become the mysticism of the masses, due in no small measure to
the writings of Martin Buber. The author moves from Buber to
the Lubavitcher movement—Chabad—then headed by the late
Rabbi Menachem Mendel Schneerson, whose representatives can
be found in virtually every Jewish community of the world.

Rabbi Schneerson was a direct descendant in the seventh
generation of Schneur Zalman, the founder of this Hasidic
dynasty. A one-time engineering student at the Sorbonne, he
spoke a dozen languages, and was considered a miracle worker by
many of his followers. Indeed, upon his death, many
Lubavitchers openly declared that he was the Messiah. Through
Weiner's accounts of his two private meetings with the Rabbi, the
reader enters a world of absolute certainty that the Torah and
mitzvot are direct commandments from God, a world in which
virtually every critical life decision may be presented to the
Rebbe for adjudication, a world of joy and celebration of the
mysteries of the universe.

Subsequent chapters outline the life and teachings of such
great mystical figures as Rabbi Nachman of Bratslav, Reb Arele
Roth, Rabbi Abraham Chen, and Rabbi Abraham Isaac Kook.
The beginning student of Jewish mysticism will find much to
ponder in Herbert Weiner's book.

PART IV

Jewish History and Anti-Semitism

42 The Apostle

Sholem Asch

Before Isaac Bashevis Singer attained world fame as a Yiddish writer and Nobel Laureate, Sholem Asch put Yiddish literature in the forefront of the public's attention. The great writer Thomas Mann discovered Asch before the days of Hitler and sponsored him.

In the midst of World War II, while millions of Jews were being slaughtered, while Hitler still had a chance to win the war, Asch wrote *The Apostle*. A product of Eastern Europe, Asch witnessed human degradation unprecedented in the history of humanity. He might well have conceived works which bespoke despair and total disillusionment. Instead, he chose to write a novel about one man who also lived in a brutal world but throughout his lifetime sought to bring hope and faith to a pagan society.

The hero of *The Apostle* is the apostle Paul, a Christian, who lived in Roman times, yet is remembered today as one of the most brilliant architects of spirituality in religious history. He, too, filled the world with propaganda, but the propaganda of goodness and ethics rather than the propaganda of evil and hate.

Anyone familiar with Christianity knows the story of Paul's life. Born Saul of Tarsus, he experienced a theophany, a revelation of Jesus. Changing his name to Paul, he then spent the rest of his days spreading the gospel in the Roman world. Asch recreates Paul's journey and his first contact with the pagan world, especially his bewilderment at their lack of gentleness and kindness.

He tells the story of the young Titus, in whom Paul had tried to inculcate the teachings of Judaism. One night they are eating in a tavern, while a group of students are enjoying a sumptuous meal at another table. A poor beggar enters the tavern, approaches the students, states that he, too, is a student of philosophy, and asks for a little food. Instead of feeding this tired and hungry man, the students mock him. They make fun of his plight, using philosophical banter to taunt him. One of the students says: "I am surprised at you, a philosopher, asking for such a thing. Do you not know that it is highly debatable whether it is preferable to live or die? If I give you food, your life will be prolonged. Is that such a good idea?" Another student continues the verbal barrage: "It would be illogical to give him good food in the light of his philosophy."

The beggar, embarrassed and shamed, starts to leave, but Titus, on an impulse, gives him some food. Paul, surprised, asks him why he did so, to which Titus responds: "I do not know. I just could not stand his misery." Through witnessing this gesture, Paul understands that his tutelage of Titus has borne fruit, that compassion and caring have begun to manifest themselves in a formerly cold and uncaring person.

As Paul travels through the pagan world, gathering companions and disciples, Asch also provides magnificent descriptions of the great cities of Alexandria and Rome. Eventually, Paul returns to Jerusalem, where he quarrels with two of the other disciples of Jesus, Peter and James. In the embryonic days of Christianity, when virtually all of its adherents were Jews, a philosophical battle raged as to the expectations of new members of this fellowship. Peter and James insisted that all new converts had to follow the mitzvot, the Torah's commandments. Paul, on the other hand, believed that practicing mercy and righteousness were sufficient, that ritual observance was not critical.

Scholars have reflected on how the world would have changed had Peter and James won out, how Hebrew might have become the language of the western world and Judaism one of the world's largest religious groups. But the result of this controversy was a compromise. Peter and James taught their approach, primarily in Jerusalem, while Paul traveled throughout the world, preaching the centrality of ethical and moral behavior to one brutal society after another. Finally, perhaps inevitably, Paul was executed, and died with the words of the Shema on his lips, "Hear, O Israel, the Lord our God, the Lord is One."

The Apostle stands on its own as a fine piece of literature. Taking the life of Paul, well known throughout the world, and transforming the facts into a historical novel was, in and of itself, a formidable accomplishment. But why would a Jewish author, a Yiddish writer, write a book such as this, lionizing a Christian whose descendants had turned their backs on Paul's teachings and brought so much pain and suffering to the author's own people?

The question is answered in part by a prayer with which Asch ends the book: "I thank Thee and praise Thee, Lord of the world, that Thou hast given me the strength to withstand all temptations and overcome all obstacles, those of my own making and those made by others, and to complete...*The Apostle*...so that I might set forth...the merit of Israel, whom Thou hast elected to bring the light of the faith to the nations of the world, for Thy glory and out of Thy love of mankind."

Asch wrote this novel for two reasons. In the first instance, he wanted to establish that the essence of genuine Christianity lay in the embrace of Jewish values and ethics. Therefore a good Christian had to eschew hate, bigotry, and oppression in order to live a life in accordance with the faith. *The Apostle* also constituted a warning to Christianity. To the Nazis, anti-Semitism was only a first step in the direction of destroying all religious systems in Aryan society. To Hitler, notions such as conscience, mercy, and justice were obstacles and potential sources of corruption of an Aryan philosophy aimed at world domination.

The Nazis accused the Jews of besmirching the world with their values. Through *The Apostle,* Asch declares that the Jews did indeed bring certain values to humanity, values that led to the emergence of Christianity, which in turn transformed a pagan world into a religious civilization. Far from corrupting the world, then, Judaism and Christianity saved the world from those who, like the Nazis, wished to remain rooted in a nihilism in which human life was expendable, in which kindness constituted weakness, and in which compassion was to be scorned and rejected. For those reasons and many more, this courageous novel, written in 1943, deserves a place on every Jewish bookshelf.

43 Our Crowd

Stephen Birmingham

The great German-Jewish families of New York City made their fortunes as bankers and merchants at a time when America was emerging as a great industrial power. Stephen Birmingham documents their rise in *Our Crowd,* which was published in 1967 and became a national bestseller.

The author chronicles the lives of such prominent families as the Loebs, Guggenheims, Lehmans, Schiffs, Seligmans, Kahns, and Lewisohns (and the various marriages between them). Birmingham, a gentile, was a roommate of John Loeb and became a family friend. He was given access not only to documents but to family members themselves. This rare perspective provided him with unique insight into an elite, private world.

Turn-of-the-century New York City was mostly barren land, and people traded paper and diamonds on the street. Regulating bodies such as the Securities and Exchange Commission did not exist, allowing banks and the cotton, steel, and railroad industries to grow at a phenomenal rate.

Family fortunes were made. They seem staggering even today, and they gave rise to the excesses of the Victorian era. A Seligman butler became a millionaire on tips alone. Marriages and business almost always went hand in hand, so that many of the families are related. As we read about the rise of these amazing men, we also learn about their interconnectedness. For instance, banker Joseph Seligman's son-in-law was Jacob Schiff, who was instrumental in financing America's railroads. One of Schiff's daughters married a Warburg, whose family was known for their banking preeminence in Germany. Their mansion on Fifth Avenue now houses the Jewish Museum.

Joseph Seligman traveled to America in steerage class, starting out as a peddler. He eventually became an international banker working with such notables as J. P. Morgan and the Rothschilds.

"The families," as this elite group of German Jews called themselves, befriended presidents and royalty. In a Seligman general store in Watertown, New York, Jesse Seligman waited on First Lieutenant Ulysses S. Grant, who was seeking a gift for his new bride. They began a friendship that lasted a lifetime.

Presidents were not the only ones impressed with the families. In 1892, the nephew of Poland's King Stanislaus, Prince André Poniatowsky, banked with the Seligmans and became friendly with them, vacationing at their summer home. He viewed them as extraordinary people who were not intimidated by his title. The prince reflected on the way they conducted themselves during their leisure time, so different from the other bankers he had met.

He declared, "Money in itself, however, had no significance for them outside of business...good rentiers, given to sport, literature, art, and especially music...contributed generously to charity and still more to the finances of their political party, and above all were devoted to family life with an intensity to be met with today only in the French provinces."

He was equally struck that, with a glance, a nod, a turn of the head, they could communicate with one another. He said, "Nature seems to have wished to compensate this astonishing race for the insecurity against which it has struggled for centuries by endowing it with an ability, which escapes us, to understand each other in silence."

The prince's open, admiring attitude was the exception. To most of gentile society, no matter how much wealth, how many accomplishments, or how much power the families obtained, they were still Jews to be excluded from clubs, hotels, and society.

The Jews themselves were also divided into two groups, the Sephardim (Spanish) and Ashkenazim (German) Jews. Tragically, it took until the Second World War for that division to fade.

There was also the Jew who didn't want to be Jewish. August Belmont, née Schonberg, the American liaison for the Rothschilds, abandoned his Judaism. A quintessential social climber, he built a ballroom in his own home and owned, rather than rented, red carpeting, which was rolled out for guests. He was also the first to elevate dining into an art, serving gourmet food rather than beef and cabbage.

The book describes how Adolph Lewisohn, a major figure in the mining industry, bought paintings by Matisse and Picasso for small sums of money and tells how banker Otto Kahn served briefly as a spy during the First World War. Kahn took his position as a member of the board of the Metropolitan Opera so seriously that he purchased most of the opera's stock, and was responsible for the great impresario Gatti-Cassazza and conductor Arturo Toscanini coming to the Met. Almost single-handedly, he shaped the Metropolitan Opera into one of the world's great opera houses. Although Jews were not allowed to buy opera boxes (they were in high demand, selling for as much as $30,000), Kahn was finally given a box. He accepted with pleasure, but never used it personally, instead reserving the space for foreign dignitaries.

Jacob Schiff was also a great philanthropist and helped form the American Jewish Committee. He was responsible for the "matching gift concept," one donor "matching" the gifts of others. He also believed in unconditional tzedakah and in the Jewish tradition of giving ten percent of his income to charity. He once startled a well-meaning woman who congratulated him on a particularly large gift by saying, somewhat abruptly, "That wasn't my money." He meant, of course, that the gift came from the one-tenth of his income that he felt had to be given away. He helped many people personally, but he also believed in the Talmudic principle that "twice blessed is he who gives in secret." Of the numerous buildings he gave to New York City, none bears his name.

In 1971, after the success of *Our Crowd,* Birmingham wrote *The Grandees: America's Sephardic Elite,* which was followed in 1984 by *The Rest of Us: The Rise of America's Eastern European Jews.*

44 The Grandees

Stephen Birmingham

In the pages of *Our Crowd,* Stephen Birmingham chronicled the great immigration of German Jews to the United States during the nineteenth century. The book was so successful that Birmingham took a step back in time to describe the emergence of a smaller wave of immigration, that of Spanish-Portuguese Jewry, the Grandees.

The Spanish-Portuguese community flourished in Spain under the Moors. But then came the Spanish Inquisition and Torquemada and Jews were forced to convert to Catholicism or leave Spain. Many converted publicly, then maintained lives as "Marranos," or secret Jews. To the outside world, they were good Catholics. But on Shabbat and holidays, they would gather in one another's basements, the floors covered with sand to muffle any sound, and recite prayers and observe rituals. Discovery meant torture and execution, and ultimately many Jews chose to leave Spain under the Expulsion Edict of 1492.

These refugees made their way to South America and the Caribbean, to places like Brazil, Aruba, St. Thomas, and Curaçao, then finally to the United States. Birmingham's account gives the reader the feeling that if one goes far enough back in one's personal family tree, a Spanish-Portuguese Jew may be part of one's ancestry. For example, author Barnaby Conrad was astonished to find that he was a descendant of the Grandees. Here was a man whose family was socially prominent in San Francisco and had always boasted of its descent from Martha Custis, the second wife of President George Washington. After discovering lineage dating back to the Levy family in Spain, Conrad shared the news with his family. His mother is reputed to have commented: "At least we were *good* Jews," a reference to the high level of ritual observance among the Spanish Jews.

The Hendricks family established the first metal factory in America, a copper-rolling mill in New Jersey. Their customers included Paul Revere and Robert Fulton. This Jewish family's name in Spain was Henriques, and in the United States they became America's first millionaires. The family is still affiliated with a Spanish-Portuguese synagogue in New York.

The author discusses the origins of various names now fairly common in America Jewry. The name Alport, for example, was in some cases formerly Alporto meaning "from Portugal." Names such as Alpert and Rappaport often reflect the same ancestry. The Seixas family made its way from Spain to Germany, where the name became germanized to Sachs or Saks. One American branch of the family retained the name Seixas, and a descendant, Vic Seixas, was long regarded as one of the world's premier professional tennis players.

In a most intriguing section, Birmingham discusses how many Jews helped Columbus on his expedition to the New World. In a striking "coincidence," Columbus sailed with the Niña, Pinta, and Santa Maria on precisely the same day in 1492 as the Jewish expulsion from Spain. Historians debate to this day whether Columbus—whose true family name was Colon—was actually Jewish, but there is no doubt that many of his key aides were.

When Columbus first mapped out his course, he used charts prepared by Judah Cresques, known as "the map Jew," and head of the Portuguese School of Navigation in Lisbon. The almanacs and astronomical tables for the trip were assembled by Abraham ben Zacuto, a Jewish professor at the University of Salamanca. The prominent Jewish banker Don Isaac Abravanel was one of the first Spaniards to offer Columbus financial backing, then he involved other Jewish bankers, including Luis de Santangel, Gabrial Sanchez, and Abraham Senior.

One of the most charming tales of the Jews and Columbus involves his Jewish interpreter, Luis de Torres. De Torres, purportedly the first of the crew to set foot on shore in the New World, is said to have spotted a rather ungainly bird. He called it by the first Hebrew word that came to his mind, "tuki." And thus, according to some historians, the turkey was named.

The book contains some fascinating chapters dealing with Spanish-Portuguese Jews who had an enormous impact on American history: Haym Solomon, who committed his personal fortune to financial support of the American Revolution; Judah Touro, the great Jewish philanthropist who built magnificent synagogues in Newport, Rhode Island, and New Orleans, and then left a famous will bequeathing his great fortune to charities helping Americans of every faith; Rebecca Gratz, the beautiful woman who is believed to have been the model for the character Rebecca in Sir Walter Scott's classic novel *Ivanhoe;* Uriah P. Levy, the first Jew to become an officer in the United States Navy and a champion of the end to practices such as flogging among U.S. sailors; Annie Nathan Mayer, the founder of Barnard College; and of course Benjamin Cardozo, who sat on the U.S. Supreme Court.

As the first Jewish immigrants to America, the Spanish-Portuguese Jews regarded themselves as an aristocracy and sometimes looked down upon others, particularly the German Jews. When Rosa Content, daughter of a pre-Revolutionary Sephardic family, married James Seligman, a German Jew from the famous international banking Seligmans, she always referred to her in-laws as "peddlers"!

The year 1868, however, changed everything for the Grandees. Temple Emanuel of New York, a Reform temple, opened its doors. The creation of New York's wealthiest German Jews, it was far more imposing than any synagogue of the Spanish-Portuguese. The *New York Times* described it as preeminent among America's Jewish religious institutions. Since then, the influence of Sephardic Jewry in America has ebbed.

In 1968, four hundred and seventy-six years after King Ferdinand and Queen Isabella ordered the Jews expelled from Spain, the Spanish government declared the order void. Of course, the Spanish-Portuguese Jews did not rush to return to Spain. Their descendants now dwell in countries throughout the world, bearers of a proud legacy of triumph over oppression and adversity.

45 Jews, God, and History

Max I. Dimont

Jews, God, and History was the first book written by Max Dimont. At the time, he was living in St. Louis, Missouri, and was a well-known lecturer on historical, biblical, and psychological subjects. Dimont spent seven years working on this history, using his family as critics and researchers in the process. The history is written with an emphasis on the uncanny ability of the Jewish people to survive the decline of many civilizations, yet continue their growth in others. Placing Jewish history in the context of world history, Dimont examines Jewish culture and events as they interfaced with the historical events of the civilizations and countries in which they occurred.

Covering four thousand years of history in a concise and simple manner, Dimont presents a very accessible story for the lay reader, while maintaining the integrity of a scholarly work. For him, the history of Jewish survival has three elements that make it unique. First, the history of the Jewish people spans four thousand continuous years during which they have been a spiritual and cultural influence. Second, Jews are a people who survived over three thousand years without a homeland. And third, they have been creative in the language of every land in which they lived, as well as their own language.

Dimont writes this work viewing history from a number of perspectives. He includes political interpretation, geographic influence, economic factors, psychoanalytical analysis, philosophical viewpoints, "cult of personalities," or the influence of great leaders on the time in which they lived, and the religious face of history. Foremost, the author believes that ideas create history and motivate people.

The book begins with Abraham and his encounter with God some four millennia ago. The Hebrews were nomads living in a pagan civilization. They remained together during the first four centuries because of their belief in one God, the rite of circumcision, and the prohibition against human sacrifice. The section continues with the life of Moses and its significance to the history of the Hebrews. The author infuses the biblical account of events with the historical explanation or psychoanalytical reasoning behind them.

Next comes the introduction of the Torah, the first foundation for all judicial law. It set the Jews apart from other peoples to an even greater extent. The Torah formulated a defined way of life for the Jewish people. The laws, which were divided into three major categories, spanned man's relation to man, man's relation to state, and man's relation to God. According to Dimont, the Mosaic Code was the actual beginning of the history of the Jewish people as it exists today and anticipates the homeland promised to Abraham by God. In addition, the American Constitution and law find their roots in the laws of the Torah.

The transition from Moses to the Greco-Roman period occurred often in exile. The Jews prospered in exile in Babylon and even multiplied. Through the teachings of the prophets Ezra and Nehemiah, they established the Jewishness that would be kept alive throughout their history.

The second section of the book moves the center of civilization from the Near East to Europe. Dimont sets the history of the Jews in the context of the rise and fall of the Greeks and Romans and the creation of a new sect of Judaism called Christianity. It was during this period, according to the author, that Jews were exposed to a complete separation of church and state. By the year 600, the Jews were the only non-Christian group remaining in a now Christian Europe. The Jews survived the turmoil of the times, and by the sixth century found themselves witnessing the emergence of the Byzantine, Islamic, and feudal civilizations.

Once again, Dimont poses the question, "How did the Jews manage to survive?" During this era, the Talmud was probably the single most important factor. Everyday Jewish life and religious orientation had changed with the evolving history of civilizations. Although the Jews had lost their independence, they gained freedom. In losing their land, they had an even greater sense of nationality. Through the Crusades and Mohammed's new creed of Islam, as well as the Spanish Inquisition, the Jews maintained a sense of their own identity.

Most Christian scholars see the Middle Ages as a time in which Jewish civilization barely existed, while Jewish scholars see it as a time that almost suffocated Jewish life. Dimont presents it as a period of interconnection with world civilization. The Middle Ages produced first the Sephardic, or Spanish Judaism, and then Ashkenazic, or German Judaism. With two distinct ways of life, literature, and philosophy, with all their differences, they worshiped the same God. Dimont's thesis is that the Jews helped bring the Enlightenment to Europe.

The modern period of history brought the discovery of the American continents for the Europeans and, with the Spanish Inquisition, the Jewish settlements there. The transition from the nineteenth to the twentieth century in Europe informally affected Jewish history. The freedom and rights of the Jews changed at the whim of Russian leaders, and anti-Semitism became a political movement. Jewish immigration to America increased as waves of German and Russian Jews found their way to freedom and the promise of a new land. The Jewish people produced many great leaders, and were responsible for many new philosophical theories and scientific discoveries. Finally, the Holocaust led the Jews to a homeland, and a new phase of history emerged.

Dimont concludes this work by posing the question of Jewish survival in the future. His conclusion is that the survival of the Jewish people rests, not on a homeland, but on the strength of Jews living in the Diaspora throughout the world.

46 Antisemitism in America Today: Outspoken Experts Explode the Myths

Jerome A. Chanes, Editor

What are Holocaust revisionists teaching about the war? What is the psychology of prejudice? How much of a threat are skinheads and white supremacists? How does the Constitution protect us? In what ways do Jews themselves use antisemitism?

Experts answer these questions as well as many others in the twenty essays included in *Antisemitism in America Today*. An invaluable reference for an overview of antisemitism nationally, this book discusses organizations that protect the Jews and those who threaten the safety of American Jewry. Edited by Jerome A. Chanes, codirector for domestic concerns for the National Jewish Community Relations Advisory Council, the essays show how the effects of antisemitism permeate our culture.

The book is then divided into five parts for the essays themselves. The essays build upon one another, often with recurring interwoven themes, so that we are able to take in large amounts of information incrementally.

One of the early essays, by psychology professor Martin S. Bergmann, describes the psychological makeup of a bigot, which includes excessive hostility, exaggerated feelings of inferiority, and even paranoia, as well as the need to project aggression onto others. Bergmann also discusses the cultural history of antisemitism and Christianity, and its logic: the Jews suffered because they rejected Christ.

Surveys about antisemitism are discussed, but their findings are not conclusive. Far more revealing, though, are the reports of actual activities taking place in the country today. We learn a great deal about the lies that Professor Leonard Jeffries of the City University of New York and Professor Tony Martin of Wellesley College are teaching. In the notes following Anti-Defamation League director Abraham H. Foxman's enlightening essay, we are also given the names of several African-American teachers and scholars who are denouncing these lies.

Among the antisemitic material Jeffries and Martin use is the Nation of Islam's book, *The Secret Relationship Between Blacks and Jews,* which claims that Jews were the major force behind slave trading. Jeffries and Farrakhan thrive in an environment where their interpretations of reality aren't contested.

When Jews see or read about Holocaust deniers in the media, we dismiss them. Most Jews, therefore, do not know specifically what lies are being taught. If we are to encounter such beliefs, we must know how history is being distorted so that we can set the record straight. Kenneth S. Stern's excellent essay, "Denial of the Holocaust: An Antisemitic Political Assault," does just that.

Stern names Holocaust deniers such as Bradley Smith, who often targets college students, and also cites examples he and others use. They claim, for example, that Anne Frank's diary was a fraud since a *copy* of the manuscript includes writing in a ballpoint pen, and the ballpoint wasn't even invented until 1951. "What the deniers don't say is that this writing consisted of emendations made later by her father, and that the original edition of the diary was published in 1947." Given partial facts, it's easy to understand why a young person who has little or no previous knowledge of the Holocaust might believe the revisionists.

Representatives of Jewish organizations refuse to meet with such people, says Stern, because "to do so suggests that their hatred is somehow not so serious, when it is really beyond the pale of what is acceptable....Refusal to debate the deniers allows them to suggest that the 'exterminationists' have something to hide. But the response is easy: credible historians debate the Holocaust all the time—just not with the Nazis."

Stern also recounts what happened when Holocaust deniers attempted to place an ad in the college newspaper, *Skidmore News.* Jens Ohlin, its editor, was planning on running the ad, but after speaking with numerous people including survivors, he wound up refusing the ad and instead publishing a sixteen-page supplement asking, "Why Are Holocaust Deniers Targeting College Campuses?" Bradley Smith's own words answered the question: "I don't want to spend time with adults anymore, I want to go to students. They are superficial, they are empty vessels to be filled."

Abraham H. Foxman's essay, "A View from the 'Defense' Agencies," is excellent, and shows how the Anti-Defamation League counters such teachings. The essay cites an historic overview of ADL activities, including its program "A World of Difference," whose goal is to reduce prejudice. Foxman also discusses hate groups and shows how the ADL drafts model legislation and helps educate law enforcement about the dangers of "extremist organizations."

Foxman recounts the full-page ad which the ADL felt compelled to run in 1994 in the *New York Times,* and later in other papers, that reprinted parts of Khalid Abdul Muhammad's speech, which he delivered at New Jersey's Kean College, "in which he drew upon virtually every antisemitic myth and slander in history." Muhammad had been espousing these ideas for more than ten years at various colleges, and the Nation of Islam was being embraced by the NAACP as well as the Congressional Black Caucus.

The ad concludes, "Minister Louis Farrakhan and the Nation of Islam claim they are moving toward greater moderation and increased tolerance. You decide." The Jewish community realized that the best way to counter antisemitism was to print the offending material without any editorial comment. Although both Muhammad and Farrakhan remain threatening forces, the ad helped identify many allies.

The book contends that antisemitism in the States is not as prevalent as it used to be but that those who espouse hate are more likely to act.

Antisemitism in America Today addresses myths and debunks them. This volume is immensely informative and a welcome addition to any library.

47 The Jewish You Wouldn't Believe It Book

M. Hirsch Goldberg

One of the classic characteristics of minority groups is the tendency to preserve a list of great achievements by their members, as well as oddities that can be shared as unique to the group. Jews are among the foremost practitioners of the "see what we've done" phenomenon, one means of building pride in Jewishness in more than a religious sense.

Contemporary books have been published on Jews in music, sports, and politics; on Jewish Nobel Prize winners; on Jews who served in the Civil War, the two world wars, and in Vietnam. There is even a book on Jewish cowboys of the old West!

The Jewish You Wouldn't Believe It Book by M. Hirsch Goldberg, published in 1986, is an updated and illustrated edition of Goldberg's *The Jewish Connection*. It provides more fodder for the Jewish equivalent of Trivial Pursuit. It affords the reader a wealth of tidbits for cocktail party discussion, one-upmanship, and general knowledge.

Goldberg begins by dashing some conventional myths. For example, the Torah never refers to the Ten Commandments as the Ten Commandments, nor does the Torah ever mention bar mitzvah! Most surprisingly, we learn that the six-pointed Star of David, commonly considered the emblem of the Jewish people, was not Jewish at all in its origins, attaining prominence only in 1897 at Theodore Herzl's Zionist Congress. Actually, the six-pointed star was originally an ornament and possible a magical sign. It appeared in civilizations as diverse as Mesopotamia and Britain, India and Iberia, and may even date back to the Bronze Age.

The reader may be surprised to learn that the word *Jew* never occurs in the Torah, and the name of Moses was Egyptian in origin, rather than Hebrew. Also intriguing is the fact that the Manischewitz wine company sells only 10 percent of its products to Jews—and actually sells more wine at Christmas than at Passover!

While America and the Arab countries are the world's great oil suppliers, the formula for petroleum was actually discovered by a Galician Jew, Abraham Schreiner, in 1853. If only he had secured oil leases to accompany his revolutionary finding! And while pizza is considered an Italian delight, it was first made more than two thousand years ago, when Roman soldiers added olive oil and cheese to matzoh!

Irony after irony fills the pages of this wonderfully informative book. We are introduced, for example, to a Russian-born Jew named Israel Baline. Born in 1888, he immigrated to America, changed his name to Irving Berlin, and composed "Alexander's Ragtime Band," "White Christmas," and "Easter Parade." And we learn that Adolph Hitler's cook was Jewish, as was his family doctor!

In a chapter entitled, "Inventors and Explorers," we find that the Jewish teacher Hillel created the first sandwich. A Jew, William Herschel, discovered the planet Uranus, while his sister, Caroline, discovered eight comets. An Austrian Jew, David Schwarz, invented the dirigible, while a German immigrant, Emile Berliner, developed the disc phonograph and made possible the modern record industry. Certainly the entire world knows of the work of Albert Einstein, but these little known inventors capture the Jewish imagination.

Jews seem to be everywhere in the world. In spite of our small numbers, we pop up at unexpected times. The Reuters News Agency was founded by a Jew. The French automobile, the Citroën, is named for a Jew. The actress Sarah Bernhardt was Jewish. And even Christopher Columbus may have been Jewish!

Columbus's actual family was a Jewish name, Colón. But while Columbus himself was probably not Jewish, many key members of his crew were: among them the ship's cook, surgeon, and interpreter. Adolph Hitler feared that he was Jewish, and Pope Anacletus II actually had a Jewish grandfather!

In one of the book's most interesting sections, Goldberg delves into the mystery of the Ten Lost Tribes of Israel. As historians know, the Assyrians invaded the Northern Kingdom of Israel in the eighth century B.C.E., carrying their prisoners into exile. The ten tribes disappeared, and, over the centuries, numerous civilizations have claimed or been ascribed a relationship with them. Among the most compelling arguments are those presented by scholars asserting that American Indian tribes derive directly from the ancient Hebrews. Some even maintain that it was the Ten Lost Tribes that discovered America over three thousand years ago.

The Yuchi tribe of Georgia and Oklahoma observes festivals and customs very similar to Jewish rituals. The Chibcha Indians of Colombia in South America have words in their language that seem to be Hebrew in origin, and have shards of pottery and stones bearing Hebrew letters. Other theories hold that Ten Lost Tribes settled in England, Japan, Armenia, Nigeria, Afghanistan, India, and Ethiopia.

Goldberg devotes an entire chapter to the ways in which Jewish words and phrases have permeated the English language. The reader will be surprised to find how many everyday expressions derive from Jewish sources: "fly in the ointment" (Ecclesiastes), "see eye to eye" (Isaiah), "the apple of my eye" (Deuteronomy), "spare the rod and spoil the child" (Proverbs), to name just a few.

The term *scapegoat* comes from the Bible, as do the terms *Jezebel* and *Satan*. If you "live off the fat of the land" or escape "by the skin of your teeth," if you act "holier than Thou" or "set your house in order," if you think that "the meek shall inherit the earth" or you speak "off the top of your head," you are quoting the Hebrew Bible.

Obviously, Jews are proud of other Jews in science. Jonas Salk, Selman Waksman, Bela Schick, and August von Wassermann were all prominent medical researchers who transformed the whole world with their dramatic discoveries in health care. And while Goldberg does not include them in this volume, Jews also take pride in their coreligionists in show business, sports, and the arts.

The Jewish You Wouldn't Believe It Book is a nonstop chronicle of how Jews have impacted human history.

48 The Invisible Thread: A Portrait of Jewish-American Women

Diana Bletter and Lori Grinker

This fascinating book portrays the diversity of Jewish women in our country, from Vermont's then governor, Madeleine Kunin, to Rosetta Buggs, whose grandfather, an African Jew, became an American slave. How does Judaism affect these women's lives? How does it make them feel different from other Americans?

Diana Bletter and Lori Grinker traveled across America in search of answers, dispelling many myths and stereotypes about Jewish women. Through individual voices, we come to know an array of personalities, each without pretense or self-consciousness. Ms. Buggs, for example, worked for a Jewish family as a cook for almost twenty-five years. "Mrs. Eisenberg made me feel right at home. She was a religious Jew who accepted me as a Jew and her equal."

The book's title derives from the widely acknowledged bond that Jewish women feel among themselves. The authors experienced it when interviewing their subjects, who took them into their homes, fed them, and treated them like long-lost family. That this immediate kinship occurred on such a consistent level surprised them.

Some themes resurface as mainstays of Judaism: the importance of family and education, a sense of humor (the authors note that all the women "shared the same quick wit"), as well as a seriousness, or, as Rusty Kanokogi, who married a Japanese man with whom she practices judo, said, "Jews are not frivolous people."

A history of oppression, coupled with the religious obligation of fulfilling one's potential, and Judaism's emphasis on tzedakah (charity) and tikkun olam (repairing the world) help create empathic, powerful doers. Shoshana Cardin of Baltimore, Maryland, is a past president of the Council of Jewish Federations. "God gave everyone in this world a role to play that includes compassion, caring, and gemilut chasadim—acts of loving-kindness. I don't think everyone needs to assume the weight of the world's problems, but if we break the world's problems down to those within our own province, everyone can assume some responsibility...I'm not ego-oriented...I'm only interested in working toward achieving tikkun olam."

The impact of racism, particularly with the Holocaust in mind, is ever present. Mickie Shuv-Ami of South Kendall, Florida, is the daughter of survivors. She wants to live in Israel and feels that it is much harder to live in America as a Jew. Even women who appear totally secure in the United States always have the Holocaust rooted in their consciousness. Ida Kohlmeyer, a New Orleans artist whose residence hasn't changed in forty years, doesn't feel as "solidly planted" as people might think; she recounts her mother's memories of surviving pogroms so vividly they seem almost her own, and Ida imagines gangsters breaking into her home in the middle of the night.

We are witness to the changing of traditional Judaism as it affects modern American women. And we have access to private moments: there are four photographs of Pamela Steinberg at a mikvah in New York. She tells of her experiences at the mikvah and explains its symbolism. Deborah Katchko-Zimmerman of Norwalk, Connecticut, continues to carry on the family tradition of serving as a cantor. She explains her reason with eloquence: "When I was in college I studied with Elie Wiesel. He had a profound influence on my commitment to Judaism. As he explained, there are six million Jews in the United States—the same number of Jews who were killed in the Holocaust. If each Jew here took on the identity of a Jew who was lost, we would live not only for ourselves but for someone else as well. Our lives would be doubly meaningful. After he said this, I found out that my grandfather had three sisters and two brothers—both cantors—who were killed; twenty other singers in my family perished. I thought about all the talented people whose lives were cut short, and I felt a strong sense of obligation. Suddenly it became clear to me that being a cantor is a way for me to fight against an enormous Jewish loss. Through my music, I'm keeping my family alive."

Such commitment to Judaism, combined with a feminist perspective, is evidenced throughout the book. Not all women feel as tied to the religion. Its weight has seemed like a burden, and several express ambivalence about being Jewish and are just beginning to search for its meaning in their lives. Some have been turned off by stereotypical behavior that they witnessed growing up in suburbia. Others know better and feel strongly attached, but also frustrated, by Orthodox Judaism's sexist tenets. Women may not be counted in a minyan, may not recite Kaddish, and may not wear tefillin.

In one of the daily prayers, the Orthodox man thanks God "for not making me a woman." In the Orthodox woman's prayer, she thanks God for "making me what I am." Some women have trouble with this prayer, but Sorah Weisman, a Hasidic butcher who "organized the first girls' yeshiva in Brooklyn," believes otherwise. "The Lord is very good to women. He made the laws lenient for us. Women get as much reward for their work—taking care of their children and supporting their husbands—as men get for learning."

A female Hasidic butcher defies stereotypes, but so do many others: a dancer in Las Vegas adorned in skimpy sequined clothes; a recently transported Iranian Jew, reminding us that religious freedom is a gift; an elegant woman named Mobilian of the Year; a remorseful inmate serving time for murder; and a farmer in Vega, Texas, who is married to a Mexican. Regardless of how each woman feels about Judaism, each is a Jew. Julie Hilton Danan, of San Antonio, Texas, explains, "The *pintele Yid* means that there is a drop of Jewishness in all Jews, no matter how assimilated they might be."

Fortunately, Jewish humor never fades. Bessie Meyerowitz, of Brooklyn, New York, who looks like a bubbie, can't help but be endearing. "Those Jews who become real religious, they're crazy! If a young fellow is in the elevator when I walk in, he turns around and puts his face up close to the wall. He doesn't want to look at me. What can I do to him? I'm an old lady in a housedress!"

And faith, too, grows old but never fades. Even those who question often believe. Fanny Wald, of Brooklyn, New York, recalls listening to Einstein talking on the radio. "Someone asked him, 'Do you think there's something out there?' Einstein said, 'Nobody could have done what God did.' If Einstein can believe something is out there, then so can I."

49 What They Say Behind Our Backs

William B. Helmreich

What They Say Behind Our Backs is a book that attempts to deal with this problem: the cruel lies that have been repeated so often, not only about Jews, but also about other groups—lies whose repetition seems to turn them into truths. The author, William Helmreich, was a professor of sociology at City College in New York. In this book he examines nine different groups: Jews, Italians, Blacks, Japanese, Chinese, Irish, Poles, White Anglo-Saxon Protestants, and Hispanics. In the case of each group, he analyzes the stereotypes that have been perpetuated about them.

In the first chapter, he lists some of these stereotypes, about Italians for example, "Everyone knows that most Italians either belong to the Mafia or have a relative who does."

About Jews: "The problem with this country is that Jews control everything! They run the TV stations, movies, newspapers, and whatever else they can get their grubby hands on."

About blacks: "The blacks think they have everything coming to them. They are lazy and shiftless! All they want to do is drink, shoot up, and play the numbers."

About the Japanese: "There you have people who are hard-working, smart and ambitious, but remember—you can never turn your back on them, even for a minute. They are really sly and treacherous. Don't forget Pearl Harbor."

The author says that prejudice is usually ingrained in us, beginning with early childhood. For example, a study of whites showed a photograph of a white man holding a razor blade while arguing with a black person in a New York City subway. The whites viewed the photo for a split second, then were asked to write what they saw on a slip of paper. More than half of the respondents said they saw a black man holding a razor blade against the throat of a white man. Their childhood prejudices had taken over!

In his chapter dealing with the Jews, Helmreich describes several stereotypes that are well known to us. For example, in a discussion of the much maligned Jewish mother, he tells the story of a mother who went to the beach with her son and daughter-in-law. The son, a physician, swam a bit too far away from shore and began struggling in the water. His mother, noticing his plight, began running up and down the beach, screaming at the top of her lungs: "Help, somebody, please help. My son, the Long Island psychiatrist, is drowning!"

Helmreich takes up the lie that is found in *The Protocols of the Elders of Zion*, that the Jews are internationalists plotting to take over the world—and he shows conclusively how false this is. He discusses the charge that the Jews crucified Jesus, and presents the arguments why this could not have happened. And he touches on the accusations that the Jews control the media, that Jews have horns, and that Jews are shrewd businessmen.

In the remainder of the book, the author deals with stereotypes and lies that have been circulated about other groups and shows conclusively that they are not true. Helmreich's book serves as a valuable workbook for any individual or group seeking to diminish prejudice through learning.

50 World of Our Fathers

Irving Howe

Stephen Birmingham has written brilliantly of the Spanish-Portuguese immigration to America (*The Grandees*) and of the German-Jewish immigration of the early to mid-nineteenth century (*Our Crowd*). Certainly these two groups of newcomers brought with them to the United States an extraordinarily high level of literacy, determination, and ambition to succeed in a land of freedom. This handful of Jews, some 450,000 over the course of two centuries, never constituted more than one half of one percent of United States population, yet produced some of America's most distinguished Jewish families in banking, industry, merchandising, law, and politics.

The year 1881, however, initiated an era unprecedented in Jewish history, when more than two million Jews from Eastern Europe began a massive immigration to the United States. In his classic work, *World of Our Fathers*, published in 1989, Irving Howe chronicles the transformation of these shtetl dwellers, many of whom were oppressed and persecuted, into citizens of America, a land of freedom and opportunity.

As the author begins this saga, he shows how Jewish life in Eastern Europe was already changing. The French Revolution had led countless Jews to enter secular society, rejecting the authority of the rabbis and embracing popular culture and customs. While this revolution by no means instantly manifested itself in Russia and Poland, the Jews living there could not help but be influenced by the news of their Western European brothers and sisters. Yiddish culture began to fade as young people left the shtetls and moved to the big cities. There they became underpaid workers, living in slums, motivated to organize and strike in response to unbearable working conditions. Then they learned that there was another option—America!

In the course of thirty-three years, approximately one-third of all Eastern European Jews left their homelands. While many Orthodox Jews warned against immigrating to "a corrupt and sinful land where the Sabbath is no Sabbath," the mass exodus began. First from Russia, then Romania, the Jews flooded into America. American Jews of German descent were not at all supportive of this mass immigration, for the Eastern Europeans were often illiterate, unskilled, and the visual stereotype of the ghetto Jew. But they had no say. The Eastern European Jews were on their way.

Most arrived at Ellis Island, worn out and emotionally drained by their two journeys: first by foot across Europe to ports of passage, then by ship under terrible conditions, crowded into steerage, deprived of food. Howe describes the medical screening and intake procedures at Ellis Island, which at best required a full twenty-four hours The Hebrew Immigrant Aid Society fought for more humane steerage conditions and gentler Ellis Island treatment.

Unlike prior Jewish immigrations, says Howe, the Eastern European influx was much more a movement of families and young people, with many adult laborers. The early arrivals were far less educated than those in later migrations, but the vast majority of newcomers made their way to the Lower East Side of New York. Almost overnight, this area became the most densely populated neighborhood in the city. Living in cramped tenements, the Jews found work wherever they could, primarily as peddlers and tailors in the garment industry. Life was hard, but the Jews persevered.

Finally, the wealthy German Jews of New York began to assume responsibility for helping their Jewish brothers and sisters. Howe tells the stories of many who gave dignity and pride to the new immigrants, among them Lillian Wald, who founded the Henry Street Settlement House. The Jewish philanthropist and banker Jacob Schiff quietly funded the settlement's activities, which initially provided nursing care, then a host of other social services. There were many problems that had to be addressed, many of them inevitable products of poverty and hunger. There were Jewish pimps and prostitutes, scam artists and vagrants, arsonists, and gamblers with nicknames such as "Spanish Johnny" and "Little Kishky"!

We see how these poor Jews began to organize labor unions, became anarchists or socialists, and created a major rift between the Orthodox Jews and nonreligious Jews. Howe shows how the Jews slowly established settlements in Williamsburg and Brownsville, while those who achieved financial success moved to Harlem.

As the years passed, many Jews made the transition from peddlers to shop owners. Others had great dreams of being in show business, and ultimately built Hollywood and the motion picture industry: Samuel Goldwyn, Louis B. Mayer, and the Warner Brothers, to name a few. Out of this era also came the rise of the Jewish mother as the preeminent force in Jewish family life. Husbands worked long, exhausting hours for paltry wages. Those who could not rise above the status of peddlers often lost their sense of self-esteem and directed their anger at their families. Many men deserted their families altogether, looking uptown for a better life. The Jewish mother, then, became the anchor of the family, the only stabilizing influence for a generation of children who needed to be fed, clothed, and educated.

Jewish religious life increased once people had enough to eat. Cantors were in especially high demand, since Jews would join the synagogue with the best cantor. Therefore, in 1897, congregations paid up to one thousand dollars to secure the services of a cantor for the High Holidays, since he would generate income and enable the shul to prosper. Since Jews value education, they also turned their attention to the establishment of schools for their children. At first they formed Jewish schools, but gradually they eased their sons and daughters into the superior public school system and then into universities such as City College.

As the Eastern European Jews became more educated and more Americanized, they began to attain a measure of prominence, especially in the labor movement. Sidney Hillman and David Dubinsky were honored by the American worker and led Jews into the mainstream of American labor negotiations. In politics, Jews slowly moved into the Democratic Party, where a majority remain to this day.

Besides the movie industry moguls, the Eastern Europeans

had their Yiddish theater, which produced nationally beloved entertainers such as Eddie Cantor, Sophie Tucker, Al Jolson, Fanny Brice, and George Burns. In every field of endeavor, Jews grew from parochialism to popularity, creating a culture and worldview that remains an influence in much of America today.

Following the restrictive American Immigration Acts of the 1920s, the Eastern European and German-Jewish communities at last had to coalesce and merge. Today, then, we have a uniquely American Jewish community. Irving Howe, however, has made it possible for students in generations to come to understand, appreciate, and respect the courage and accomplishments of our Eastern European ancestors.

51 The Teaching of Contempt: Christian Roots of Anti-Semitism

Jules Isaac

For 1900 years the Christian church preached peace, yet often practiced violence against the Jewish people.

Then in the 1960s, the tumult and the shouting faded away, and the battle seemed to have ended. Christian clergy of virtually every denomination were giving friendly sermons on Judaism and conducting serious seminars in order to bring about an understanding of the Jewish faith. The war against Judaism gave way to a war against anti-Semitism.

Therefore the question naturally arises: "Why this sudden change?" Many scholars have attempted to answer this question, among them a remarkable French Jew named Jules Isaac.

Jules Isaac was born in Rennes, France, in 1877. His grandfather served in Napoleon's army. His father was a colonel in the French army, but Jules decided against a military career. Instead, he became a historian. His books on French and European history became the standard textbooks in all French secondary schools. He was a man who believed in liberty, logic, fraternity, and enlightenment. He believed that the world was moving forward, to knowledge, to understanding, and to idealism.

This historian, who believed in culture and man's future, was away from his home during the German occupation. He returned to find that the gestapo had killed his wife, daughter, and other members of his family. Aside from his personal bereavement, his faith in human nature was shattered. The murder of innocent women and children, who had nothing to do with the war, shook him deeply. He was determined to search out the origins of this irrational brutality and hatred. Being a great Latinist, he gathered church catechisms and church teachings and drew up an indictment of what was taught in the seminaries and parochial schools about the Jews. Christian children were taught, for example, that Jews were "the deicide people," and that the Jews were dispersed throughout the world as a punishment for the crucifixion.

He compiled anti-Semitic statements found in textbooks used by parochial schoolchildren. For example, "Jerusalem and the Jewish people were visibly punished by the hand of God.... The Temple of Jerusalem was destroyed, and with it the religion of Moses ceased to exist. From that time the Jews wandered homeless, exiled, over the face of the earth." Or, "Were Jesus' prophecies fulfilled? History teaches us that in the year 70...the survivors were scattered, and from then on the 'Jewish race' never succeeded, despite all its repeated efforts in rebuilding a nation." And still another, "From that time [the year 70 C.E.) the Jews lived scattered all over the world. They should realize only too well that they had succeeded in killing the Lord." He gathered all this material in a book entitled *The Teaching of Contempt: Christian Roots of Anti-Semitism*.

Several of Isaac's friends who were Catholic leaders read the book. Deeply moved, they were determined to rectify an ancient wrong. In 1959, Pope John XXIII eliminated the word *perfidis* from a prayer which referred to the perfidious Jews, the treacherous Jews—from the Good Friday liturgy. And then in 1960, in a private interview with the pope, Jules Isaac requested that the head of the church publicly condemn the teaching of contempt. Thus, at the Ecumenical Council, a statement on the church's attitude to the Jews was distributed to the bishops.

The committee, under the chairmanship of German cardinal Bea, was confronted by a delicate problem. The gospel account in the New Testament is violently anti-Jewish. It depicts the Jews crying out, "Crucify him, crucify him." The passages could not be deleted from the New Testament or the Gospel rewritten. But the teaching that the Jews in all the ages are guilty of that crime is not in the Gospel. And Jules Isaac points out not only how harmful this generalized accusation is to Christian children, but also that it is historically false.

He writes: "At the time of Jesus, there were two million Jews in Palestine and five million Jews outside of Palestine." At the most, he reasons, there were one thousand people in the mob. The remaining one million, nine hundred and ninety-nine thousand Jews in Palestine weren't there. Nor were the five million Jews outside of Palestine. They were not guilty, nor were their descendants and their descendants after them.

And then there is a theological difficulty. If it was God's will that Jesus was to be sacrificed to redeem humankind for its sins, then those who crucified him were merely instruments of God's will. They were predestined to perform this task. How can they be held guilty? And so, point four in the schema on ecumenism asserts that it is wrong and harmful to blame the Jews for the crucifixion of Jesus. The Jesuit magazine *America* wrote: "To blame the passion (the suffering) of Jesus upon the Jews is a scandal."

When Jules Isaac's wife was arrested by the Nazis, she managed to write a note to her husband: "You must save yourself for your work. The world is waiting for it."

Jules Isaac died in 1963 at the age of eighty-six. Although he did not live long enough to complete his task, he died with the assurance that his efforts were beginning to bear fruit, that those who had been moved by his determined campaign would continue his struggle against hatred.

52 The Crucifixion of the Jews

Franklin Littell

For many centuries, the Jews tended to look within themselves for flaws which would explain the mindless oppression they endured. Maybe, our ancestors wondered, it's because we're so different from others. We talk differently. We dress differently. So let's become like everybody else. We should learn to speak without an accent, dress like others, shave off our beards, and assimilate. Then we will be accepted and anti-Semitism will end.

It seemed like a logical solution. And then they saw how the most integrated and assimilated Jews anywhere in the world—the Jews of Germany—were the first victims of Nazism.

Dr. Franklin Littell, professor of theology at Temple University, has written a different kind of book about anti-Semitism. *The Crucifixion of the Jews,* published in 1986, is an indictment of the failure of Christians to understand the Jewish experience, written for Christians by a great Christian scholar.

Littell begins by stating that the cornerstone of Christian anti-Semitism is the displacement myth. This is the myth that the mission of the Jewish people was finished with the coming of Jesus Christ. The author says: "To teach that a people's mission is finished, that they have been relegated to the limbo of history, has murderous implications." In other words, if Judaism is no longer valid, then Jews are expendable.

The murder of six million Jews during the Holocaust by baptized Christians, from whom church membership in good standing was never withdrawn, raises the most compelling question of the credibility of Christianity. And, says Littell, "the existence of a restored Israel, proof positive that the Jewish

150

people are not annihilated...is substantial refutation of the traditional Christian myth about their end in the historic process."

Littell says that if a dialogue between Christians and Jews were to take place, then Christians would have to give up their traditional practice of trying to convert Jews. This has been Christianity's relationship to the Jews for centuries. Christians have invited the Jews to give up being Jews, and when they did not, anti-Semitism blossomed. The author shows us just how this happened with Martin Luther and the Jews, attacks then used by the Nazis in their anti-Semitic propaganda campaign. Luther, frustrated in his attempt to convert Jews, wrote: "First, their synagogue or school is to be set on fire, and what won't burn is to be heaped over with dirt and dumped on.... Second, their houses are to be torn down and destroyed.... Third, they are to have all their prayerbooks and Talmuds taken from them.... Fourth, their rabbis are to be forbidden to teach...to praise God, to thank God, to pray to God, to teach of God among us and ours."

Littell then discusses the great churchman, Dietrich Bonhoeffer, who was murdered by the Nazis just three days before American troops reached the prison where he was incarcerated. A pastor who opposed the racist church in Germany, Bonhoeffer is regarded as a martyr. Yet Littell quotes these words that he declared openly from his pulpit: "The Church of Christ has never lost sight of the thought that the 'chosen' people (the Jews) who nailed the redeemer of the world to the cross, must bear the curse for its action through a long period of suffering....The conversion of Israel will be the end of the people's period of suffering."

Dr. Littell points out that if the churches had used the spiritual power at their disposal, called the Nazi leaders to repentance, and excommunicated them for failing to respond, history might have been different. Instead, the Nazis remained church members, and the church even honored mass murderers. Adolph Hitler died a Roman Catholic, and an annual mass is celebrated in his memory in Madrid! Herman Goering died a Lutheran, and Dr. Littell comments with these startling words: "The murder of European Jewry by baptized Christians...raises the credibility of Christianity. Was Jesus a false messiah? Can one be a true messiah if one's followers feel compelled to torture and destroy other human beings who think differently?"

Littell calls to task virtually every civilized nation for its failure to intervene, to rescue those who could have been saved. He affirms that the Holocaust is the "unfinished business" of the Christian churches and suggests that Christian congregational worship memorialize the six million who were murdered. He concludes with his belief that Christians have a great deal of atoning to do.

Although this book was written primarily for Christians, every Jew should read it. It is reassuring to know that people like Dr. Littell possessed the courage and integrity to confront the church which has nurtured anti-Semitic teachings for so many centuries.

By the same token, perhaps it is time for Jews to take a critical look at the virus of prejudice that still exists within Judaism. In emulating Dr. Littell's example, we Jews, victims for so many centuries, can now transform ourselves into activists for understanding.

53 Great Jews in Music

Darryl Lyman

Until the present generation, virtually every Jewish child received some form of musical instruction. Along with a good public school education, Jewish parents strove to equip their sons and daughters with a sense of culture. Accordingly, Jewish neighborhoods reverberated with the sounds of pianos, violins, and other instruments on virtually every day of the week. Piano students often listened to recordings of Arthur Rubinstein and Vladimir Horowitz, while aspiring violinists listened to the seemingly effortless playing of Isaac Stern and Jascha Heifetz.

In *Great Jews in Music,* Darryl Lyman has assembled over one hundred snapshots of the greatest Jews in music, their tragedies and their triumphs. In his introduction, he points out that Jews once had only two primary musical outlets. Those Jews who sang became cantors in the synagogue, while those blessed with instrumental ability became klezmer musicians. *Klezmorim,* often poor Jews, traveled the circuit of weddings and bar mitzvahs, adding festive or sentimental music to the occasion, depending upon the moment. Lyman points to Salamone Rossi as the first Jewish composer who crossed over into general society's music during the seventeenth century.

After the French Revolution and Emancipation, many talented Jews left the ghetto behind for the acceptance afforded to those who assimilated. Felix Mendelssohn and Gustav Mahler were two of the great composers who took this route. Other Jews, however, gained fame and adulation, as Jews, purely on the basis of their talent. With the coming of the Holocaust, many Jewish artists fled Germany, many to the United States, a handful to Palestine and other countries. Especially in America and the State of Israel, Jewish composers and artists have flourished, helping to

153

shape the musical idiom of the lands where they have now settled in freedom.

One obvious choice for inclusion in the book is Irving Berlin, America's most beloved songwriter. Originally named Israel Baline, this son of a Russian cantor was born in Russia in 1888. At the age of fourteen he tried street singing, made a few pennies, and became enamored of show business. Working as a singing waiter on the Lower East Side, Baline, who by now had changed his name to Irving Berlin, started writing songs. During the course of his sterling career, he wrote dozens of hit songs, including "Alexander's Ragtime Band," "God Bless America," "A Pretty Girl Is Like a Melody," "Easter Parade," and "White Christmas." The cantor's son became an American institution.

A more contemporary musical genius, Leonard Bernstein, was American born and raised. He loved the Hasidic tunes sung by his father and the melodies of his local Massachusetts synagogue. His love of piano led to an interest in conducting, and ultimately to an apprenticeship and friendship with Aaron Copland that extended for some fifty years. At the age of twenty-five, he became assistant conductor of the New York Philharmonic, a launching pad for his international fame as both a conductor and composer. He is best known in popular music circles for his beautiful score of *West Side Story,* which has become a classic of American theater and film. In recognition of his commitment to the State of Israel, he received the honor of being invited to conduct the Israeli Philharmonic at a 1967 concert on the top of Mount Scopus in Jerusalem, just one month after Israel's dramatic victory in the Six-Day War.

Millions of Americans love Barbra Streisand and have seen the movie "Funny Girl." Fans sometimes forget, however, that Streisand portrays the legendary performer Fanny Brice. Born in New York in 1891 as Fanny Borach, Brice began her career in show business by singing in her father's saloon. George M. Cohan hired her as a chorus girl at the tender age of fifteen. Four years later she began her professional relationship with Flo Ziegfeld in the Ziegfeld Follies. After her tumultuous marriage to Nicky Arnstein ended in divorce, she married and then divorced Broadway producer Billy Rose. Two of her signature songs, "My Man" and "Second Hand Rose," are beloved to this day, and her later-life portrayal of Baby Snooks is still considered a radio gem. Brice was one of the first celebrities to have plastic surgery performed on her nose. She died in 1951 at age fifty nine, a show business legend who gave others much pleasure, though her own life was filled with much pain.

The Gershwin brothers, George and Ira, composer and lyricist, electrified audiences around the world with their unconventional style. The brothers grew up in a poor section of New York City's Lower East Side, but parlayed their musical talent into an important place in musical history. George had his first song published at the age of seventeen. At the age of twenty-one, he wrote "Swanee" and rose to Broadway prominence. "Rhapsody in Blue" was first performed just five years later. George and Ira collaborated on such hits as "Fascinating Rhythm," "'Swonderful," "I Got Rhythm," and "Embraceable You." Two years after the first performance of *Porgy and Bess,* George Gershwin died at age thirty-eight of a brain tumor. Though Ira continued the Gershwin legacy for many more years, America had lost a musical genius.

"You ain't heard nothin' yet!" was the proud declaration of the great Al Jolson. Born in Lithuania as Asa Yoelson, his rabbi/cantor father brought the family to America. Jolson sang in the streets, in restaurants, in burlesque shows, then graduated to the vaudeville stage. By 1911, Jolson was on Broadway in blackface, and a year later introduced the runway that extended into the audience, enabling him to reach out and touch the people with songs like "My Mammy," "April Showers," and "Sonny Boy." Jolson starred in the first significant sound movie, "The Jazz Singer." At his death in 1950, Jolson's $4 million estate went to worthy charities of every orientation.

Great Jews in Music is filled with page after page of delightful biographies, little-known facts, and nostalgic reminiscences of songs America loved and loves.

Eddie Cantor is there, as is Arthur Fiedler. The great violinists Jascha Heifetz, Yehudi Menuhin, Isaac Stern, and Itzhak Perlman, are included, as are opera singers Jan Peerce, Robert Merrill, Roberta Peters, and Beverly Sills. If you like popular music, there are sections on Bette Midler, Barbra Streisand, Bob Dylan, Barry Manilow, Sophie Tucker, Dinah Shore, and Simon and Garfunkel.

And then, of course, there is a portrait of Arthur Rubinstein, possibly the single most recognized pianist in history. Born in Poland in 1887, Rubinstein played the piano by ear at age three.

Convinced that he would never be a success, Rubinstein attempted suicide at the age of twenty-one, but survived. Then began a long road to "overnight success" in his forties. In 1949 he joined with violinist Jascha Heifetz and cellist Gregor Piatigorsky as part of what *Life* magazine dubbed "The Million Dollar Trio." A passionate supporter of the State of Israel, Rubinstein performed there frequently, and established a chair of musicology at the Hebrew University of Jerusalem. A triennial International Piano Competition in Israel also bears his name. When Arthur Rubinstein died in 1982 at the age of ninety-five, the entire world mourned his passing.

The reader who enjoys music will find this book informative and entertaining.

54 Response to Modernity

Michael M. Meyer

Dr. Michael Meyer is professor of Jewish history at the Hebrew Union College, Jewish Institute of Religion. He is also a product of the Reform movement, which is the subject of his superb book *Response to Modernity*.

Today, Reform Judaism is arguably the most dynamic and fastest growing of the three major movements within American Judaism. With over nine hundred congregations and a combined population nearing one and a half million men, women, and children, Reform is at the zenith of its popularity. This achievement comes after less than two decades of existence.

Meyer begins by establishing that until the eighteenth century, many Jews regarded their religion as external. The Written and Oral Laws were, in their view, both revealed by God to Moses at Mount Sinai. Thus, all subsequent evolutionary changes were seen as elaborations on the Sinaitic covenant. Inasmuch as the covenant came "from heaven," no human being could simply change it, regardless of societal circumstances. During the eighteenth century, the French Revolution and the Enlightenment enabled Jews to enter the larger society, to encounter new crosscurrents of culture and science that in turn led to a reexamination of previously held absolutist assumptions.

A man by the name of Israel Jacobson was the founder of the Reform movement. A wealthy and Jewishly literate layman, he established a trade and agricultural school for poor boys in 1801 in Seesen, a small town in Germany. Along with the school, Jacobson built a sanctuary for worship, instituting then-revolutionary reforms such as an organ, liturgy in both Hebrew and German, German hymns, and a sermon in German.

Jacobson's bold experiment resonated with those Jews already

157

bent on reform in other European cities. The *Wissenschaft des Judentums,* the scholarly study of the Jewish religion and people, emerged a decade after Jacobson dedicated his school. Radical thinkers such as Samuel Holdheim and Abraham Geiger argued that the modern Jew had to make a complete break with Orthodoxy in order to enable Judaism to enter the new world. Geiger called his new approach "Prophetic Judaism." Values, social justice, social morality, and a vision of universal peace far outweighed the value of the law in Geiger's mind.

Orthodox opposition to Geiger and his Reform colleagues was immediate and predictable. After all, the whole authority base on which Orthodox Judaism was built had been challenged. Calling upon both religious and civil authorities where possible, Orthodox leaders sought to stifle the rise of Reform and called on their colleagues to do likewise in neighboring lands. Over time, while pockets of Reform flourished in a number of communities in Germany, France, and England, the intervention of secular authorities blocked Reform's full potential for dynamic growth.

That was not the case in the United States. With no entrenched Orthodox structure, America was ripe for a modern manifestation of Judaism, assuming strong leadership and vision to launch the movement here. And, as is often the case in Jewish history, the laity led the clergy in that reforming process. Dr. Meyer tells the story of congregation Beth Elohim in Charleston, South Carolina. A group of members wished to have more English in the service, a weekly sermon, shorter services, and elimination of the sale of "honors" in the synagogue. Rebuffed by those in power, the group, led by a layman named Isaac Harby, formed their own congregation in January 1825, the Reformed Society of Israelites. The congregation published its own prayer book, and today is recognized as the first Reform congregation in the United States.

Twenty-one years later, in 1846, the man known as the architect of Reform in the United States, Isaac Mayer Wise, arrived on these shores. While other more scholarly reformers had preceded him, Wise had both the vision and persuasive powers to win over key people to his radical positions. At his first pulpit in Albany, New York, he introduced a coed choir, confirmation, and German and English hymns. After an ugly public episode in Albany, during which Wise was assaulted by a congregant on the pulpit, he came to Cincinnati, Ohio, to a congregation which would ultimately bear his name.

The author takes us through the Civil War, which saw a Jewish community divided as America was divided. Isaac Mayer Wise, anxious to have one Jewish presence in the United States led by American-trained rabbis, saw his chance following the end of the conflict. In 1873, thirty-four congregations formed the Union of American Hebrew Congregations. Two years later, in 1875, this congregational body established the Hebrew Union College, the Reform seminary of which Wise had dreamed. By 1889 there were a sufficient number of rabbinic alumni to form the Central Conference of American Rabbis, the Reform rabbinical association.

In 1885, a group of nineteen rabbis met in Pittsburgh to draft a platform for this embryonic movement. The resulting document, "The Pittsburgh Platform," rooted Reform in moral and ethical values while downplaying adherence to Jewish law except insofar as it was meaningful to the individual.

Dr. Meyer traces the years from those early beginnings, showing the growth of Reform groups such as the Sisterhood and Brotherhood. The reader sees how Reform rabbis led the movement into the realm of social justice, fought on behalf of labor, grappled with the issues of interfaith marriage and Zionism, and revolutionized Jewish education under the influence of Emanuel Gamoran. In 1937, the Central Conference of American Rabbis adopted a new platform in Columbus, Ohio, which included a pro-Zionist platform. Rabbis like Abba Hillel Silver, Stephen S. Wise, and Leon Fram courageously argued for the platform, with a vision brought to fruition by the establishment of the State of Israel in 1948.

Meyer shows us the growth of Reform Judaism abroad, in communities now ready for its message. Furthermore, the period of explosive growth in Reform following World War II is carefully documented: the expansion of HUC-JIR to four campuses; the move of the UAHC to New York City; the involvement of Reform in civil rights and anti-Vietnam War protest; and the ordination of the first woman rabbi in 1972. As the twenty-first century approaches, the Reform movement stands poised to lead world Jewry. As its second century of existence draws to a close, it can point with pride to a record of achievement unmatched in many generations.

55 The Source

James Michener

The novels of James Michener are sui generis, one of a kind. There is a massive amount of research that clearly precedes the writing of a single line: facts, people, customs, language, natural environment, and the like. But Michener, unlike virtually any author of recent centuries, takes those facts and builds a story line spanning history. Where hard facts are skimpy, Michener uses his fertile imagination to create credible explanations of why things happened as they did and crafts full-blown characters who move the story along from the unknown to the known.

Such skills have made Michener one of the most widely read writers of historical fiction in the twentieth century. Both *Hawaii* and *Alaska* are moving chronicles of two of America's least known states. For the generation of the 1960s, *The Drifters* captured the essence of the hippie generation, young men and women traveling abroad to "find themselves" in exotic locales.

For Jews, however, Michener's novel *The Source* is a treasured piece of literature on the history of the Jewish people. Whatever its factual inaccuracies, *The Source* remains a staple of Jewish homes and libraries more than thirty years after its initial publication in 1965.

The story begins when an archaeologist named Dr. Cullinae undertakes an excavation of Tell Makor in Israel. In ancient times, certain sites stood out as obvious places upon which to build a settlement or town. The site may have been close to water or set on high ground, making it a perfect place for a military encampment. Over many thousands of years, a cycle ensued in which a settlement was razed, captured, or abandoned. The locale itself, however, remained valuable. And so it was that generation after generation built settlement upon settlement, in the process creating a tall mound which contained centuries of history within its remnants. Such a mound is called a tell, a virtual source of living historical evidence about those who dwelt there. Tell Makor was just such a place, a site, we are told, that would take a full ten years to excavate.

Cullinae undertakes the dig, and almost immediately finds objects of increasingly ancient evidence, beginning with a bullet from a British rifle from about 1950. Then, in fairly rapid succession comes a Turkish gold coin from the year 1875, a golden menorah from 1550, a Crusader seal from 1290, a Crusader headstone from 1125, a Muslim piece from 640, a stone from a synagogue in 350, a coin from 70, a piece of glass from 5 B.C.E., a piece of Greek statuary from 165 B.C.E., a Babylonian piece dated 600 B.C.E., clay pots from 1400 B.C.E., a clay figure of the Canaanite goddess Astarte from 2000 B.C.E., and ultimately, a flint sickle from 10,000 B.C.E.

This gradual series of random finds, carefully supervised by an Israeli government representative named Dr. Eliav, enables Michener to use the flint sickle to flash back to the origin of the tell in 9831 B.C.E. and to tell its story, then subsequently to utilize each piece in turn as a focus for a chapter leading to the present.

As we begin, in the year 10,000 B.C.E., Michener's storytelling genius moves into high gear as we are first introduced to a well, named Makor, the source. A beekeeper named Ur is presented as the tell's first resident, a man who gathered honey and tended fields with the primitive sickle found in the tell. Tragedy befalls him, as the elements and wild animals claim his family. As the chapter ends, Ur confronts the mysteries of life and death.

We move forward eight thousand years to a time represented by the clay statue of Astarte. Makor is now a town with seven hundred inhabitants ruled by its own king. It survives as an untroubled community because of its small size, having never attracted the attention of Egypt or Mesopotamia. In the past it had been destroyed many times—its men killed, their wives raped, and their children enslaved. The current village leader is a man named Urbaal, a direct descendant of the original Ur.

Like others in the village, Urbaal worships idols, and so buys the statue of Astarte to help assure a good crop. The people are required to offer their firstborn sons to the god Melak to protect them in times of war. Urbaal's son is burned at the altar, but Urbaal is given a fertile young maiden with whom he has intercourse in public, the hope being that he will have a new child soon. Urbaal falls in love with the prostitute and wants to marry her, but such a marriage is forbidden. He kills another man who is chosen to have intercourse with the maiden, and flees to the altar of a man named Joktan, where he claims refuge. Joktan, a monotheist, tries to protect Urbaal, but fails. Urbaal is executed. Nevertheless, Joktan travels to Makor, bringing monotheism into the world of the tell.

Six hundred years pass, and it is now 1419 B.C.E. In a scene reminiscent of the burning bush tale in Exodus, a character named Zakok is commanded by God, now named El-Shaddai, to conquer Makor. A man named Uriel now governs Makor, and sees Zadok and his men approaching. A temporary peace gives way to slaughter, Makor is defeated, and all but nine of its inhabitants are destroyed.

An engrossing style characterizes each succeeding chapter, as the relics from the dig take us slowly from the past to the present. Each section echoes faint reminders of a great biblical moment, then the destruction of the Temple and the Ten Lost Tribes. Many of the Jews are taken into exile, but the Jews of Makor remain as a constant presence in what is now Israel.

Michener takes us into the Jerusalem of King Herod, where Jesus is crucified by the Romans and the blame is laid at the feet of the Jews. We witness the destruction of the second Temple, the fall of Masada, the enslavement in Rome, and the rise of the little school at Yavneh whose students preserved the Jewish people and tradition. The Mishnah, also known as the oral law, is committed to writing as a companion to the written law, the Torah. The synagogue replaces the Temple in Jerusalem, while the rabbi becomes the head of the community in place of the high priest. Christianity arises, and Makor is razed to make way for the church.

Then come the Muslims in the seventh century, the Crusades in the eleventh and twelfth centuries, the Ottoman Empire in the sixteenth century, the Zionist settlers of the nineteenth and twentieth centuries, Israel's statehood, and the War of Independence. All these great events in Jewish history are captured through Michener's telling, the events based on this simple mound of earth.

As the book concludes, another relic is discovered, indicating that Makor is far older than anyone could have ever anticipated—perhaps dating back to 200,000 B.C.E. The implication is that the dig will go on, striving to discover an ever greater Jewish historical past.

56 Jewish Cooking in America

Joan Nathan

As you leaf through the pages of this book, you can almost smell a brisket simmering or imagine people arguing at the Carnegie Deli in New York. With over three hundred kosher recipes, *Jewish Cooking in America,* published in 1994, provides mouthwatering illustrations, quotes, and anecdotes about Jewish food and life.

The author is as interested in people as she is interested in the food itself, and the pictures are as diverse as the recipes and people behind them—from old advertisements to a photograph of immigrant farmers in Connecticut. Next to an early Maxwell House coffee ad for "Shabbos Coffee," Nathan explains that Jews thought coffee was forbidden during Pesach (like other beans), until a rabbi explained that coffee beans were technically berries.

Traveling around the country, Nathan ate family meals and shared family histories, which unfolded through stories of food. Eating is central to Jewish life, and just as certain foods represent love, such as chicken soup, others represent specific holidays. What would Purim be without hamantaschen, or Chanukah without latkes? These recipes are included, as are new interpretations of traditional foods, such as Curried Sweet Potato Latkes. Reflecting geographical influences are Moroccan Brisket with Olives, Adafina Georgian-Jewish Southern Fried Chicken, and Argentinean Potato Meat Pie. These creative versions illustrate how Jews have adapted their recipes to their environment along with the rest of their lives. Fortunately, Nathan has reduced the fat and sugar content whenever possible, without compromising on taste.

Other standard American Jewish fare, such as kugel, gefilte fish and dill pickles, are here as well. Of equal interest are recipes that sound a bit odd—brisket made with Coca-Cola, or a mouthwatering Dumpling Cake Soaked in Caramel Sauce. There is also an easy, delicious brownies recipe for Pesach that you'll want to make year round. Nathan introduces us to many restaurateurs, including Abe Kirschenbaum, who, along with his mother and brother, owns Levana, a kosher restaurant on New York's Upper West Side. They specialize in contemporary food; Nathan ate Cornish hens with morels and wild rice there.

Certain Jewish foods, such as the bagel, have been woven into the American consciousness, which makes them very popular in the food industry. In the chapter on breads, for example, you learn that making bagels is a fun way to start a Sunday, and also get to read about Murray Lender, whose father founded Lender's Bagels, as he reflects on bagels in America. In the fifties, bagels were thought of as primarily a Jewish food; non-Jews had little interest in eating them. Today, however, many bagel businesses aren't even run by Jews anymore; H and H Bagels in New York, for example, is operated by a Puerto Rican family.

Kosher food has also become an incredibly popular commodity, and almost all kinds of ethnic foods are served in kosher restaurants in New York and Los Angeles. Nathan even includes a recipe for South Indian Kosher Cauliflower, Potato, and Pea Curry from a defunct Indian restaurant in New York, which served only kosher, vegetarian food.

Well-known chefs share their recipes, including Molasses Roast Quail with Savoy Cabbage and Kasha from Anne Rosenzweig of New York's Arcadia. Chef Rosenzweig remembers the influence of her grandmother, a cook in the Catskills. (While she worked, her grandfather was busy at shul!) Moishe Mizrachi of Moishe's Falafel is a first-generation falafel maker. Regarded as "the best stretch pushcart in New York City," Moishe's stand is located in the diamond district (46th Street and Sixth Avenue in Manhattan). Not only does Moishe give tips on how to make the best falafel—he divulges his own falafel recipe!

Nathan couldn't believe it when she first learned about Zingerman's Deli in Ann Arbor, Michigan. It's "not really a deli but more of an international food emporium like New York's Zabar's, but with a definite Jewish touch." Well known not only in Ann Arbor, but also in metropolitan Detroit, Zingerman's makes outstanding sandwiches and soups. She includes their Mushroom and Barley Soup recipe, which calls for porcini mushrooms.

This book also offers a political history of food; a page is devoted to "Dining Kosher in the White House." Here we learn that "State dinners with multiple kosher meals began during the Carter Administration." Henry Haller remembers the Camp David Peace Treaty dinner in 1978 when he was a White House chef. "Later, a kosher state dinner for one hundred and eighty guests was served to Prime Minister Menachem Begin on April 15, 1980." He recalls the menu, which included, in part, "cold Columbia River salmon with sauce verte and golden twists, roast duckling with glazed peaches...."

In a tribute to Jewish-American cooking, Nathan includes a page on the history of *The Settlement Cook Book*. This cookbook, still widely regarded as essential in Jewish homes today, began as a pamphlet with 100 recipes to help immigrants new to America. First published as a book in 1902, by 1925 it had readers in Australia and China. In that same year, fifty thousand dollars was raised from sales of the book and used to build a new Jewish community center.

Clearly, *Jewish Cooking in America* is far more than a cookbook. It is a joy to read even if you never intend to cook.

57 Guess Who's Jewish in American History?

Bernard Postal and Lionel Koppman

How old is the American Jewish community? Older than the original thirteen colonies. Who was the first Jewish doctor to practice in America? Dr. Jacob Lumbrozo, who came to Maryland in 1656! This book is a compendium, full of short biographies with interesting facts, covering many remarkable men and women whose names aren't well known today, but who made significant contributions to American culture.

The reader will also find fascinating information about well-known figures, such as Emma Lazarus, who died without knowing that her sonnet would become famous and grace the Statue of Liberty. Levi Strauss, a secondhand-goods peddler, failed in the California gold rush and turned to making special pants for miners. This easy-to-read book also makes browsing fun, with more than twenty pages of photographs, including pictures of such notables as Emma Goldman, Joseph Pulitzer, and Dr. Jonas E. Salk.

The book includes sections about "Arts and Journalism," "Women," "Science and Medicine," "Labor," "Business and Banking," and "Sports." "Curosia and Eccentrics" is another heading, as is "Nobel Laureates," and "The Presidency and Jewry"—which provides a unique look at how various presidents have treated Jews and the State of Israel. For example, civil servants were first guaranteed the right to observe the Sabbath under Pres. Rutherford B. Hayes.

The introduction places Jews in historical context within America. Rather than merging fully into American culture, Jews have maintained both cultures. Although Jews lived and worked under harsh conditions as new immigrants, there were fewer instances of crime, drunkenness, or illiteracy in the Jewish community in comparison to other groups. Ford Maddox Ford, the English literary critic, visited America in the '20s and said: "The intellectual vividness is partly due to the immense Jewish population...the only people who really loved books with a passionate yearning that transcended their attention to all terrestrial manifestations."

The presence of Jews at American political events is noted as a means of demonstrating the recognition of Jews as part of America. In 1789, when George Washington was inaugurated as president, Rabbi Gershom Mendes Seixas, spiritual leader of the Spanish and Portuguese Synagogue, was one of the guests invited. In a special section toward the book's end, entitled "Documents of Honor," three letters Washington wrote to different Jewish congregations on the occasion of congregational celebrations are reprinted.

Eight thousand Jews served in the Civil War. As for the Jewish stance on slavery: in general, Jews behaved as the people around them did. The first rabbi to open the House of Representatives with prayer was a well-known anti-abolitionist named Morris Jacob Raphall, who delivered a sermon saying that biblical law sanctioned the right to have slaves. He was bitterly opposed by Jews and non-Jewish liberals in the North. Rabbi David Einhorn, of Baltimore, not only fiercely denounced the sermon and slavery, but as a result had to flee mob violence.

As for music, we learn that Irving Berlin came to the States with his family when he was only four years old, and as a child sang in the street for pennies. Berlin composed two of the most well-loved American tunes: "White Christmas" and "Easter Parade." Aaron Copland, Leonard Bernstein, and Beverly Sills are also included.

Evolving American Judaism is addressed in "Religions," along with brief profiles of those who initiated change. Rabbi Isaac Mayer Wise, who helped found the American Reform movement, is included, as is Felix Adler, who helped shape the New York Society for Ethical Culture. When Leo Tolstoy was asked how he felt about the "American literary scene," his response was negative, except for the pleasure he derived from the writings of Felix Adler.

There are also examples of great heroism. During World War II, four chaplains, including a Jew named Alexander David Goode, went down aboard a troop transport. The ship was torpedoed, and the four men went on deck, prayed with the fearful passengers, helped them into their life jackets and lifeboats, removed their own life jackets, and gave them to others. Then the men stayed on deck, arm in arm, praying aloud as the ship sank.

The section on "Women" shows the influence of strong Jewish women, and includes fascinating biographies. One of those included is Dr. Rosalyn Sussman Yalow, who won a 1977 Nobel Prize in medicine. Another remarkable woman profiled is Henrietta Szold, who founded both Hadassah and the Youth Aliyah, which saved more than 13,000 Jewish adolescents from the Nazis. In the chapter's opening, it is reported that "Jewish women were engaged in commerce and trade in early Colonial America. Mrs. David Hays, whose husband was serving with the Revolutionary forces in Westchester County, New York, was still in bed with a newborn infant when she defied the demands of the British forces to disclose the hiding place of a party of patriots."

At the book's end, a special section, "Did you know?" asks many interesting questions, including "Who donated the world's largest art collection to the American People?" and "Who is one of the greatest bullfighters in history?" Joseph Hirschhorn, a Russian immigrant, is the answer to the former; Sidney Franklin, from Brooklyn, was the bullfighter.

Among the writers, Dorothy Parker receives a prominent note. When reviewing theater, her clever reviews had the power to close a show. Of Katharine Hepburn she wrote, "She ran the gamut of emotions from A to B." Before she died in 1967, Parker suggested the one-liner "Excuse My Dust" for her epitaph.

58 The Last of the Just

André Schwarz-Bart

There is a remarkable legend promulgated by Jewish mystics regarding thirty-six righteous men for whose sake the world is preserved in spite of its evil. According to the mystics, these thirty-six righteous individuals, known as the *lamed-vav-niks*("thirty-six" in Hebrew numerology) do not know who they are. What they share in common is absolute goodness, kindness, caring, and concern.

At first glance, André Schwarz-Bart would seem to have been a rather unlikely author for a volume as profound and powerful as *The Last of the Just*. He was a man of no philosophic education and very little formal education. Born into a Polish-Jewish family who immigrated to Germany and then to France, Schwarz-Bart's parents were murdered by the Nazis when the author was fifteen years old. With no family to help him, the young André joined the maquis, the French underground, to resist Nazi tyranny.

In his spare time, André read detective stories, until he found Dostoyevsky's *Crime and Punishment*. This classic novel awakened a literary impulse within him, a desire to write a book that dealt with the meaning of life, perhaps to make sense of the chaos that filled his own. Subsequently, he was introduced to the legend of the thirty-six righteous men. It gripped him, but also left him with a dilemma. The thirty-six are unknown. How can you write a novel about an unknown hero? Therefore, Schwarz-Bart transformed the legend and wrote, not of individuals, but rather of the Levi family, a family of saintly people whose merit sustained the world.

The story begins in England in the year 1031, after the Bishop of York has preached a sermon arousing the populace against the handful of Jews in the city. The local residents burn the synagogues and Jewish homes, while the survivors flee into a tower, with their leader Aaron Ha-Levi. He tells them that it is their lot to endure sufferings in this evil world, and thereby to enable the world to continue. The whole group commits suicide rather than being dragged to forced conversion. Aaron Ha-Levi, the book says, is the first of "the Just."

One child of Aaron Ha-Levi, Aaron Levi, is smuggled safely to France, where he, too, becomes known for his saintly character. He is ultimately thrown, by anti-Semites, into a bonfire of Jewish manuscripts in the streets of Paris and dies, but a descendant escapes to Spain. And so, through the family, down through the ages, the author traces the family of "The Just," until we find them in a Polish town, a family of workmen, crystal polishers.

We first meet Mordecai, a giant of a man, a field worker who is not afraid to fight the Polish peasants. He becomes a peddler and meets and marries his Judith. After the pogroms begin, Mordecai's son, Benjamin, a tailor, flees to Berlin and from there to a small village in West Germany. Now operating his own business, Benjamin sends for his parents, marries, and has two sons; Moritz and Ernie, the hero-victim of the novel.

As the Hitler period begins, Schwarz-Bart shows us the mental torture of Jewish schoolchildren and the wave of suicides among them. Ernie slashes his wrists and spends two years in bed, after which the family moves to Paris to escape the Nazis. The Nazis occupy France, and Jews are murdered. Ernie joins the army to fight the occupation, but soon realizes that resistance is to no avail.

How can this be, he asks himself? Raised with the teaching that he is destined by God to bear the sufferings of the world, he decides that he no longer wants to live. Pathetically he takes on the persona of a dog—barking, walking around on all fours— symbolic of the fact that he has thrown off, not only faith, but humanity. It is only after a Christian blacksmith recognizes his eyes of suffering as proof that he is a Jew that he returns to the Paris ghetto to rejoin his people.

He meets a young crippled girl and decides to marry her, but she is taken by the Nazis before they can wed. He tries to find her in a Paris concentration camp, but is beaten and left in the street to die. He finds a girl, named Golda, at last, and joins her on a bus with children destined for Auschwitz. It is here at Auschwitz where the book ends, as Ernie insists on entering the gas chambers with a group of women and children. He is the last to die, and the narrator of the book declares:

"Nothing left, no one to mourn them, not even a dog to howl at their absence. They have become part of the dust in the skies of Europe.... I still cannot believe that my friend Ernie Levy is dead. I know where he went and I know what was done to him, but sometimes as I walk, I feel a presence, and sometimes from the heavens, from the clouds, there drops a tear."

The most troubling aspect of Schwarz-Bart's title, *The Last of The Just,* is the implication that Hitler destroyed all goodness in the world along with six million Jews. If Ernie is "the last," then there will be no more righteous individuals willing to endure pain and preserve a sense of hope in the ultimate triumph of the human spirit over any evil.

Or perhaps Schwarz-Bart reminds us that while humanity died in the gas chambers of Europe, men, women, and children of goodwill still have the opportunity to begin again. The Jewish mystics maintain that the lamed-vav-niks are with us still, unknown and unrecognized, yet still serving God—and us. If that is true, then we can look forward to a time when "the Just" will include, not just one family, but thousands, determined to transform society.

59 The Merchant of Venice

William Shakespeare

William Shakespeare was the foremost playwright of his day. Born in 1564, the son of a tanner, he demonstrated his writing proficiency at an early age. By 1599, he was one of the owners of the Globe Theater in London. Then, about 1608, he acquired a piece of the Blackfriars Theater. As the author of at least thirty-seven plays, virtually all of which have reached tens of millions of theatergoers over the centuries, he is considered a true genius of the world theater.

The one Shakespearean play that has troubled and angered Jews over time has been *The Merchant of Venice,* due to its perceived unflattering, even vicious, portrayal of Shylock the moneylender. That image of the Jew has permeated society on many levels, some subtle, others overt. To this day, phrases from the play are used as English colloquialisms. Someone bent on vengeance is spoken of as demanding "his pound of flesh," while mob moneylenders charging high interest rates are called "Shylocks" or "Shys."

Was Shakespeare anti-Semitic? Did he truly hate Jews? Or was he merely reflecting the reality of the society of his day?

The play begins with Antonio, a leading merchant of Venice, a wealthy, respected, and popular man. His young friend Bassanio owes Antonio a great deal of money. Bassanio intends to repay the loan by marrying a wealthy young heiress but needs to borrow additional funds with which to impress her. Antonio is a bit short of cash himself, but says that he will refer him to a local moneylender named Shylock.

Shylock, who secretly hates Antonio, agrees to lend Bassanio the money he needs. As a seeming gesture of goodwill, he agrees to forego his usual interest rates but stipulates that he will cut one pound of flesh from Antonio's body if Bassanio fails to repay the loan on time. Antonio, Bassanio's guarantor, anticipating an influx of cash well before the due date, agrees.

Now the plot thickens. Lorenzo, a close friend of both Antonio and Bassanio, elopes with Shylock's daughter, Jessica, taking a great deal of her father's money with her. Infuriated, Shylock vows revenge, just as Bassanio sets off to win the hand of the wealthy heiress Portia. Bassanio meets Portia, and the two young people fall in love. He even succeeds in passing the test that Portia has devised to weed out her suitors. They make plans to be married, as do their two servants, who also fall in love.

All seems to be well until Antonio sends news that his ships, the source of his income, have been lost at sea. He bids Bassanio farewell, since he assumes that he will die once Shylock has cut the agreed-upon pound of flesh from his body. Portia agrees to pay the bond to save Antonio's life, and Bassanio returns to Venice. But Shylock wants revenge, not just money. Lorenzo stole his daughter and his money. He takes Antonio to court, refuses double the money agreed upon, and demands his pound of flesh.

At this point, Portia enters the court disguised as a lawyer and offers Shylock triple the money due, while entreating him to be merciful. Shylock again refuses. Then, in a twist of plot, Portia becomes the aggressor. Interpreting the agreement according to the letter of the law, she puts Shylock on the defensive. Yes, he may have his pound of flesh, one pound exactly. However, he is not entitled to spill a single drop of Antonio's blood. That was not in the agreement. If he does so, she declares, all of Shylock's land and possessions will be confiscated. Shylock, recognizing his perilous position, agrees to accept triple the money, but that offer is no longer on the table. He backs off further, agreeing to accept the original bond. Again, Portia refuses. He insisted on a strict interpretation of the law, and he shall have it.

The law of Venice held that since Shylock sought the life of a Venetian citizen, all of his wealth was to be divided between his intended victim and the public treasury. Furthermore, he himself is subject to the death penalty. The judge, a Duke, rules with Portia, sparing Shylock's life but confiscating all of his possessions. Antonio agrees to forego his share of the money if Shylock agrees to convert to Christianity and leave his money to his daughter, Jessica, and her beloved Lorenzo. Shylock, broken and defeated, agrees to all these conditions and leaves the court.

Portia, discarding her disguise, marries Bassanio, three of Antonio's ships arrive safely in port, and the story ends happily, except for Shylock's disgrace.

So what do we make of Shylock? Is he truly a villain? Or is he just one of the Jewish people, denied an opportunity to engage in any meaningful occupation other than moneylending in the Venice of his era? Most critics believe that the role of Shylock is not anti-Semitic, that his character was merely a device which Shakespeare employed to create a barrier to the true love that lies at the heart of this romantic comedy.

Usury was forbidden by Christians during the Middle Ages, but they could own property, ships, and businesses. The Jew was proscribed from any of these business endeavors. Jews did what they needed to do in order to survive. Historically, Shakespeare dealt with individuals, not groups, in his plays. The moneylender fit the intent of the drama. Shakespeare presents Shylock as evil at times, sympathetic at others, but never compassionate, kind, or understanding. As a result, he loses everything: his religion, his daughter, and his money—not as a result of his Jewishness, but because of his cruelty. He is a tragic, selfish figure with no redeeming qualities. Though evil was done to him, he did evil in return, and that destroyed him.

Had Shakespeare's plays not attained classic status, the figure of Shylock might have been relegated to minor status in world literature. As it is, regardless of Shakespeare's intent, the character of Shylock and the stereotype of the Jew that his character occasioned remain a source of concern and anger for many Jewish readers today.

60 Great Jews in Sports

Robert Slater

American-born Robert Slater has lived in Jerusalem since 1971. Serving first as a Jerusalem correspondent for UPI, then *Newsweek* and *Time* magazines, Slater, a first-rate journalist, wrote biographies on Yitzhak Rabin and Golda Meir. At heart, however, Bob Slater is a rabid sports fan, and *Great Jews in Sports*, published in 1983, salutes those Jews who have become superstars in all areas of athletic endeavor.

The foreword, written by legendary Boston Celtics coach Red Auerbach, reminds the reader that for Jewish young people, athletics was once often a way out of a life of poverty. In the same way in which minority youngsters today transcend their modest upbringing through their sports talent, many Jews became professional athletes to escape Lower East Side tenements and star in major league arenas and ball fields.

As Jews entered the mainstream of American life, however, upwardly mobile parents no longer viewed sports as something that nice Jewish boys should do. Many promising athletes never made it to the big leagues due to parental vetoes.

Slater recalls his grandfather, who relished watching Jewish ballplayers succeed. But, as the author notes, approval of participation by Jews in sports is a rather recent phenomenon. Traditional Judaism rejected a sports culture, especially in Greek and Roman times, since sports were associated with pagan worship. Therefore, as centuries passed, Jewish parents encouraged their children to become lawyers, doctors, teachers, and writers. During the nineteenth century, however, the tide began to turn. Jewish parents were still not eager for their youngsters to participate in sports, but ended their absolute taboo.

Slater profiles about one hundred figures in the book, drawn

176

from a vast spectrum of sports. In order to qualify for consideration, an athlete had to be born of a Jewish mother. In addition, Americans are emphasized over athletes from other countries. Nevertheless, Slater's first entry is British sprinter Harold Abrahams, a gold medal winner in the 1924 Paris Olympics, who became a lawyer, and who was immortalized in the film about his life, "Chariots of Fire."

One of the more fascinating figures in the book is Moe Berg, a major league baseball catcher for the Brooklyn Dodgers, Chicago White Sox, Cleveland Indians, Washington Senators, and Boston Red Sox. Berg was considered the most educated man ever to play the game of baseball. He spoke twelve languages. After retiring from baseball, he earned a law degree, then entered the service of his country during World War II as a counterintelligence agent. Some students of his life conclude that he worked for the CIA in his later years.

The most unusual sportsman in the book is certainly Sidney Franklin, the first Jewish bullfighter. Born in 1903, Franklin became one of Spain's leading matadors, and was especially acclaimed during the 1930s. How does a Jewish boy become a bullfighter? Having changed his name from the original Frumkin to Franklin, the policeman's shy son originally wanted to be an actor. He studied Spanish at Columbia University, then journeyed to Spain, ostensibly to study Mayan art. Once there, he started a poster business, focusing on art designed for bullfight fans.

Determined to achieve a measure of realism in his posters, he attended a bullfight and was hooked. In spite of warnings from friends that he could never succeed in mastering the sport, Franklin studied with a great matador, Rudolfo Gaona. He entered the ring for the first time in 1923, slipped twice, but killed the bull. Ultimately, Franklin became a star in Spain, Portugal, Mexico, and South America, earning close to one hundred thousand dollars a year.

University of Michigan football fans will enjoy reading about Benny Friedman, "football's first great passer," described by Coach Fielding Yost as "the quarterback who never makes a mistake." A two-time All-American at Michigan (1925–26), Friedman played professional football for seven years (1927–34), and won All-Pro designation four times. After his retirement, Friedman grew increasingly bitter at his lack of recognition, and died in 1982 of a self-imposed gunshot wound.

What baseball fan has not heard of Hank Greenberg, one of baseball's greatest right-handed hitters? He played for fourteen seasons, primarily with the Detroit Tigers, and ended his career with a .313 batting average and 331 home runs, including 11 grand slams. Greenberg was the first National Leaguer to earn one hundred thousand dollars a year. He was named Most Valuable Player in 1935 and 1940, and was selected to the All-Star Team for four consecutive years. In 1934, Greenberg refused to play in a critical game on Yom Kippur out of respect for this holiest day of the Jewish year. It was then that Edgar Guest penned these immortal lines: "We shall miss him in the infield and shall miss him at the bat. But he's true to his religion—and I honor him for that!"

No book on Jewish sports heroes would be complete without the inclusion of Sandy Koufax, the youngest player ever admitted to the Baseball Hall of Fame. He pitched four no-hit games and won the Cy Young award three times in four seasons. In the 1963 season he compiled a record of 25–5, and in 1966 improved to 27–9 with an earned run average of 1.73. Arthritis cut short his career at its peak. But Sandy Koufax remains one of America's true Jewish sports legends, not only because of his talent, but because of his steadfast refusal to pitch on Yom Kippur during the World Series.

Finally, Slater examines the career of the greatest Jewish swimmer of all time, Mark Spitz. Between 1965 and 1972, Spitz won nine Olympic gold medals, one silver, and one bronze. During those years he set thirty-three world records, and was designated "World Swimmer of the Year" in 1967, 1971, and 1972. Spitz attained his greatest fame at the 1972 Olympics in Munich, where he gave the greatest swimming performance in Olympic history. In just eight days he won seven gold medals. The murder of eleven Israeli athletes by terrorists in Munich overshadowed any athletic performance at that Olympics, but with the passage of time the enormity of what Spitz achieved has been duly acknowledged in the annals of sport.

These are just a few of the dozens of Jews in sports to which Bob Slater gives careful attention. It is important for Jews to realize that their fellow Jews produce great sports heroes.

PART V

Israel and the Holocaust

61 Heroes and Hustlers, Hard Hats and Holy Men

Ze'ev Chafets

Born in Pontiac, Michigan, in 1947, Ze'ev Chafets moved to Israel just after the Six-Day War of 1967. A bright, articulate, and politically-savvy young man, he secured a position in the Israeli civil service system, working for Menachem Begin's Herut Party. When Begin, after losing eight campaigns, unexpectedly won Israel's 1977 election and became prime minister Chafets was appointed director of Israel's Government Press Office. There he supervised world press coverage of Egyptian president Anwar el-Sadat's dramatic visit to Jerusalem, making Chafets a national figure less than a decade after his arrival in Israel.

Subsequent to his departure from government life following the 1982 war in Lebanon, Chafets became a journalist and author, writing nonfiction books and novels.

Heroes and Hustlers, Hardhats and Holy Men, Chafets's second book, takes readers inside what he calls the real Israel. In a style reminiscent of Jack Kerouac and Charles Kuralt, Chafets introduces us to famous—and not so famous—Israelis who have enriched their society in a variety of ways. The author's talent for storytelling, humor, and gentle irreverence often leaves the reader laughing out loud at the mental images evoked by Chafets's style.

For example, Chafets describes his first flight to Israel in August 1967, on his way to a college junior year abroad at Hebrew University. He fantasizes himself in a flowing robe, wandering through the Galilee, a pioneer, a soldier, helping to liberate Jerusalem while the strains of the "Theme from Exodus" play softly in the background. As he descended from the plane, he writes, he even kissed the ground, winding up with grease stains from the steaming tarmac all over his clothes, hands and face, as the ground crew convulsed in laughter.

Chafets enables us to see Israel through the eyes of a first-time visitor: the geography of a land where every site is drenched in history; the mix of Jews from countries throughout the world; the Holocaust survivors and the Hasidim. He concludes with his own decision to remain and be part of Israel's future.

The book's title, *Heroes and Hustlers, Hardhats and Holy Men*, derives from the book's three divisions. The section on "Heroes" contains a detailed account of Menachem Begin's stunning 1977 political victory. During the campaign, Chafets served as the coordinator of the Herut Information Department. Begin had suffered a heart attack, and General Ezer Weizman ran the electoral effort on behalf of the "Old Man." Begin rejected all attempts to utilize Madison Avenue advertising techniques, consistently describing himself as "an old Jew." Still, on May 17, 1977, Israelis voted him into power. Chafets describes the elation that filled campaign headquarters: screaming, back-pounding, tears, disbelief, and pure joy. But Begin's decisive actions following the victory reveal part of the inner man.

The author tells us that Begin chose Gen. Moshe Dyan of the opposition Labor Party as his foreign minister. Begin had true admiration and respect for generals. In his years as a member of the Irgun, Begin never participated in violent operations, but he admired the military men who "got things done." Gen. Yigael Yadin became part of his inner circle, as did Gen. Ezer Weizman and Gen. Ariel Sharon.

During the latter years of his first term, Begin spent Thursdays at the Defense Ministry with the generals. Chafets tells us "the dandy-ish prime minister would appear with an open collar instead of his customary tie and jacket, and one or two of his less reverent aides began referring to this as his 'Clint Eastwood outfit.'" Menachem Begin left government in 1983, having established his place in history by making peace with Egypt.

The second division of the book, "Hard Hats and Holy Men," focuses in part on the rise of Oriental Jews, or Sephardim, to positions of prominence during the Begin years. Chafets also describes the vast array of Orthodox Jewish groups in Israeli society who wield enormous power in both religious and political life. "There is a separate Orthodox public school system for Jews, and private, state-funded academies for the hyper-Orthodox; but even in the non-religious, secular public schools, Bible, Talmud, rabbinic literature and Jewish history—and of course Hebrew—are required subjects."

Chafets describes one tension-filled moment when Orthodox guidelines and diplomacy clashed. Less than a month after Anwar Sadat's visit to Jerusalem, an Israeli delegation went to Cairo for preliminary peace negotiations. The delegation, led by Eliahu Ben-Elissar, now Israel's ambassador to the United States, was brought to a seafood restaurant for lunch.

Israeli officials abroad are not allowed to eat non-kosher food at public functions, and the world press was there:

"Red-jacketed waiters began to serve...huge shrimps fresh from the Mediterranean. Our hosts—unaware that shrimp are not kosher—glowed with pleasure at the treat they had prepared for us."

Ben Elissar hesitated, assessed the political damage that refusing the meal might cause, then took a bite of the prohibited shellfish. Chafets recalls impishly: "I wolfed it down, bathed in the special glow that comes from personal sacrifice in the cause of international understanding."

The author clearly resents the power of the Orthodox over the lives of Israeli citizens. He portrays many of Israel's "most venerable rabbis" as "power brokers who cut deals with the secular pols over money, legislation, and patronage with all the restraint and dignity of Tammany ward heelers." He harshly criticizes the absence of spiritual pronouncements from many of the rabbis, and says, "Religious courts have a Judge Roy Bean ambience in which the letter of the law often takes precedence over common sense and common decency."

The final section of the book, "Hustlers," is an endearing look at some of the entrepreneurs who have brought a piece of the outside world to Israel, among them Shaul Evron, who first introduced Wild Turkey whiskey to the Holy Land, and Danny Sanderson, who brought Israeli rock 'n' roll music to prominence with his first group Kaveret—the Israeli Beatles—and who once remarked in a radio interview, "Doo-wop is Zionism, too."

Chafets concludes this intriguing, funny, revealing book with a serious assessment of Israel's future:

"Mostly, Israel is a country of ordinary people who get their kids off to school every morning and go to work, people who want security and prosperity and a little fun. Like everyone else they are confused by confusing situations, fear and dislike their enemies, have fine impulses and dark ones. For two thousand years, religion and communal solidarity and the world's hostility held the Jews together, but in this century, Zionism has rendered a country out of prayers and poetry. These influences—religion and ideology—are still potent forces in Israel. But in recent years the state has been increasingly taken over by its own people, and it is they who will determine what Israel will be when it finally grows up."

62 My Father, His Daughter

Yael Dayan

There is an old proverb which says: "Worship your heroes from afar; contact withers them." What it means is that nobody, not even a hero, is perfect; that if you come closer and examine their inner lives, you will probably become disappointed and disillusioned. That may be the reader's experience after finishing the biography of Moshe Dayan written by his daughter, Yael.

Moshe Dayan was born in 1914 on Israel's Kibbutz Deganya, which his parents had founded. At fourteen he joined the Haganah—the Jewish underground defense force. In 1934 he married Ruth Schwartz, a girl from Jerusalem, whose parents were fairly well-to-do; both of them were college graduates.

Moshe was unhappy with kibbutz life and joined a local British police training course, from which he graduated as a sergeant. In 1939, the first of his three children was born, a baby girl named Yael, who wrote his biography and who had a strange love-hate relationship with her father. She describes his imprisonment by the British. He was sentenced to ten years but released after two, so that he could participate with the Allied Forces during World War II. While he was standing on a roof to man a machine gun, he put binoculars to his eyes to locate the position of the enemy. It was then that an enemy bullet smashed the glasses and caused the loss of his left eye. The surgeon informed him that the metal and glass fragments could not be removed, and would be forever embedded in his head. He went through a lengthy period of recuperation and wore a black patch over his left eye for the rest of his life.

In 1946, Dayan and another young man by the name of Shimon Peres (who became the prime minister of Israel), were selected to attend the Zionist Congress in Basel, Switzerland. A year later, on

185

November 29, 1947, the United Nations General Assembly voted to partition Palestine between Arabs and Jews. And six months later, on May 14, 1948, the prime minister of Israel, David Ben-Gurion, read Israel's Declaration of Independence to the world. Here was the culmination of two thousand years of Jewish hopes and prayers. It should have been a time of happiness. Instead, it became a time of anxiety, as all the Arab countries attacked the newborn state.

Moshe Dayan was immediately selected to organize and train an elite commando battalion. Literally overnight, Dayan became a national hero. He was assigned the task of defending Jerusalem. He was given the title of lieutenant colonel. Wherever he went, he took his ten-year-old daughter, Yael, with him. He adored her, and she idolized him.

It was no secret that Dayan was Ben-Gurion's favorite general. In 1952, he was sent to England to attend a senior officers school. It was obvious that someday he was to become chief of staff of Israel's army.

By this time, two additional children were born to the Dayans—both boys—but Yael was clearly the favorite. In the book she describes her father's sense of humor. When he was caught speeding, he said to the policeman: "I have only one eye. Do you want me to look at the road or at the speedometer?" She describes his courage. He would say: "Officers of the Israeli army do not *send* their men into battle. They *lead* them into battle." She describes his poor relationship with his sons. Early in their lives they were embarrassed about being his children and tried to conceal the fact that their father was the famous Moshe Dayan.

In June 1967 another war seemed imminent. Nasser of Egypt was boasting: "Egypt will destroy Israel." Immediately, mobilization began, and throughout Israel there were demonstrations with placards saying: "We want Moshe Dayan." Dayan was fifty-two at this time, somewhat removed from army life. But his country needed him, and he immediately responded.

By this time, Jordan and Syria had joined Egypt. This book contains an exciting description of the events that followed, culminating in the capture of the Old City of Jerusalem. At the Western Wall, Dayan was asked to say a few words to be broadcast to the entire nation. After scribbling a prayer on a small piece of paper and inserting it into a crevice into the Western Wall, he said: "We have returned to the holiest of our sites, and will never again be separated from it. To our Arab neighbors, Israel extends the hand of peace—and to the peoples of all faiths we guarantee full freedom of worship."

After Dayan's divorce from Ruth, his new wife, Rachel, introduced many changes in his life. Whereas in the past he was rather indifferent to material possessions, he now became preoccupied with earning money. Everything had a price tag. He wore designer clothes; the two of them attended cocktail parties. He led a far more active social life than he had led with his first wife.

Toward the end of the book, there is a description of Anwar el-Sadat making his historic journey to Jerusalem. At the ensuing Camp David meetings Henry Kissinger's complimentary description of Dayan was: "War was Dayan's profession. Peace was his obsession...history will record him as a principal architect of the peace treaty with Egypt."

Moshe Dayan died on October 16, 1981. After the shivah period—the seven days of mourning—his will was opened and read. His estate was sizable, and so it was expected that he would leave a portion to his second wife and that the bulk of the estate would go to his children. Instead, he left virtually everything to his second wife and almost nothing to his children. He also requested that no one was to take the will to court to question or dispute it.

His daughter, the author of this book, wrote a scathing letter, addressed to Dayan's widow, Rachel, in which she describes her father in the most unflattering of terms. The letter was circulated only among the members of the family, but his son Udi wrote an equally critical letter which was published in the Israeli newspapers. It was entitled: "A Letter to a Dead Father." In it he vowed that he would never say Kaddish for his father. And on that note the biography ends.

63 The Diary of a Young Girl

Anne Frank

Anne Frank's beloved diary was first published in 1947 and has become a classic; it has been read in schools and performed on the stage all over the world. This story humanized the Nazis' chokehold on Jewish life in Europe for millions of people worldwide. *The Diary of a Young Girl: The Definitive Edition* first appeared in 1995 and includes previously unpublished passages from Anne's original diary.

In actuality, Anne kept two diaries; one she began in June of 1942; the other diary was her own edited and expanded version of the original—a diary she thought she would turn into a book after the war. This new, definitive edition—a combination of writings—shows Anne as an even brighter, more mature adolescent, whose maturity is quickened through her circumstances. It includes about thirty percent more writings than the earlier version, passages Anne's father, Otto Frank, had hitherto left out, including those concerning Anne's tumultuous relationship with her mother and her own feelings about her budding sexuality.

The reader comes to know Anne, a popular, quick-witted girl just turning thirteen. She and her family left Germany during Hitler's early years. She is full of quick insights into classmates and family members—many of which aren't particularly complimentary. Anne's concerns are those of any ordinary adolescent, with a few references about the inconveniences of being Jewish woven in. More troubled times are something she suggests, but clearly not something she ponders deeply on a regular basis. That her initial concerns are so ordinary is what makes the diary so striking: Anne's voice represents the universal voice of millions of children who were never heard.

Soon after she begins her diary, which she has named "Kitty," the family goes into hiding. Anne reports on the intimate details of leaving home, the absurd layers of clothes, and her amazement upon entering their now famous secret annex above her father's office building/warehouse in Amsterdam, behind a bookcase that swings open.

The annex consists of five rooms, and houses eight people: Anne's parents; her older sister Margot; Mr. & Mrs. Van Daan and their son, Peter; and soon after the Franks' arrival, a dentist named Dussel with whom Anne shares a room. Anne reports on the daily lives of the annex's inhabitants. There are also five devoted family friends without whose help the family would not have been able to hide, most of whom work in the building: Mr. Kugler, Mr. Kleiman, Miep Gies (and her husband, Jan), and Bep Voskuijl. These heroic Dutch people risked their lives to help the family.

This particularly poignant diary isn't just about being a Jew during the war, but about the maturation of a young girl coming to terms with her changing body, trapped in an environment that forces her to grow more quickly than she would have chosen. We're also taken on her emotional ride, accompanying her in her adolescent obsession with Peter Van Daan, and the reckoning of her own needs and desires. She also details, with a reporter's eye, the limited foods to which they have access, as well as the tensions of hiding, and the constant fear of being discovered.

But there is also the resiliency of the young in her tone and in her outlook: she knows this experience will strengthen her and has already changed her into a better person. There are celebrations in the annex, too: birthdays, particularly, seem cozy and indulgent, and although there is general tension among its inhabitants, there's also a sense of camaraderie in their small world. She describes the importance of obeying the annex's rules, and the way that the imposed order provides a sense of security and routine—as it does in all our daily lives.

Her writing is often eloquent, startlingly wise for a girl of her age. It is Anne's innate optimism and her keen eye that has kept this diary alive for so many years, loved by millions of readers. Although the diary is most famous for her lines, "I still believe, in spite of everything, that people are truly good at heart," there are numerous other passages that touch the reader, either by their kernels of wisdom or their purity of heart.

Anne Frank comes to a similar conclusion about responsibility and anti-Semitism that scholar Daniel Jonah Goldhagen arrived at in *Hitler's Willing Executioners,* which takes an academic, objective approach to the Holocaust. Each book demonstrates how anti-Semitism helped fuel the war and acknowledges that ordinary Germans carried out the crimes. Frank writes: "I don't believe the war is simply the work of politicians and capitalists. Oh no, the common man is every bit as guilty; otherwise, people and nations would have rebelled long ago! There's a destructive urge in people, the urge to rage, murder and kill. And until all of humanity, without exception, undergoes a metamorphosis, wars will continue to be waged, and everything that has been carefully built up, cultivated and grown will be cut down and destroyed, only to start all over again!"

Although there are other subjects in which Anne reveals this more mature side of herself, she never loses her humor for long, and works at her optimistic nature, constantly putting her hiding in perspective (considering the alternative). She writes more than once that she would just like to be a normal teenager, and wants more than anything time alone—and time outside.

We also have the sad benefit of hindsight: Anne questions whether she can write anything of lasting value. On August 1, 1944, Anne wrote her last entry; the annex was raided on August 4. The Frank family had been in hiding for over two years. In 1945, both Margot and Anne died in Bergen-Belsen concentration camp. The only member of her family to survive was her father, Otto Frank.

Miep Gies and Bep Voskuijl, the two secretaries working in the building, found Anne's diaries strewn all over the floor; Miep Gies tucked them away in a desk drawer for safekeeping. After the war, when it became clear that Anne was dead, she gave the diaries, unread, to Anne's father, Otto Frank. Anne Frank's diary is one of the most moving works to emerge from the Holocaust and will continue to enlighten and inspire millions of readers for generations to come.

64 Hitler's Willing Executioners

Daniel Jonah Goldhagen

First published in 1996, this book has not only become a bestseller in the United States, but its recent German edition of forty thousand copies sold out within a week. The book is dedicated to the author's father, a survivor of a Romanian ghetto; his father is now a professor at Harvard where the author is an associate professor. The book's foundation was Goldhagen's dissertation, an outgrowth of his obsession with the Holocaust.

His objective is "to explain why the Holocaust occurred, to explain how it could occur." Unlike other studies which focus on the Nazi Party and its leaders, this book zeroes in on the ordinary Germans who carried out the mass killings, whether they were police in battalions, guards in the camps, or guards on the death marches. Goldhagen sets the stage by placing anti-Semitism in a historical context, and studies German society under the Nazi regime and its institutions.

Goldhagen's ideas are backed by solid research, culled from historical documents and war testimony from the men themselves. It includes much information about the nature of nineteenth- and twentieth-century German anti-Semitism before the war and the evolution of what Goldhagen terms "elimination anti-Semitism" in Germany.

Excerpts from speeches by pastors and texts from children's books show that anti-Semitism was sanctioned at every level of society (from school to church to state). It was composed of actual Jewish characteristics along with fantastic ones, extending supernatural powers to Jews. These included, but were not limited to: Jews not only rejected Christ but also killed him; they were parasites instead of workers; they were the devil's children (as a children's book taught); they controlled government, and were

191

responsible for the loss of World War I, as even Protestant leaders claimed. Germans viewed Jews not as human beings but rather as members of a demonic race who destroyed all they touched; it was therefore imperative to abolish this evil race in order for Germany to live.

Goldhagen clearly demonstrates that Hitler didn't turn a nation into Jew-haters; hatred of Jews permeated their society long before his rise to power. What Hitler did, though, was channel the hatred into a systematic plan of annihilation. Many of the ordinary Germans who became killers in police battalions or as camp guards were not S.S. or even Nazi members—but their hatred for Jews was a "great equalizer."

In showing the progression of eliminationist anti-Semitism, from verbally assaulting Jews to their exclusion from society both socially and financially, Goldhagen allows us to see how Jews became socially dead beings. Physically removed by being placed in the ghetto, they were no longer seen as part of society. Laws fell into place with a German public eager to enact them, from wearing the mandatory yellow Star of David (which allowed Germans to readily identify, then taunt, all Jews, even children) to mandatory death sentences, such as the shoot-to-kill order—which required the immediate killing of any Jew found outside the ghetto.

The Protestant and Catholic churches were key players, helping the eliminationist cause. When the Nuremberg Laws of September 1935 went into effect, defining who was a Jew, local churches supplied genealogical records to aid the cause. (Even Jewish converts to Christianity were considered intrinsically evil, in spite of their intent.)

Goldhagen also studied Police Battalion 101, a unit of the Order Police comprised of ordinary, "decent" Germans who didn't make it into the army and had no formal training to kill. Contrary to the myth of naive youths blindly following orders, these men were primarily family men in their thirties and forties. Using quotes from the men's own testimony, we learn that their commander, Major Trapp, even gave them the option not to kill, without penalty, but the overwhelming majority eagerly accepted the role, performing the gruesome task with astounding cruelty. It was not uncommon for "brains, blood and bone" to explode on them during the killing.

In Poland, they barbarically massacred entire Jewish villages, including children and the elderly, one by one. Germans didn't merely want Jews to die; they had to suffer in doing so: whether Jews were locked in a synagogue and burned to death, or Jewish children were picked up by the hair and then shot in the head. Proud to rid the world of vermin, they often took pictures of their kill, and, even more astoundingly, some of the men even brought along family members to watch the murders! They celebrated their fine work afterwards.

Goldhagen looks at camp guards with equal care, and the concept of "work" in the camps. The camps were distinct creations of the Holocaust, totaling more than ten thousand in number. These women and men executed their orders with extreme passion, deriving great pleasure in the power they had over their victims.

Who were the Germans who became guards at these camps, and what made them willingly follow their orders with unimaginable cruelty? Contrary to logical assumptions, guards in the work camps did not utilize the workers' productivity to the best of their ability. Instead, they purposefully weakened them and killed them. Teasing and humiliating Jews were equally common, extending their suffering as long as possible, because Jews deserved not only to die but to suffer for having lived. Since the guards believed Jews were innately slothful, work was futile and often solely punitive; prisoners labored at useless tasks such as building a wall, only to tear it down the next day. Jews were constantly treated worse than other prisoners.

Why, in the death marches at the end of the war, despite Himmler's orders to stop killing the Jews, did the guards continue to do so? Comprehending German anti-Semitism is fundamental to understanding these war crimes, Goldhagen asserts, because it is what motivated ordinary people not only to kill but to do so with deep inner conviction and sadistic pleasure.

The section of the book entitled "Explaining the Perpetrators' Actions: Assessing the Competing Explanations" dispels the most common rationalizations for the Holocaust, instead supporting Goldhagen's theory that the majority of ordinary Germans were willing killers. They were not blindly following orders, as readily witnessed in their open opposition to the Weimar Republic, so "German's conditional regard for authority should be the truism." In Weimar, the day after Kristallnacht, close to one hundred thousand ordinary citizens gathered in an anti-Semitic rally—proof of widespread German approval.

That Germans committed crimes through peer pressure is also a faulty argument; if indeed there had been peer pressure, it would have "sustained their individual and collective resolve to avoid the killing." That people did this for their own self-interest (career and financial benefits) is also false; the men who constituted the police battalions, as well as others, "had no bureaucratic or career interests to advance by their involvement."

It is also true that the "tasks were so fragmented that they either did not comprehend the real significance of their actions or, if they did, that the alleged fragmentation then allowed them to displace responsibility of others," since many of the Germans were shooting Jews face-to-face. Most people clearly knew what was happening, Goldhagen writes.

He shows that individuals chose to participate in genocidal slaughters because they believed they were doing the right thing. As the filmmaker Jean Renoir said in his 1939 film, *Rules of the Game,* when playing the character Octave, "There's only one terrible thing in this world. That everyone has his reasons." Goldhagen makes a definitive case for understanding the reason that so many ordinary Germans became Hitler's willing executioners.

65 To Touch a Dream

Aviva Hellman

Countless scholarly books have been written about the history of modern Palestine and the creation of the State of Israel. Aviva Hellman's *To Touch a Dream,* however, is one of the few books addressing that complex period of history in the form of a novel.

The author, who grew up in Israel, and whose late husband, Yehuda Hellman, was the executive director of the Conference of Presidents of Major American Jewish Organizations, tells the story of Palestine and Israel through four generations of a family named Danziger.

The Danzigers had left a comfortable life in Romania to settle in Palestine during the early 1900s, committed to helping establish a Jewish homeland. We meet the three Danziger children—Raphael, and his two beautiful sisters, Tamar and Deborah, around whose lives the story revolves. The time is World War I, when Turkey and German were Allies. Most Jews in Palestine remained loyal to the Turkish Empire, which controlled Palestine at the time. Not so the Danziger family.

Raphael decides to align himself with the British, and establishes a small spy network to collect military information. His sister, Deborah, and her husband, David, join him in this enterprise. Ultimately, David is arrested on charges of espionage, and the Turks discover that the Danziger home is the headquarters of the spy ring.

Tamar, the second Danziger daughter, is captured and tortured, but refuses to reveal any information. Rather than face the pain of further interrogation, she commits suicide, leaving behind a son, Gidon, the child of Tamar and her great love, Thomas Hardwicke. David is subsequently murdered by a band of Bedouins. Therefore, when 1918 comes and with it victory for the Allies, the Danziger family has already been shattered by tragedy.

The family's saga continues against the backdrop of the Balfour Declaration, which promised a homeland for the Jews of Palestine. Gidon is sent to live with his biological father in London, but returns to Palestine when his father is killed in a motorcycle accident. By 1929, he bears witness to the Arab riots and the issuing of the infamous British "White Paper," which forbade further immigration to Palestine and which called for eventual partition of the country. In the meantime, Hitler's plans for the Jews are becoming evident, but the Jews who wish to leave Germany find Palestine closed to them.

Gidon, now an adult, becomes a member of an extremist militant group fighting the British. He marries, has a daughter named Tanya, but then is asked by a leader of the underground to leave his family and enlist in the British army so that he might advise the underground regarding British plans and strategies. Gidon continues his extremist activities, and eventually murders a British colonel Cartwright, whom he blames for his father's death. He flees, but ultimately dies in a raid, and is buried next to his mother, Tamar.

Of the original three Danziger children, only Deborah is left. She goes to the cemetery to visit the graves of her siblings and her nephew, Gidon, wondering aloud if the dream of building a Jewish homeland was worth this terrible price. By now World War II is over, and the grim evidence of Nazi genocide is known throughout the world. The United Nations takes up the issue of statehood, and on May 14th, 1948, the British mandate ends, and the State of Israel is born.

The reader sees the War of Independence through the eyes of the Danzigers, the bloodshed and the ultimate survival of the infant country. We see the hope of peace dashed time and time again by the Arab determination to "drive the Jews into the sea" and take all of Palestine for themselves. Hellman takes us through the 1956 Suez Campaign, when Israeli conquest of a major portion of the Sinai was stopped only by a direct order to Israel from Pres. Dwight D. Eisenhower. We read about the Six-Day War of 1967, when Israeli forces struck so quickly in response to menacing Egyptian gestures that the victory and retaking of old Jerusalem after two thousand years was accomplished before any outside pressure could be applied to stop the Israeli juggernaut.

Members of the Danziger family embody in their own lives and loves the search for a way in which Arab and Jew might coexist in peace. One of Deborah Danziger's granddaughters, Alexandra, visits Paris on vacation, where she meets and falls in love with an Arab man. Once he learns that she is an Israeli, Edward vilifies her, calls her a "Zionist whore," and declares that his life is dedicated to the destruction of Israel. The Yom Kippur War of 1973 ensues, a war in which Israel came perilously close to defeat.

Alexandra, now working in a camp in Lebanon called Shattila, meets Edward again after a long separation. Their passion leads to her pregnancy, but her refusal to convert to Islam results in Edward treating her cruelly. When Lebanese Christians enter the camp in the great slaughter at Sabra and Shattila during the war in Lebanon, Edward shoots and kills Alexandra, and is in turn killed by soldiers in the camp. Edward and Alexandra both lie there dead, as if symbolic of the dead hopes that Israelis and Arabs might live in peace.

The novel ends with Deborah's eighty-fifth birthday and the birth of a child who would have been her sister Tamar's great-granddaughter. As Deborah cradles the little girl, we are left to wonder what the future in the Middle East will bring. Aviva Hellman holds out the hope, at least symbolically, that future generations might realize the dream so elusive to her own.

66 The Wall

John Hersey

John Hersey, the son of Protestant missionaries, was raised in Tientsin, China, among people very different from himself.

After working under the mentorship of the great Sinclair Lewis, Hersey wrote *A Bell for Adano* (1944), the first gentle and caring novel about those whom the United States conquered in Italy during World War II. He subsequently exhibited great courage in writing *Hiroshima,* a compassionate treatment of the Japanese. Years after Japan's defeat, Hersey set aside the demonization of "the enemy" and instead wrote the story of simple people, most of whom were victimized by circumstances beyond their control. It was not surprising that Hersey chose the victims of the Warsaw Ghetto as the subjects of a third novel, *The Wall,* somehow finding in this mindless tragedy the triumph of the human spirit over adversity.

The Wall, published in 1961, is written in the form of a diary of the ghetto's last days. The novel begins with an editor's introduction, which many believe to be based upon actual facts. Hersey describes an expedition into the ruins of the Warsaw Ghetto in 1944. The seven-foot wall surrounding the twenty-five city blocks remained intact, but the ghetto itself had been turned into rubble. Within the confines of the wall, one million men, women, and children had died, bombarded by Nazi artillery, deprived of food and water, and gassed by poisonous fumes. A few had survived, among them Benjamin Meed, who founded a Warsaw Ghetto survivors organization in New York, and saw to it that a moving memorial service for victims of the Holocaust was conducted in a prominent Manhattan location every year.

But those entering the ruined ghetto in 1944 had a very specific goal: to find and bring to the world the archives of the

Warsaw Ghetto, recorded in detail by an old scribe, Noah Levinson. He had told a few survivors where the archives were buried. He understood that the ghetto was doomed in spite of the valiant resistance movement, and further knew that if the world were to remember those who died, evidence was essential. Almost as if anticipating revisionist anti-Semitic writers who would claim that the Holocaust never occurred, Levinson set about collecting personal diaries, stories, poems, and financial records, supplemented by his detailed written observations about daily ghetto life. The resulting chronicles totaled twenty-five bundles, wrapped and buried in the ashes of the ghetto. In a bitter irony, the twenty-five bundles, wrapped in linen sheets reminiscent of shrouds, amounted to one bundle of memories for each block of the ghetto, the lives of one million human beings reduced to two dozen packages.

In 1944, after the defeat of the Nazis, two Warsaw city engineers accompanied by two survivors, Rachel Apt and an old Socialist named Rappaport, went into the ghetto ruins. With the help of a surveyor, they found the spot and dug up the parcels. Some were sent to Jerusalem and others to the United States, where John Hersey studied and translated them into living history. Noah Levinson's archives in effect became the narrative outline for *The Wall*. In one particularly powerful section, the ghetto fighters are resisting the massed might of the German army surrounding the wall. Word comes to them from Stalingrad that Hitler's army is beginning to falter, that the tide of war has turned, that for the first time there is hope that Germany will be defeated. Instead of joy, however, the news brings only greater despair. For the Warsaw Ghetto is not Stalingrad, and its heroic resistance movement hardly the equal of the Russian army. There are no supplies, no place to retreat and regroup, no time to be rescued by those who would ultimately emerge victorious. The Warsaw Ghetto fighters could count only on death and defeat.

Their courage in the face of hopelessness permeates *The Wall*. Hersey illustrates how this mass of human beings, faced with almost certain destruction, retained their dignity until the very end. Lovers still walked arm in arm along the streets. Mothers sang lullabies to their children at bedtime. Businessmen still adhered to tight ethical principles. Jews still sang and prayed and lived. This, demonstrates Hersey, was a heroism the likes of which humanity was not yet aware, a heroism that has not been sufficiently praised or glorified by writers and poets. This was something much more important in human life; the heroism of the humble, the courage of the obscure, the power of simple people to bear whatever they had to bear.

From where did this heroism emerge? The diary entries seem to reflect an answer. The people of the Warsaw Ghetto maintained their religious traditions and values, and therefore continually looked to the future. They never surrendered that most precious of gifts, their unconquerable mood of hope.

At the very end of the book, Rachel Apt steps out of the ghetto into the forest, a survivor, surrounded by all the memories of bitterness, bloodshed, tears, murder, close friends dying, and is able to say: "Well, what is the plan for tomorrow?"

Through John Hersey's literary genius, he recaptures the lives and deaths, the agony and ultimate destruction, of a community of Jews, who in spite of their fear and impending doom, were nevertheless able to say each day: "Well, what is the plan for tomorrow?"

67 Schindler's List

Thomas Keneally

The name of Oskar Schindler has become familiar to tens of millions of people through the movie *Schindler's List*. The internationally acclaimed Steven Spielberg film has been accorded virtually every honor possible, and has brought new luster to the careers of those actors and actresses fortunate enough to have been included in its cast.

Many people, however, forget that *Schindler's List* is also a book. Written by Thomas Keneally in the form of an historical novel, the volume gives depth and texture to the story of a man who came to understand how each of us has the responsibility and power to affect eternity.

The real Oskar Schindler was significantly less virtuous than his portrayal in the film. Married to a woman in Moravia, Schindler kept a German mistress in Cracow and maintained a love affair with his Polish secretary. A heavy drinker, he was ambitious for wealth and possessions. He felt that his charm, good looks, and quick thinking would take him far.

But this was the adult Oskar Schindler. The little boy, born in 1908 in Austria into a Catholic family, lived in a modern villa. His childhood friends included a number of Jewish youngsters, including the two sons of his next door neighbor, the liberal Rabbi Felix Kantor. Oskar loved motorcycles, and even raced them in high-level competition. Married in his early twenties, Schindler served in the army, then returned home, where he neglected his wife and partied late into the night.

By 1939, Schindler's mother had died, and his father's business had gone bankrupt. The National Socialist German Workers Party ruled Germany, and the black market flourished in a world war environment. Oskar traveled to Cracow, seeking a chance to make his fortune. We encounter Itzhak Stern, the accountant who became Schindler's right-hand man and business manager, who assisted him in purchasing a faltering factory, organizing it for wartime production, and supervising the workers, virtually all of whom were Jewish ghetto inhabitants.

By 1942, Schindler's factory was doing well, even though the hate campaign against Jews was escalating. Plans for crematoria were already on the drawing boards, and very soon would begin claiming thousands of Jewish lives. There was no attempt to hide contempt for Jews. The book captures one incident in which Schindler, out for a horseback ride with his mistress, witnesses the savage beating of Jews by Nazi soldiers. Reports begin to circulate regarding the gassing and burning of Jews, of places named Treblinka and Birkenau and Auschwitz. Finally, representatives of Jewish groups quietly approach Schindler to plead for his help. As a manufacturer whose products were important to the war effort, he could protect his workers from deportation and almost certain death.

The book makes clear that Schindler may have acted initially because it was in his best interest to do so. A stable workforce meant a steady stream of product and minimal training time. Since Schindler also felt a sense of disgust at vicious Nazi behavior, he agreed to try his best to protect his workers. That meant dealing with the psychotic Commandant Amon Goeth, whose idea of a good time included summarily executing prisoners when his whim prompted him to do so.

Schindler finally persuaded the authorities to allow his workers to live on the factory's premises, in effect in his own compound. Constantly adding to his employment rolls under the guise of increased production, Schindler saved the lives of many men and women who had absolutely no technical skills. Through bribes of money and liquor, he was even able to rescue some Jews who were not working for him and who had been sentenced to death. The vicious Goeth, however, remained his greatest obstacle and threat. Only after Goeth was himself arrested by the SS and taken to jail for mismanagement and fraud could Schindler safely accelerate his efforts to save more Jewish lives.

At long last, Oskar Schindler secured his own factory camp, even though the thirty-two thousand dollars he paid to the authorities each week far exceeded any possible profit he could expect. The women assigned to work in the factory were sent to

Auschwitz in error. Arrested and interrogated by the SS for days before being released, Oskar Schindler persevered and secured the reassignment of the "Schindler women" to the new "munitions factory" which never produced anything! "All" it did was save Jewish lives.

With the coming of peace Oskar Schindler closed the factory and made his way to Munich. Amon Goeth was hanged for war crimes. Schindler moved to Argentina where his nutria farm went bankrupt, then lost another business—a cement factory—in Germany. Those whom he had saved, however, had not forgotten their savior. Hearing of his business reversals, Schindler's former employees living in Israel brought him to Tel Aviv, where he was honored by the municipality, and then to Jerusalem, where he was declared one of "the righteous Gentiles" at the Holocaust memorial Yad Vashem.

Oskar Schindler died in 1974 at the age of sixty-eight. His last wish—to be buried in Jerusalem—was honored. His legacy lives on in the dreams and accomplishments of the descendants of "Schindler's Jews."

68 While Six Million Died

Arthur Morse

During World War II, Hitler's legions swept across Europe, occupying one country after another in a grand scheme that aimed at creating "The Thousand Year Reich." Faced with the alternatives of death or surrender, virtually all of Germany's targets became subordinate to Nazi power.

As the Nazis gained acceptance among German citizenry, the National Socialist Party found it politically expedient to blame the Jews of Germany and the world for its embarrassment in World War I, claiming that the Jews were traitors to the Reich, and therefore had to be treated as such. Restrictive legislation, Jewish disempowerment, nationalization of Jewish businesses and property, ghettoization, and pariah-like isolation ultimately led to "The Final Solution," the torture and murder of six million Jewish men, women, and children, simply because they were Jews.

As World War II came to an end, as the concentration camps were liberated, as the truth became known, the world expressed horror and pleaded ignorance of what had transpired. In part in response to the genocide, the United Nations voted to establish the State of Israel by the narrowest of margins, including an affirmative vote cast by the United States.

In the aftermath of the war, however, many painful and troublesome questions remained for the freedom-loving citizens of America. Was the U.S. government aware of the concentration camps? If so, what provisions did our country make to save the innocent from certain death?

In a profoundly disturbing indictment of United States policy, Arthur Morse's *While Six Million Died* chronicles American action and inaction in response to the greatest instance of mass murder in human history. Chilling and indisputable facts emerge in this volume, drawn from public and secret documents, then unavailable to the American public.

In August of 1942, Hitler's gas chambers had not yet been constructed. Hundreds of thousands of Jews had already been executed by Nazi soldiers, but the systematic annihilation of European Jewry was yet to begin. Gerhart Riegner, a young representative of the World Jewish Congress living in Switzerland, received indisputable evidence of Nazi plans, and attempted to let the world know so that the United States and Great Britain might react. Riegner cabled Rabbi Stephen S. Wise in New York, feeling that Wise's leadership in the American Jewish community and personal relationship with President Roosevelt might prove important. Riegner's cable to Rabbi Wise was suppressed by the U.S. government, but reached Wise through other avenues. When Wise sought an audience with the president, he was urged to keep silent. At last, President Roosevelt himself received the cold hard facts of Jewish death. He promised action "to bring the criminals to justice," but only via a War Crimes Commission that would be convened *after* the war.

The shameful account continues for hundreds of pages. We see documented how information on genocide was kept from the American public, how the American government refused to lift immigration quotas so that Jews fleeing for their lives might find refuge, how a conference in Bermuda chose to ignore the last pleas of the Jews in the Warsaw Ghetto. One hundred and seventy thousand Romanian Jews were slaughtered because no country would take them.

To his everlasting discredit, Rabbi Wise succumbed to the charm of his "friend" President Roosevelt, who expressed sympathy for Jewish suffering but declined to act. Only after a document was published in 1944 accusing the State Department of "acquiescence in the murder of the Jews" did Roosevelt establish the War Refugee Board. Four million Jews had already died.

A careful examination of Morse's documentation helps in part explain why the State of Israel is so loath to accept any governmental guarantees for safe and secure borders. If the world's greatest democracy could turn away the 936 passengers of the ship *St. Louis,* forcing them to return to certain death in Europe, if the President of the United States most beloved by Jews could refuse to bomb the railroad tracks to Auschwitz to save the lives of twenty thousand Jews each day, who is to criticize Israeli caution?

Though the United States indeed stopped Hitler and won World War II, history will also record that American inaction may have cost millions of Jewish lives that might otherwise have been saved.

69 Ship of Fools

Katherine Anne Porter

If the late 1940s and 1950s saw a proliferation of novels illustrating the insanity of war and horror of the Holocaust, the 1960s was a time of societal upheaval and fundamental questioning of authority. The Civil Rights movement, Vietnam, and a cultural revolution generated music, books, and films, many of which asked: "How can our world be the way it is?"

The 1960s were also a decade in which writers had a chance to reflect on what the world might have learned from World War II. Korea and Vietnam dispelled any illusion that war was now obsolete. Katherine Anne Porter's novel *Ship of Fools,* published in 1962, cast similar doubts on any hope that hate was any less virulent two decades after the war had concluded.

In an era in which there were virtually no heroes, where the anti-hero reigned supreme in popular culture, Porter crafted a novel with sixty characters, none of whom possessed heroic qualities—a novel without a hero or anti-hero! She sets the stage for her story by placing all of the characters in a confined space, on a ship, then examines each of their personalities in turn. The Austrian novelist Vicki Baum used a similar method in *Grand Hotel,* as did Chaucer with his pilgrims in *The Canterbury Tales* and Boccaccio in *Decameron.*

Porter's attitude toward her characters is indicated by the book's title, *Ship of Fools,* drawn from a fourteenth-century German novel, *Das Narrenschiff,* in which the author described his society as a ship of fools, steered by fools to a fool's paradise. Porter outlines her characters in this modern *Ship of Fools* with an acid pen. Everyone is a minor character, but each awakens in the reader a major dislike. It is clear that the author herself does not like any of them except, perhaps, the ship's doctor.

The story begins in 1931 as the passengers, most of whom have been teaching in various schools in Mexico, board the ship at Veracruz. The ship, a German vessel, will ultimately take them to Bremerhaven in Germany.

A big, middle-aged, shrieking woman named Lizzi Spockenkieker, hangs around with a short, chubby, German magazine publisher who is a primitive anti-Semite. Professor Hutten and his wife are childless, but they have a little bulldog whom they adore and who is constantly seasick. Herr Baumgartner had been a successful lawyer, but developed some physical pains that were not clearly diagnosed and now drinks heavily. His wife, irritated at what has happened to him, and therefore to her, has become a strict disciplinarian of their son. Frau Schmitt, the widow of an educator, takes her husband's body back to Germany for burial. A young German engineer named Freytag is aboard, accompanied by his Jewish wife. He loves her, but hates Jews, and so is constantly in inner turmoil.

Porter also acquaints us with the crew: the captain, a stern disciplinarian; the ship's doctor, a man with a weak heart; the purser; and various young officers. A Swiss family Lutz is aboard, as is an American couple, David Scott and Jenny Brown. Both painters, they live together, love each other madly, but torment each other endlessly. Finally, there is William Denny, from a border town in Texas, who hates Mexicans yet is pursuing a Mexican-Spanish girl throughout the voyage.

The author paints this unflattering picture of the passengers: bigoted, ostentatious, pretentious, lusting after one another like animals in heat, angry, and drunk. Their pursuit of degradation is led by the ship's dance company, eight gypsies, who are intent on exploiting the passengers in any way possible.

As if this collection of ugly characters were not sufficient, the ship takes on nearly nine hundred Spanish workers and their wives, who are being sent back from Cuba to their homes because of a drop in sugar prices. They are crammed into steerage— miserable, sick, and constantly quarreling. In short, the ship is filled with tension, anger, and resentment, often expressed in the most graphic language.

The most obvious undercurrent throughout the volume is the deep-rooted anti-Semitism among Germans of all classes. The story takes place in 1931, before Hitler truly established his power. Germans, cultured and refined, are already prepared to establish a policy reflecting their hatred of Jews.

The Jews on board the *Ship of Fools* blithely ignore the palpable anti-Semitism surrounding them. They willingly return to a Germany that would claim the lives of most of their families and friends. Finally, the author reminds us of the tenuousness of life. The ship on ocean waters is subject to many dangers. The same is true of our own lives. We never know when tragedy may strike. Therefore we must live in the present, thankful for what we have, but never taking that bounty for granted. If we do, we are no better than the passengers on the *Ship of Fools*. We have become fools ourselves.

70 Out of the Shadows: A Photographic Portrait of Jewish Life in Central Europe Since the Holocaust

Edward Serotta

Edward Serotta, a Jewish photographer raised in Savannah, Georgia, set out to memorialize Jewish life in Central Europe, but in the process discovered that Jewish life, although irreparably scarred by the Holocaust, remained a vibrant force. The photographs span a five-year period beginning in 1985. After talking with a survivor in Prague, who spoke optimistically about the ensuing political changes, he began reassessing his initial intent:

"Here was a woman who had gone through enough to make Job wince and she was looking toward tomorrow. And that got me thinking about this so-called epitaph. Who was I to be writing on their tombstones when they had no intention of climbing into the grave? Better yet, the question was turned back on me: 'What grave?'"

Still, in this wonderfully conceived book, the inclusion of memorial photographs signifying the loss of Jewish lives is important. They include various types of cemeteries, a mass grave, tombstones in varying conditions, and a particularly eerie picture from a morgue of recently unearthed jawbones, with teeth lined up in rows like ribs, from the little Majdanek ghetto in Poland.

Serotta divides his chapters by countries: Hungary, Czechoslovakia, Poland, Romania, Bulgaria, Yugoslavia, and the German Democratic Republic. He begins each chapter with a detailed essay of the country's history and the people he has met there.

From these essays we gain a good sense of the various Jewish communities and their inhabitants. Following each essay are the photographs themselves, in which we witness Jewish life today and meet many of the people about whom Serotta has written.

His essay on Hungary, for example, begins with a description of a hotel in Budapest filled with three thousand Jews attending a Chanukah dance. Hungary has the largest population of Jews in postwar central Europe—at least eighty thousand. Through the pictures, one easily imagines widespread Jewish life before the war. A compelling reminder of how it appeared before Hitler's rise is seen in photographs of several synagogues, including the Grand Synagogue of Szeged in Hungary, which was built at the turn of the century, fell into disuse after the war, then was restored by an anonymous donor. The structure is so huge and ornately detailed—with Gothic arches and domed ceilings—that it looks permanent, as if it has been there for centuries and will always remain so. In contrast, the Spanish Synagogue of Prague is now used only for storage.

"This baroque jewel of a city" describes Prague, where Jewish intellectuals played a vital role in the arts in the prewar era (most of them considered themselves simply European artists and did not speak Yiddish). Serotta quotes Milan Kundera about Central Europe and its Jews: "that they were 'its intellectual cement, a condensed version of its spirit.'"

Prague's old Jewish cemetery is beautifully photographed; it is fantastic—the tombstones are crowded so tightly that "it looks like a sculpture garden." The reason: "for hundreds of years this was the only place Jews were allowed to be buried so bodies were buried in layers up to twelve deep."

The portraits of survivors are equally moving. Jiri Lauscher, who has an incredibly sweet face, holds a charming wooden puppet he made while at Theresienstadt concentration camp. Made for children of German soldiers, the puppets "kept him from being deported to the death camps," since so many Nazis wished to give his puppets as gifts to their children. And we meet Petyus, a double amputee resident of the Budapest Jewish hospital, who witnessed the death of his entire family at the hands of the Nazis, and never recovered from the shock. Petyus sits upright, shirtless in bed, surrounded by "those things he found most precious: prayer books, postcards of Israel, even a key to a synagogue far away."

In Poland, anti-Semitism remains strong while education is still weak. Under Communism, Jewish suffering was not included when teaching about the Holocaust. Serotta recounts a discussion with a nun who teaches children in the village of Sandomierz. While looking at seventeenth-century oil paintings of Christians being tortured, she explains with sincerity that the paintings are about "Jews killing Christian babies to make their matzoh." One of the saddest, most revealing photographs is of the yard in a priest's home in Poland. Upon first perusal, the picture looks mundane: a building, two people, a yard. This makes it even more horrifying when we learn that the stones paving the yard are Jewish gravestones. In case we begin to draw negative conclusions about all Poles, Serotta introduces us to Artur Krol, whose family hid a Jewish family for four years "under penalty of death" because they were good Catholics, and it was the right thing to do. In spite of the country's anti-Semitism, the Poles saved more Jews during the war than the citizens of any other Nazi-occupied country.

Bulgaria has a history of ethnic tolerance, and the Jews have long had a history there, dating back to Roman times. In 1910, the Czar helped dedicate the Synagogue of Sofia. Things changed during the war, when all Jews had to wear stars, and their businesses were confiscated. The Jews were sent to internment camps, but the government ultimately refused to deport its forty-five thousand Jews. In Romania, the Jewish population is small and strong; many make aliyah; they are grateful for Israel's presence and understand its importance.

In Yugoslavia, the Jewish population is about a tenth of what it was, but Jews hold well-respected positions in every facet of life and the "Jews there have created the most active small community in the whole of post-Holocaust Europe." In October of 1989, the Zagreb Jewish kindergarten opened with seven students. In the German Democratic Republic, Jews are busy advancing their careers due to the allure of capitalism. "Unlike anywhere else in the world, Jews living in Germany are defined as much by their country as by their identity as Jews."

With the emergence of democracy in former Communist nations, Jews are finally able to explore their roots openly. This book, ultimately, is about hope, and Jewish life being lived fully in places where only the most optimistic person could have conceived that it could emerge again.

71 The Pledge

Leonard Slater

The year 1998 marks the fiftieth anniversary of the establishment of the State of Israel, and therein lies a dilemma. For those born prior to and during the 1940s, Israel's creation was nothing less than a miracle, a piece of living history. After two thousand years of wandering and exile, after six million Jewish men, women, and children were annihilated in genocidal Nazi crematoria, that generation of Jews watched in awe as the United Nations declared Israel a sovereign country, a homeland for any Jew who wished to live there in freedom.

Five decades have come and gone. The giants of Israel's history are dead. And sadly, the very real possibility exists that this miracle of the human spirit will fade in significance as the years between the event and the present increase, and as David Ben-Gurion, Golda Meir, Moshe Dayan, Menachem Begin, and countless others, personages once well-known on a personal basis to thousands of American Jews, have their life stories converted to library studies, distant and remote from a new generation.

This stark possibility makes books such as Leonard Slater's *The Pledge* must reading for any person wishing to recapture the drama of Israel's creation in its golden anniversary era.

Originally published in 1970, *The Pledge* chronicles the heroic efforts of both Jewish and non-Jewish Americans to enable the Jews of Palestine to survive as a nation, the first Jewish Commonwealth in over two thousand years.

Slater's captivating retelling of the epic saga begins in 1945 at the now famous Hotel 14 on East 60 Street in New York City. There a small group of seventeen Jews gathered to hear David Ben-Gurion speak of the grim Nazi Holocaust of the present and his absolute determination to realize the establishment of a

Jewish State in Palestine, where six hundred thousand Jews and one million Arabs then resided.

Projecting an end to the British mandate in Palestine, Ben-Gurion told his listeners that the Jews would fight. No one else wanted the survivors of the concentration camps. The new Jewish State would be their safe haven.

We come to know the conveners of that first meeting, the wealthy, aristocratic Rudolf Sonneborn and Henry Montor. We also meet the "can-do" Haim Slavin, who came to the United States with only a dream and broken English, yet established Israel's first military arms factory. With his band of recruits, Slavin not only assembled the machinery required, but succeeded in getting it shipped to Palestine any way possible, welcoming the help of any person who was willing to assist.

By 1946, Rudolf Sonneborn had formed the Sonneborn Institute, primarily to coordinate fund-raising to buy materials, including a ship that would become the famous *Exodus*. Working first with Slavin, then Jacob Dostrovsky and Shlomo Rabinovich, Sonneborn assembled an unlikely collection of funders and workers, all imbued with a passion for Jewish statehood. The cast of characters included West Point graduate Colonel David "Mickey" Marcus, who became a trusted adviser to the Israeli military.

Wiretapping, cryptography, combat techniques, and demolition were taught at the headquarters of Jewish organizations. The book relates wonderfully bizarre tales of Jewish gun collectors spontaneously emerging throughout America: attorneys, an amusement park owner, an art dealer, and even members of Murder Incorporated. Through their efforts and those of thousands like them, Israel was provided with the arms, ammunition, ships, planes, and even tanks with which to fight for its survival during the 1948 War of Independence.

The Pledge reminds the reader that Israel was not always—as it is today—a strong and prosperous nation with one of the most powerful armies in the world. Its very existence hung by a thread for decades of its half-century history. The quiet heroism of average American men and women, Jewish and Christian, made the ultimate difference between survival and destruction.

Long before they attained their almost mythic proportions, these Americans worked with Jerusalem's famed mayor, Teddy Kollek, then a farmer from Kibbutz Ein Gev; with Golda Myerson, an immigrant to Israel from Milwaukee, who would become Golda Meir, Israel's prime minister; and with Aubrey Eban, one day to be recognized as Israel's most articulate spokesman, Abba Eban.

Where are these American heroes of Zionism today? Many have died. Others are retired, now living quiet lives far removed from their dramatic and often dangerous tasks in pursuit of a Jewish state that would serve as a safe haven for any Jew, anywhere, who needed a homeland. Leonard Slater has assured that their courage will never be forgotten, that honor will be accorded to them for all of Jewish history, that they will be remembered for their willingness to act when most of the world remained silent, and that generations of their families yet to come will tell the story of how "our family" wrested dignity and freedom from one of the darkest hours of the epic two-thousand-year-old journey from Abraham to modern Israel.

72 Maus I

Art Spiegelman

73 Maus II

Art Spiegelman

These remarkable nonfiction memoirs about the life of Vladek Spiegelman, the artist's father, a survivor of Dachau and Auschwitz, prove that even comic book drawings can be made into a powerful artistic medium. History is reenacted through anthropomorphic characters—Jews are mice, Nazis are cats, Poles are pigs, and Americans are dogs. Art's story is woven into the text as well, as he tries to make sense of his father's past and the generational effect of the Holocaust.

The structure of the first book is based around the author interviewing his father. As his father recounts the past, Art takes notes and reminds him to stay in chronological order.

Art's voice is hip and colloquial; we're not struck by his eloquence, even though the text is well written, but by the story itself and the means through which he tells it. The author finds humor—and often irony—in the present and points it out to the reader. *Maus I* won the Pulitzer Prize in 1992, but it would not be complete in itself: *Maus II* completes the story.

Many stories intertwine. There is the story of Art's father, and his mother Anja's unfinished one (she survived the war but later killed herself), and Art Spiegelman's account of surviving his father, whose tormented memories were casually recalled with unexpected candor during his childhood. Equally important, there is the haunting memory of Richieu, Anja and Vladek's first son, who was poisoned by his aunt just before the Nazis were to take them to Auschwitz.

The black-and-white drawings have a timeless quality, which brings the animal images into the present so that the story takes on an immediacy. There are many instances of the books' graphic power—from huge mice limply hanging with nooses around their necks to Anja and Vladek walking down a street shaped like a swastika.

Maus I is subtitled "My Father Bleeds History," and opens with Hitler's quote: "The Jews are undoubtedly a race, but they are not human." When reading, one might be inclined to substitute "Nazis" for "Jews" in Hitler's quote, yet even that is untrue. Since Spiegelman portrays animals as people, there is an underlying suggestion that no one is really human. The one constant theme, when Spiegelman cuts to the present, with his father in Rego Park or his rented Catskills bungalow, is that even though the war is over, it never ended.

Chapter One, entitled "The Sheik (mid-1930's to Winter 1944)," opens with Art visiting his father in Queens to research his book. "The Sheik" covers the early years, and his parents' courtship. Framed by the real love story, complete with details about a past girlfriend who tried to prevent the marriage, we come to know Vladek. He moved from one part of Poland to the other to marry Anja, and was set up in business by his wealthy father-in-law.

In Chapter Four, Vladek recalls when the Nazis took over early on; his business associate Cohn and his son were arrested for trading in the black market; they were used as examples and hanged in public, where their bodies remained for a week. Recalling them, Vladek cries, and although one of his eyes is glass, that eye tears as well.

In "Mouse Holes," the fifth chapter, Art learns that Vladek and his second wife, Mala, have read a cartoon which Art drew years ago that appeared in an underground comic book he thought his father would never see. Entitled "Prisoner on the Hell Planet," it recounts his mother's suicide, and Art's massive guilt.

Since each chapter opens with Art portraying Vladek speaking in the present, there is also the subtext—what Vladek is like now that he has survived the war. Art expresses his concerns to Mala. "It's something that worries me about the book I'm doing about him....in some ways he's just like the racist caricature of the miserly old Jew."

Art tells Mala, "I used to think the war made him that way...." to which she replies, "Fah! I went through the camps.... All our friends went through the camps. Nobody is like him!"

Vladek's voice, ironically, is most sane when describing the war. It is calm and consistent, and interruptions—whether he's dropped the pills he's counting or getting off his exercycle—bring us back to the present. In other ways, Vladek seems immensely kind—even heroic in the way he puts himself on the line for a fellow prisoner who is also a friend.

One can't help but admire his constant ingenuity, as he reveals numerous episodes of quick thinking that helped him survive. Early on he built bunkers and hid with his family in them. He instructs Art on how to build one: "Such things it's good to know exactly how it was—just in case."

Art's diagrams are fascinating—revealing false walls and sometimes people behind them. Later, on a crowded train car, he takes his blanket and attaches it to hooks in the ceiling, creating a hammock in which he rests. Above the crowd, he can breathe and eat snow off the roof of the train.

One night, in Srodula, when the family was hiding in an attic bunker (the opening was behind the chandelier), they left it in search of food and discovered another Jew in the house. Skeptical, they questioned him and kept him overnight. He was searching for food for his wife and baby. They sympathized, and in the morning, gave him food and let him go. He was a traitor and turned them in. Anja's parents were taken to Auschwitz, where they were gassed.

When Vladek and Anja were in the ghetto, Vladek was given work in a shoe shop. He learned skills that would help him in the camps later: he did favors for Nazi officers by repairing their boots. In one shoe shop, a cousin showed him where they would hide when the Jews were evacuated. He was amazed to discover the room, made with shoes piled to the ceiling, with a tunnel and a room inside. And this is where they hid.

After the ghetto was emptied, Anja and Vladek left the inside of the shoe pile and hid in various other places, eventually making their way to Hungary—but were captured en route. *Maus I* ends with Vladek and Anja's arrival at Auschwitz: "We knew the stories—that they will gas us and throw us in the oven. This was 1944....We knew everything...and here we were."

Vladek tells Art: "Anja and I went each in a different direction, and we couldn't know if ever we'll see each other alive again."

Maus II: A Survivor's Tale/And Here My Troubles Began brings us up to date on the Spiegelmans' lives, beginning with Art and his wife, Françoise, vacationing in Vermont with friends. Vladek leaves a phone message that he's had a heart attack, and the couple quickly call back. They learn that he hasn't really had a heart attack, but that Mala has left him. Feeling manipulated, they go to see him at his Catskills bungalow.

In the car, Art tells Françoise, "When I was a kid I used to think about which of my parents I'd let the Nazis take to the ovens if I could only save one of them....Usually I saved my mother. Do you think that's normal?" Françoise replies, "Nobody's normal."

Speaking of Richieu, he says, "I wonder if Richieu and I would get along if he was still alive." "Your brother?" she asks. "My ghost-brother, since he got killed before I was born. He was only five or six. After the war my parents traced down the vaguest rumors, and went to orphanages all over Europe. They couldn't believe he was dead. I didn't think about him much when I was growing up....He was mainly a large, blurry photograph hanging in my parents' bedroom....The photo never threw tantrums....I couldn't compete....It's spooky, having sibling rivalry with a snapshot!"

In *Maus I,* when Vladek posed as a Pole, he wore a pig mask; when Art writes about *Maus I* and its success, he portrays himself wearing a mouse mask. He brings us up to date on how unprepared he was for the success of *Maus I,* which brought an onslaught of publicity and profiteering. He also tells us that Françoise is pregnant, and he can't believe that he is going to be a father. The shifting of time isn't confusing because it's clear early on where we are: Art is writing at his desk wearing a mouse mask, with Françoise, his father, or his doctor, or back in the war, with all the mice in striped uniforms in the camps.

Maus II is also filled with the technical details of running a concentration camp. In the same way that Art drew diagrams of bunkers, he shows how a crematorium operates from various perspectives, including an aerial view. Here Vladek gives an enormously detailed account of working at the crematorium, including what he heard the bodies looked like after struggling. These are the most disturbing parts of the whole book, because they are vivid and utterly repulsive. ("Their fingers were broken from trying to climb up the wall...and sometimes their arms were as long as their bodies, pulled from the socket.") One picture shows a diagram with the ovens, an elevator for the corpse lift, and a room for melting gold fillings. "To such a place finished my father, my sisters, my brother, so many."

Maus II also deals with Art's attempts to come to grips with his past through therapy. He speaks with his psychiatrist who is a survivor, too. In sessions, both wear mouse masks. He tells his doctor he is having trouble working and can't imagine what it felt like to be at Auschwitz. "What Auschwitz felt like? Hmm.... How can I explain?.... BOO!" This answer startles Art. "It felt a little like that. But always! From the moment you got to the gate until the very end."

After the war, Anja returns to her hometown. There, she consults a gypsy fortune-teller. Everything she tells Anja is true, including that her husband is alive, that he had typhoid, that there is a dead child (Richieu), and that there is a new life, another little boy.

Maus II ends after showing Vladek and Anja reunited. "More I don't need to tell you. We were both very happy, and lived happy, happy ever after." At his father's request, Art stops his tape recorder. Vladek is tired, and rests. The last frame is Vladek and Anja's shared tombstone. Anja died May 21, 1968; Vladek on August 18, 1982.

74 Sophie's Choice

William Styron

Until the 1960s, the chief protagonist in most novels was a hero. The main character struggled against poverty, tragedy, or physical limitations to attain a dream, a goal, or material success. With the coming of the sixties, however, a new genre of literature emerged, the rise of the anti-hero.

The anti-hero, far from grappling with life, stands at a distance, sneering, perhaps suffering, giving up before the battle even begins. There are those who explain the rise of the anti-hero as an inevitable consequence of our modern society. The pressures, they say, have become unbearable, the attainment of great success too difficult, the expression of faith denigrated. Therefore, we have the anomaly of a hero fighting without hope of a victory, and a novel comprised of four hundred or so brokenhearted pages.

Sophie's Choice by William Styron won a vast readership, in large measure because this talented author created a novel with no heroes, which nonetheless conveys a profound and poignant message. The story is told by a character named Stingo (who is really William Styron) during 1947. Stingo, a twenty-two-year-old aspiring writer who has just lost his job at a publishing firm, rents a room in Brooklyn in a house filled with Jewish tenants. No sooner has he settled in when he hears a terrible commotion on the floor above him, passionate lovemaking followed by yelling, doors slamming, then silence, except for a phonograph playing Beethoven's Fourth Symphony.

Subsequently, he befriends his neighbors: Nathan, a thirty-year-old research biologist, and his girlfriend, Sophie, a beautiful blonde with a number tattooed on her arm. Clearly, Nathan has

221

manic-depressive tendencies. He can be kind and tender to
Sophie one moment, then vicious, abusive, and angry the next.

As the novel unfolds, Sophie confides her story to Stingo, even
as he gradually falls in love with her. She was born in Cracow; her
father was a university professor and her mother was a pianist.
Sophie married a math instructor, but both her husband and her
father were executed by the Nazis as dangerous intellectuals
when the Germans invaded Poland. In 1943, we learn, she was
arrested and sent to Auschwitz for twenty months for trying to
smuggle meat to her dying mother. She survived, came to
America, and met Nathan following a fainting spell in the library.

Nathan nursed her back to health and saw to her every need.
She fell madly in love with him and he with her. Yet he is
constantly accusing her of being a "whore," for surviving Auschwitz only by sleeping with every soldier.

The sick relationship, it turns out, also includes a potential
suicide pact and frequent bouts of drugs (by Nathan) and alcohol
(by Sophie). Still, Stingo remains loyal to his friends, and especially to Sophie.

One day, Nathan announces that he and Sophie will marry, and
asks Stingo to be the best man. Stingo agrees, but then receives a
phone call from Nathan's brother, Larry. Nathan, he says, is not a
research biologist and has no degree. His whole life is a masquer-
ade. Larry begs Stingo to stop the wedding and to be certain that
Nathan takes his antidepressants.

After Nathan beats up Sophie, Stingo spirits her away, this in
spite of Nathan's threat to shoot them both. They flee, take a
train, and plan to go to Virginia to live on a farm. The lovesick
Stingo asks Sophie to marry him, but she puts him off. They then
check into a hotel, where Sophie becomes drunk and at last tells
her terrible secret to Stingo.

At Auschwitz she stood in the selection line with her two
children. It was clear that those who went to the right would live,
while those sent to the left would die. The doctor making the
selection told Sophie that she could keep only one of her children.
It was her choice, and she made it—Sophie's choice. She never saw
either child again, she weeps. She is sure that they are both dead.

Shortly thereafter, Sophie, in a drunken stupor, makes love to
Stingo. But when he wakes up she is gone, leaving only a note
attached to the hotel room mirror. Stingo goes back to New York
to the rooming house, to find that Sophie has returned to

Nathan, then together, with him, committed suicide. They are buried together in a nonsectarian cemetery, and thus the story ends.

What makes this extraordinary novel even more exceptional is that both the author and the main character are not Jewish. In other words, for the very first time a Holocaust novel reflects the perspective of a Polish Catholic, Sophie. It serves to convey a sense that the hatred touches us all, that no group dare be silent in the face of another's oppression.

Sophie's Choice presents us with two non-heroes, Nathan and Sophie, who have given up on life before their story ever begins. Life has brutalized them to the point where their wish to die cannot be reversed. In truth, Sophie really had no choice. Her first choice regarding her children was made under terrible duress. Her second choice—to die—was made out of guilt and emotional illness.

The lives of these two characters enable the reader to glimpse, not only the horror of the Holocaust, but its devastation on the lives of those who survived. This is the lost generation of Holocaust survivors. In a very few years there will be none left to tell the story and thereby to warn humanity. *Sophie's Choice,* however, a bestseller when it was first published, will continue to bear witness so long as books are read and stories are told.

75 Exodus

Leon Uris

Exodus, Leon Uris's account of the liberation of the State of Israel, parallels the story of deliverance of the Israelites from slavery in Egypt to freedom in their own land. A work of fiction, it draws its story from actual events.

After suffering the atrocities of the Holocaust, thousands of Jews fled their homelands for Palestine, in the hope of reaching a place where they would be welcome and protected. Instead, the British put them in detention camps, reminiscent of the concentration camps the Jews had known during the war. The novel begins in one of these camps on the island of Cyprus.

During World War II and at the Nuremberg trials, Mark Parker had served as a news correspondent for the American press. Before traveling to Palestine to cover the creation of the Jewish state, he stops in Cyprus for a much-needed break, and to visit Kitty Freemont, the widow of his best friend.

Kitty had married Mark's friend before the war. Immediately after he was killed on Guadalcanal, her daughter died of polio, leaving her alone. She spent the remainder of the war helping injured children, and when they meet, she is working with the United Nations to establish orphanages for young survivors of the war.

Parker tells her, "There's going to be a war, Kitty. Some people are out to resurrect a nation that has been dead for two thousand years. Nothing like that has ever happened before. What's more, I think they're going to do it."

As Mark and Kitty sit in the dining room of the Dome Hotel, Mark glances over Kitty's shoulder and freezes. "Mark, you look as though you've seen a ghost," Kitty says.

"I have, and he's just about here. We are going to have a very

224

interesting evening," Mark replies. He has just recognized the man approaching their table as Ari Ben Canaan, leader of the movement to smuggle Jews into Palestine illegally by boat. Ben Canaan makes a deal with Parker that he will get exclusive rights to the story if he will be the first to write about it. Perhaps in doing so he can end British immigration policy that denies Jews the right to live in Palestine.

Parker's help is not the only assistance that Ben Canaan seeks. Kitty, a highly skilled nurse, has passed up working in the refugee camps on Cyprus. The detainees are Jewish, and as a Christian, she feels uncomfortable among them. Ari Ben Canaan persists in urging her to serve, since as a Christian volunteer she can pass in and out of the camp and carry messages vital to those seeking to help the refugees. Kitty reluctantly agrees to visit a camp where thousands of refugees are being detained. Ben Canaan takes her on a tour of the camp and introduces her to some of the people there, including Karen Hansen Clement. Karen, not even in her teens, was the only one in her family who survived the Holocaust. Because of her age, her appearance, and her kind disposition, Karen reminds Kitty of her own daughter. Kitty becomes committed to helping the refugees, hoping to convince Karen to return to the U.S. with her, as her adopted daughter.

With the assistance of both Mark and Kitty, Ari's plan succeeds. Three hundred refugee children are smuggled out of the camp under the guise of being relocated to another camp, and board the ship *Exodus*, waiting in the harbor. As soon as Parker alerts the British officials, at Ben Canaan's instructions, British vessels aiming to block the ship from leaving port encircle the *Exodus*. The British are informed by Ben Canaan that massive amounts of explosives are aboard the boat, and that if any attempts are made to board her, the *Exodus* will be blown up.

Just as planned, the international media soon publish the story of a boat full of Jewish refugee children surrounded by British warships in a foreign harbor. The British are portrayed as villains, who would endanger the lives of hundreds of children rather than grant safe transit to Palestine.

The children of the *Exodus* soon begin a hunger strike, thereby increasing public pressure and lowering public opinion of the British. As children faint from lack of food, they are carried up to the deck for the world to see. After a desperate promise by all aboard to commit suicide if they are not let out of the port, the British finally accede to their demands, and release the *Exodus*.

After arriving in Palestine, Kitty, Ari, and Karen find their way to the Gan Dafna youth settlement, named after Ben Canaan's martyred childhood sweetheart. It becomes evident that Kitty is falling in love with the land of Palestine and Ari Ben Canaan. After convincing herself that she cannot become attached to Ben Canaan because she is afraid of losing him, she decides to stay in Palestine through the War of Independence. In a terrible tragedy, Karen dies near the end of the battle. In her grieving, Kitty sees that Ari, too, is devastated over again losing someone he cared about. He finally accepts his love for Kitty and his need for the love of another human being. They decide to spend the rest of their lives together in the newly liberated land of Israel—home of the Jewish people.

Exodus is more than just the story of numerous personal victories and defeats; it vividly depicts the quintessential struggle for survival of the Jewish people. As Kitty joins Ari's family in their Passover Seder, the leader reads: "Why is this night different from all other nights of the year? This is different because we celebrate the most important moment in the history of our people. On this night we celebrate their going forth in triumph from slavery into freedom." And so *Exodus* ends, the metaphorical story of the Jews' deliverance from bondage into the Promised Land, where they can live in freedom.

76 The Janowska Road

Leon Wells

Why do certain fairy tales live? Why are fairy tales written in every language? The answer is that they fill a hunger in the human heart. Consider the fairy tale of Cinderella—dressed in rags, sitting by the fire covered with ashes. She has her moment of glory when the prince dances with her, and then it is gone at the stroke of twelve, and finally restored again. That Cinderella dream is the consolation dream of all the dispossessed. You might say that the daydream is the opiate for human sorrow. Isn't that a perennial need in every land, with every group? That is why the Cinderella story lives.

Now sometimes it happens that it is not only a fairy tale that lives, but also a particular event that becomes the subject of endless legend. Today, fifty years after the Holocaust, there are people who have asked: Did the Nazi nightmare actually happen, or was it just an evil dream? Some people are already beginning to say that it is exaggerated, that it is an unbelievable myth, that human beings could not descend to such depths of depravity. It is precisely for that reason that many survivors who lived through the terrible nightmare of the concentration camps have written books describing their journey through hell.

One of these writers is the author of *The Janowska Road*. Leon Wells grew up in Poland, in the village of Stojanov. The village had a population of two thousand, and over one thousand were Jews. His father was a timber merchant, a wealthy man who had interests in other enterprises. Both his parents were learned. There were seven children in the family. They belonged to a Hasidic sect, and Wells gives a very interesting description of the beliefs of Hasidism.

In 1933, when he was eight years old, his family moved to the city of Lvov. In 1938 he entered the gymnasium, the high school, which he attended from eight in the morning until two in the afternoon, then went to the yeshiva from three in the afternoon to eight at night. It was a secure, serene existence.

In the following year, in August 1939, black clouds began to appear on the horizon. On September 1, 1939, Germany declared war on Poland. The Red Army immediately occupied part of Poland. Wells describes the hardships, the rationing. His father's business was taken over, but there was no religious discrimination. In June 1941 he applied for admission to the Technical Institute in Moscow and was accepted. The future still seemed secure.

On June 22, however, Moscow radio announced that the German army had invaded Russia. At two o'clock that afternoon, Lvov was bombed. Yet, even then, there was no cause for alarm. After all, Germany was a civilized country. Eight days later, when the Germans marched into Lvov, they were even cheered by the inhabitants of the town.

In a few days, however, ugly rumors began to circulate. Jews were being beaten, arrested. Entire families had been taken away. Ukrainian militiamen were bursting into Jewish homes, rounding up all males, beating them mercilessly with their rubber truncheons. Leon and his father were taken to a field. After being whipped for no apparent reason, they were told to go home.

Leon Well writes, "A 'farewell stripe' from the Ukrainian whips as we made our way through the exit left no impression whatever on us. All I could see was that beyond the gate my mother was waiting, and all I could feel was that, weeping copiously, she had her arms about me."

In the weeks that followed, the terror increased. All Jews were compelled to wear a Star of David on their arms. It was extended to those who had one grandparent who was Jewish.

Systematically, Jews were forced into a ghetto. Rumors spread that thousands of Jews had been killed. But the rumors were never confirmed. After all, Leon and his father were safe. They had work permits, and were not molested. Even when Leon was sent to the Janowska concentration camp, he and his parents were not overly alarmed. After all, how long could the Germans withstand the opinions of the free world? It was a foregone conclusion that they would be defeated. But the Germans were not defeated, and the brutality increased.

The author writes, "It is said that people get 'hardened' to pain. I believe from my own experience that this is so. Without realizing it, one gradually begins to apply what is called 'self-hypnotism' to shut off certain connections between the brain and the body. In time, one begins to witness the most brutal and degrading scenes without reacting; a person may be killed before one's eyes, and one views it without reacting emotionally, simply records it as a machine might. The same process applies to personal beatings. As the amount of the beatings increased, one consciously felt them far less."

He describes the conditions that prevailed in the concentration camp, the beatings, the shootings, the torture—for example, making each man urinate into another's mouth, and if the man spat out the urine he was immediately shot; the typhoid, the dysentery, digging graves for friends who had been shot, bribing guards for a piece of bread.

On two occasions, he escaped. While he was free, he learned that his mother and four little sisters had been shot, betrayed by a Polish neighbor woman. Then he learned that his father had been killed. Immediately after that, Leon was recaptured. "My youngest brother, Jacob, tried to hide, and crept up to a fence. He tried to make himself quite small, hoping the SS men would not notice him. But they did. They shot him."

Leon again managed to escape. He found refuge on a farm owned by a Polish farmer. He was led into a cellar directly under the barn and found that there were twenty-three Jews living there. There is a gripping description of how they lived, the various personalities and temperaments. Finally, in May 1944, the Russians arrived. Leon went to Lvov. In 1941, there had been one hundred fifty thousand Jews in Lvov. In 1944 there were 184 Jews left.

He went to see the Polish woman who had betrayed his mother, and asked her why she had done it. "More often we spoke of how our own 'good' non-Jewish neighbors had betrayed us. Why? We didn't expect them to help us, but why did they so enthusiastically help to murder us? I found out where the gentile neighbor who had betrayed my mother now lived, and went there. I was greeted with the familiar, 'I knew that some of you would survive.' I asked the woman why she had given my mother's hiding place to the S.S. man after having lived on good terms next door to her for so many years. To this she replied: 'It wasn't Hitler who killed the

Jews; it was God's will, and Hitler was his tool. How could I stand by and be against the will of God?' I walked away stunned. I hadn't expected that kind of answer. She did not feel that she should repent or even deny her deed. She was a woman in her sixties."

Wells ends the book by explaining why he had written it. "The last wish of my people, each as he died, was to let the world know what had happened. They felt and hoped that the world cared about them and their fate. Does the world care?"

77 The Gates of the Forest

Elie Wiesel

For nineteen hundred years, Jews have wandered the face of the earth. During this time, Jews have wondered when humanity would become civilized. In every generation tyrants rose up to destroy us, culminating in the Nazi brutality of the 1930s and 1940s. But there is one significant difference: in the past, the persecution was religious, which meant that Jews could escape by conversion. Under the Nazis, the persecution was racial, which meant that there was no escape, because you cannot abolish your ancestors.

In 1944, at the age of fifteen, Elie Wiesel was taken to Auschwitz with his parents and an eight-year-old sister. Adolph Eichmann personally supervised the deportation of ten thousand Jews from the little Hungarian town of Sighet. Wiesel's mother and sister were killed, and his father died in Buchenwald. The United States army arrived in time to rescue Wiesel from the ovens. And so this boy who had witnessed the destruction of so many of his fellow Jews resolved to keep their memory alive. In *Gates of the Forest* he gives us insight into the odyssey of his soul.

The book is divided into four parts. It is a small book—two hundred and twenty-six pages. You will read it in two hours, and you will remember it forever. He begins by describing a Jewish boy who is seventeen, hiding in a cave from Hungarian soldiers. A stranger comes to the cave—nameless—and the boy gives his name to the stranger. His original name was Gavriel, and now he assumes for himself the name Gregor. The stranger tells Gregor that the Jews are being systematically liquidated. He says to Gregor:

"Are you listening?"

"Yes, I'm listening."

"You won't forget?"

"No, I won't forget."

"You won't forget the calls to prayer and the prayers of my companions when they were face to face with their impassive executioner?"

"I won't forget."

"They looked him straight in the eye, you know, without flinching. They might have thrown themselves at his feet and tried to win his pity. That is what others would have done, but not they. A pride that came down to them from an earlier age prevented them from bowing down even before God, who was there behind the executioner."

"I know, Gavriel, I know."

"And the fragile and heart-rending silence of the children at the hour of their death, you'll remember that?"

"I'll make it mine."

"And that Zaddik who sang as he walked to the ditch where the corpses of his townsmen were piled up, will you remember him?"

"I'll remember him always. His song will be my guide; I'll follow it and shall never let it die."

He tells the boy that one night he confronted the prophet Elijah. He pleaded with Elijah to send the Messiah, and this is what he said: "If the Messiah doesn't hurry, he may be too late; there will be no one left to save."

In the second part of the book, Gregor makes his way to the hut of a woman who had once been the family maid. Her name is Maria. She gives him shelter and offers a plan to save him. She had had a sister, Ileana, a very beautiful, charming girl, to whom every man was a challenge. She had virtually seduced every man in the village and had left some twenty years ago. Her whereabouts are unknown. Maria says that Gregor will be called the illegitimate son of her sister Ileana. To further protect him, he will assume the role of a deaf mute.

Everyone accepts Gregor in this role. As a matter of fact, he becomes the most popular person in town. Everyone goes to him to confess. Who could be safer than a deaf mute? Even the priest comes to him to confess. All goes well, until a schoolteacher, a middle-aged man, Constantine Stefan, decides to present a passion play at the end of the school year. There is only one problem: no one wants to play the role of Judas. It suddenly occurs to the schoolmaster that Gregor would make a perfect

Judas. "A silent Judas, a Judas struck dumb by God." Maria is opposed to this, but all her arguments are futile. Gregor is cast in the role of Judas.

In the third act, when Judas is accused of betraying Jesus, suddenly (and this happened all too frequently in Europe during the Middle Ages), the audience becomes a mob and surges onto the stage. "Kill him, kill him...." Gregor, beaten and bloodied, summons up his last remaining strength and speaks. The mob is stunned. The peasants are convinced that this is a miracle. They are frightened too. After all, he knows all their secrets.

Gregor forces them to admit (in what is one of the strongest and most dramatic portions of the book) that Judas, not Jesus, is the victim; that Judas, not Jesus, is the crucified. But when he finally tells them that he is a Jew, they become enraged and are about to kill him. Just as he is about to be murdered, a stranger, Count Petruska, takes him by the hand, puts him in his carriage and rides away to safety. He leads him to the Jewish partisans who are hiding in the forest, and whose struggles are chronicled in part three.

By part four, the war is over. Gregor goes to Paris and by chance meets his friend Clara. He proposes marriage to her. She tells him that she cannot marry him because she still loves his friend Leib who was killed. She says: "Would you want to feel that every time I was with you that I thought of Leib? I love him, even though he is dead."

He persuades her to marry him, however, and they settle in New York. It is a poor marriage. Clara cries constantly, calling out in her sleep for Leib.

Gregor decides that he will leave Clara, but then one day he visits a Hasidic synagogue in Brooklyn. A young boy from the yeshivah leads him to the sanctuary, where Kaddish is being said. "What is your name," asks the boy. "Gregor, I mean Gavriel." As soon as Gavriel assumes his real name, and takes on his Jewish identity, he begins to live again.

Wiesel teaches us that we don't know where God is, we don't know where the Messiah is. But the Jewish approach is to keep on struggling, because perhaps even God needs our help. He affirms that you can remember the dead, but that it is wrong to live with the dead. And so, even though he is tempted to remain in the forest, which symbolizes a removal from life and love, he finally walks away from the gates of the forest, and decides to walk in the land of the living.

78 Night

Elie Wiesel

In *Night,* Elie Wiesel chronicles his life with a cinematic sensibility, starting in 1941 at the age of twelve, when he lived with his parents and three sisters in the tiny village of Sighet in Transylvania. We follow Wiesel and his family through the war years until the beginning of 1945. Detailing unimaginable horrors, made even more incomprehensible by their magnitude, this account cuts so deeply that the reader can't help but weep during Elie Wiesel's journey.

And the reader understands how Wiesel, the most reverent of boys, would lose his faith in God. A prisoner confides, "I've got more faith in Hitler than in anyone else. He's the only one who's kept his promises, all his promises to the Jewish people." The foreword, written by François Mauriac, is equally moving.

Wiesel opens with a description of Moshe the Beadle, a poor man who was "a past master in the art of making himself insignificant." He taught Wiesel Talmud ("He explained to me with great insistence that every question possessed a power that did not lie in the answer"), and spoke with him about Jewish mysticism. Then one day, many Jews were expelled: suddenly Moshe was gone. There was talk that the deportees were in Galicia, working and happy. Subsequently, Moshe the Beadle returned and told the truth: "The train full of deportees had crossed the Hungarian frontier and on Polish territory had been taken in charge by the Gestapo...to a forest. The Jews were made to get out...dig huge graves. Without passion, without haste, they slaughtered their prisoners. Each one had to go up to the hold and present his neck. Babies were thrown into the air and machine gunners used them as targets....How had Moshe the Beadle escaped? Miraculously. He was wounded in the leg and taken for dead."

Neither Weisel nor anyone else believed the unbelievable, which they hadn't witnessed. Moshe the Beadle went from household to household repeating the story. He is mistaken for a madman. The power of denial is never again seen so innocently. "I have been saved miraculously," he tells Wiesel. "I managed to get back here. Where did I get the strength from? I wanted to come back to Sighet to tell you the story of my death. So that you could prepare yourselves while there was still time."

Life returned to normal temporarily until the Fascists came to power; soon after, German troops entered Hungary. At first, the Germans didn't appear brutish; they seemed well-mannered, sometimes even gracious. But soon, all pretense of cordiality ended abruptly. Jewish leaders were arrested and Jews were quarantined.

On the occasions when Wiesel's fate could have been different, each option seemed too extreme in the context of disbelief: the young Wiesel asks his father to emigrate to Israel, and an old servant tearfully pleads for the family to join her in her village where they could find a safe refuge.

The Germans load the Jews of Sighet, including the Wiesels, aboard cattle cars bound for Birkenau and Auschwitz. At the camps, Wiesel is separated from his mother and sister: "For a part of a second I glimpsed my mother and my sister moving away to the right. Tzipora held Mother's hand. I saw them disappear into the distance; my mother was stroking my sister's fair hair, as though to protect her, while I walked on with my father and the other men. And I did not know that in that place, at that moment, I was parting from my mother and Tzipora forever."

Elie and his father continue on, as prisoners at Birkenau ("reception center for Auschwitz"), on to Auschwitz, and then Buna. Upon his arrival at Auschwitz, Wiesel saw: "Babies! Yes, I saw it—saw it with my own eyes...those children in the flames.... Was I still alive? Was I awake?...How could it be possible for them to burn people, children, and for the world to keep silent?" His eloquence heightens the pain: "Never shall I forget that night, the first night in camp, which has turned my life into one long night, seven times cursed and seven times sealed. Never shall I forget that smoke. Never shall I forget the little faces of the children, whose bodies I saw turned into wreaths of smoke beneath a silent blue sky.... Never shall I forget those flames which consumed my faith forever.... Never shall I forget that nocturnal silence which deprived me, for all eternity, of the desire to live. Never shall I forget those moments which murdered my God and my soul and turned my dreams to dust. Never shall I forget these things even if I am condemned to live as long as God Himself. Never."

At Auschwitz Wiesel became number A-7713, which was tattooed into his arm. At Buna he encountered the infamous Dr. Mengele, but was not singled out by him for medical experiments conducted on live prisoners. He had his crowned tooth removed with a rusty spoon because the foreman wanted the gold, and he was whipped repeatedly until he fainted. He witnessed hangings, including that of a young boy, so light he didn't die right away, but struggled "between life and death, dying in slow agony under our eyes. And we had to look him full in the face."

Leaving Buna, as the Russians approached, Wiesel tells of running in the snowy night, along with his father, whose presence helped keep him alive. He forgot his body; if he couldn't keep up he knew he would be shot by the S.S. or trampled on by the "thousands of concentration camp inmates running behind them. Reaching Buchenwald, death permeated everything: "We trod on wounded faces. No cries. A few groans. My father and I were ourselves thrown to the ground by this rolling tide.

"'You're crushing me...mercy!'...

"...That voice had spoken to me one day....I struggled to disengage myself beneath the weight of other bodies. I could hardly breathe. I dug my nails into unknown faces....Suddenly I remembered. Juliek! The boy from Warsaw who played the violin in the band at Buna!"

The journey weakened his father so that he was on the verge of death. A few days later "...I had to go to bed. I climbed into my bunk, above my father, who was still alive. It was January 28, 1945....I awoke on January 29 at dawn. In my father's place lay another invalid. They must have taken him away before dawn and carried him to the crematory. He may still have been breathing."

Death, both of individuals and of human morality, make this haunting recollection our story of loss as well, which is what the Holocaust truly is.

Elie Wiesel was liberated from Buchenwald by the Allies, then lived and wrote in France before moving to the United States. A Nobel Peace Prize Laureate, his articles and books are now read and studied throughout the world.

79 Max and Helen

Simon Wiesenthal

A generation ago, the Italian dramatist Luigi Pirandello wrote a famous playlet with the provocative title *Six Characters in Search of an Author.*

Indeed, the world is full of interesting personalities who have not yet been discovered, thousands of people who lived influential lives, others who lived lives of tragedy, all of whom remained anonymous unless the time came when an author told their story.

Simon Wiesenthal, author of *The Sunflower*, has made it his life's work to bring Nazi criminals to justice, thus remembering the lives of martyrs who might otherwise be forgotten. He is already responsible for the arrest of over one thousand Nazis, including Adolph Eichmann.

Whenever he is asked why he became a Nazi hunter, he is fond of relating a story of one Sabbath when he was a guest at the home of a friend who had been in the same concentration camp with him and who was now a wealthy jeweler. After dinner, his host reflected on the fact that had Wiesenthal pursued his original occupation of building houses, he would have become a millionaire. Wiesenthal responded: "I know that you are a religious man, and that you believe in life after death. Some day, when we die and come to the other world, we will meet the millions of Jews who died in the camps, and they will ask us: 'What have you done with your life?'

"There will be many answers. You will say: 'I became a jeweler.' Another will say: 'I built houses.' And I will say: 'I didn't forget you!'"

Wiesenthal wrote a book based on actual events, entitled *Max and Helen*—no last names, just Max and Helen—two characters in search of an author. Wiesenthal tells their story in a most intriguing way.

The book begins as Wiesenthal is traveling by train from
Vienna to Budapest. A man sits down and confides that a top
executive at a factory they are passing was the commander of a
Nazi concentration camp during the war. At the next stop the
man gets off without further comment.

Wiesenthal learns that Werner Schulze is married to the
factory president's daughter. He is in charge of personnel at the
factory, and Wiesenthal discovers that Schulze is reputed to have
a violent temper. Wiesenthal senses that Schulze might have been
the commander of Zaleskie camp. He has Schulze photographed
and circulates the picture, but no one recognizes him. It seems, he
is told, that no Jews survived Zaleskie. All were put to death.

One day he learns of a doctor named Max who lives in Paris
and had been an inmate of the Zaleskie camp. He finds the
doctor. Upon seeing the picture, Max tells Wiesenthal that
Schulze was indeed the camp commandant, but that he is
unwilling to testify against him. Bewildered by this unprecedented lack of cooperation, Wiesenthal meets Max in a Zurich
hotel, and learns the story of Zaleskie camp.

Born in Poland, Max dreamed of becoming a doctor. In high
school, he met Helen. The two planned to marry, but the war
intervened. The Nazis occupied Poland and built Zaleskie. Max
and Helen could have escaped, but refused to leave Helen's sister,
Miriam, who was too frail to travel.

Max describes Schulze's brutality as commandant, ascribing his
survival to his status as the camp doctor. Helen also survived as
Schulze's maid. One day, Max devised an escape plan, but Helen
refused to desert her sister. They vowed to find each other and
marry after the war. Max escaped, but wound up in a Russian
prison for thirteen years. All this time he was sustained by two
thoughts: he will find Helen and bring Schulze to justice!

After his release from prison, Max completed his medical
training, received a degree, and was employed in a hospital
laboratory. He carried Helen's picture and showed it to everyone,
hoping that someone might recognize her and know where she
was. Even when he was told that all the Jews in Zaleskie were
murdered, he refused to give up.

One day in a restaurant in Cracow, he recognizes a woman who
had been Helen's high school friend. She tells him that Helen is
alive and living under an assumed name in West Germany. After
all these years, Max steals into West Germany, finds out where

Helen lives, climbs the stairs to her second-floor apartment, and with his knees shaking, rings the bell.

The door opens, and there stands a boy who looks exactly like Schulze! Helen sees Max and embraces him, weeping. She tells how Schulze beat her, raped her repeatedly; how when she became pregnant he sent her to a convent where the baby was born; how she raised this boy as a Jew, telling him that his father had been killed fighting the Nazis.

Max listens, then tells Helen that he loves her but cannot marry her or see her again. She is the mother of Schulze's child, and he cannot bear to be near her. She begs him to stay, but her plea fails to move Max, who leaves.

He will not testify against Schulze, he tells Wiesenthal, because it would destroy the lives of both Helen and her son. He cannot be with her, but he will not be an instrument of further pain in her life.

Wiesenthal goes to see Helen, and when she, too, pleads with him not to bring Schulze to trial, he drops the case, the only Nazi criminal he ever let go.

Nine years go by, and Wiesenthal visits Max to inform him that Schulze has been killed in a car accident. He urges Max to return to Helen, but Max cannot bring himself to do so. Three years later, Wiesenthal sees Helen. She tells him that her son is engaged to a Jewish girl from Toronto, that they will make their home in Canada. Wiesenthal tells her: "When you return from Canada, write to Max and just say, 'Max, I am alone now.'"

The reader is not told whether Helen ever writes to Max or whether Max ever replies.

80 The Sunflower

Simon Wiesenthal

Rabbi Abraham Joshua Heschel tells the story of a man who boarded a train in Warsaw. The man was a great rabbinic scholar, but small in stature and not distinguished-looking in the least. Ushered into a small compartment in the train, he saw a group of salesmen playing cards. The salesmen, unaware of the identity of the man to whom they were speaking, invited him to join, but the rabbi remained aloof. The salesmen became annoyed and demanded that he either join or leave. When the rabbi steadfastly refused, he was forcibly ejected from the compartment and stood for the rest of the trip.

When the train reached its destination in the city of Brisk, the famous rabbi was greeted by hundreds of disciples. Realizing that he had shamed a great teacher, one of the salesmen approached and asked him for forgiveness. The rabbi refused. He next went to the rabbi's house with a gift of three hundred rubles and a plea for forgiveness. Again, the answer was no. Finally the salesman went to the synagogue to ask forgiveness. Still the rabbi refused. As he told his disciples: "I cannot forgive him. He did not know who I was. He offended a common man. Let him go to that common man and ask for forgiveness."

And Heschel concludes by saying: "Since that is impossible, it is equally impossible to say that anybody alive can extend forgiveness for the suffering of the six million who perished. God can only forgive sins against *Himself;* not against *Man.*"

Simon Wiesenthal's *The Sunflower* reopens the question of forgiveness of the Nazis from the perspective of a man with rather extraordinary credentials. Wiesenthal achieved a reputation for bringing Nazi war criminals to justice as the head of the Jewish Documentation Center in Vienna. Eighty-nine of his relatives died at the hands of the Nazis, and he himself was imprisoned in a camp, then liberated in 1945 by American troops.

This slim, two-hundred-page volume begins with the story of its hero, named Simon, a concentration camp prisoner assigned to a daily work detail. Every morning they leave the camp to work, returning at evening to their dismal quarters.

One day the prisoners are brought into town to work at a hospital. A nurse approaches Simon and asks, "Are you a Jew?" When Simon answers in the affirmative, he is brought to a hospital room where there is a wounded soldier, his head and face completely bandaged, with openings only for his mouth, nose, and ears.

The soldier knows he is dying, and tells Simon his story. Now twenty-one years of age, he was raised a Catholic, but joined the Hitler Youth and became a storm trooper. One day, his company entered a Jewish village, forced two hundred men, women, and children into a house, set the house on fire, and watched as these innocent people died. He looks up at Simon and says: "I have been asking to talk to a Jew....I am asking you to forgive me...without your answer, I cannot die in peace."

In the book, the character Simon says nothing. He leaves the room and the Nazi soldier dies without the slightest response to his entreaty. Thus, the question remains: should he have forgiven?

Now Wiesenthal did something very interesting. He sent the manuscript to thirty-two leading scholars and asked them for their opinion. The second half of the book consists of their answers.

Milton Konvitz, professor emeritus of law at Cornell University responded in part: "I cannot speak for your victims. I cannot speak for the Jewish people. I cannot speak for God. But I am a man. I am a Jew. I am commanded, in my personal relations, to act with compassion. I have been taught that if I expect the Compassionate One to have compassion on me, I must act with compassion toward others...my broken heart pleads for your broken heart."

Herbert Marcuse, professor of philosophy at UCLA, wrote: "I think I would have acted the way you did, that is to say, refused the request of the dying S.S. man. It always seemed to me inhuman and a travesty of justice if the executioner asked the victim to forgive....I believe that the easy forgiving of such crimes perpetuates the very evil it wants to alleviate."

A British journalist, Christopher Hollis, urged forgiveness, as follows: "According to an old medieval legend, the apostles assembled together in heaven to recelebrate the Last Supper. There was one place vacant, until through the door Judas came in and Christ rose and kissed him and said, 'We have waited for thee.'"

These answers and twenty-nine more offer the reader a spectrum of modern responses to this painful conundrum. Of course, in the final analysis, there can be no one answer on which everyone agrees. Furthermore, the individual responses may change with time.

We are left, however, with yet another question. Why did Wiesenthal title this book *The Sunflower*? It appears that this flower may be a symbol of our mandate to remember the Holocaust, not to let flowers, however beautiful, cover up the graves and the history that goes with them. There may be a question as to who should forgive, but there can be no question that we must never forget. Was Wiesenthal's story autobiographical? Is the Simon character a reflection of his personal experience? Wiesenthal does not say.

PART VI

Fiction and General Works on Jewish Themes

81 Getting Even

Side Effects

Without Feathers

Woody Allen

I don't want to achieve immortality through my work....I want
to achieve it through not dying," Woody Allen said years ago. Part
of the appeal of Allen's humor is that often his characters
verbalize what everyone is thinking but no one will actually say.
And his quintessentially Jewish-American persona, as the neurotic intellectual, appears nonthreatening; he's a small, balding
man—a zany and charming worrier. His contributions to American film and writing are unique.

His earlier off-the-wall comedies included a multitude of
ridiculously perfect scenes. Who can forget the famous scene in
Annie Hall where Marshall McLuhan actually steps out from
behind a poster in a movie theater to correct a pretentious man as
he pontificates about McLuhan's intentions?

Fortunately, Allen's talents are not limited to the screen. His
fiction, mostly comprised of short stories, is found in three
volumes: *Getting Even* (1978), *Side Effects,* (1980) and *Without
Feathers* (1986). *Getting Even* is probably the funniest.

There is lightheartedness to Allen's written humor, evocative of
his early films. The writings comprised in these three books were
produced fairly early on in his career (*Manhattan* was his most
recent film when the last volume, *Side Effects,* was published as a
collection). The situations are absurd, and he plays them out to
their fullest extreme.

Opening lines are tremendously important in fiction, much like first impressions in real life. *Side Effects* begins with a short story, "Remembering Needleman": "It has been four weeks and it is still hard for me to believe Sandor Needleman is dead. I was present at the cremation and at his son's request, brought the marshmallows, but few of us could think of anything but our pain."

In *Side Effects,* "The Kugelmass Episode" is one of the funniest stories. Sidney Kugelmass, a professor of humanities at City College, is on his second marriage, to a woman he wed because she had both potential and money—but she's let herself go and looks like a beach ball. Unhappy and lusting, Kugelmass confides his desires to his analyst, who tells him he shouldn't act out these feelings, but rather explore them in therapy. Kugelmass quits therapy.

Soon he gets a call from Persky, a magician who had learned of his desires. In Persky's apartment, Kugelmass stares at a poorly lacquered Chinese cabinet with rhinestones glued on it, which, Persky explains, is a time machine. Meet any woman in literature, Kugelmass tells him, by getting into the cabinet with the book in which the woman appears, and you'll join her in its pages.

Soon Kugelmass finds himself in Emma Bovary's house in Yonville, where their love affair begins. Of course, there are glitches, and things don't wind up as smoothly as Kugelmass was told. (Meanwhile, another professor is reading about a character named Kugelmass in *Madame Bovary!*)

Another classic Woody Allen story is *The U.F.O. Menace,* in which various sightings are reported. Allen's tongue-in-cheek tone is delivered deadpan, as he creates one-of-a-kind characters who are either so unappealing or ridiculously absurd that one can't help but laugh. Regarding a U.F.O. sighting: "One of the eeriest accounts occurred in August 1975, to a man on Montauk Point, in Long Island: 'I was in bed at my beach house, but could not sleep because of some fried chicken in the icebox that I felt entitled to. I waited till my wife dropped off, and tiptoed into the kitchen. I remember looking at the clock. It was precisely four-fifteen. I'm quite certain of this, because our kitchen clock has not worked in twenty-one years and is always at that time. I also noticed that our dog, Judas, was acting funny. He was standing up on his hind legs and singing, "I Enjoy Being a Girl." Suddenly the room turned bright orange.'"

This silly, lighthearted humor is typical of all three volumes, which can be easily read in short spurts. The first section of *Side Effects* is entitled "Selections From the Allen Notebooks," and includes his pondering: "Should I Marry W.? Not if she won't tell me the other letters in her name."

Allen's characteristic irreverence also occurs in his treatment of biblical passages. For example, in *Without Feathers,* one chapter, entitled "The Scrolls," has Allen's versions of biblical stories, including the following anecdote: "And it came to pass that a man who sold shirts was smitten by hard times." He prays to God, and the Lord tells the man: "Put an alligator over the pocket." Lo and behold, his shirts began to sell....

In *Getting Even,* there is a chapter entitled "Hassidic Tales." A man with a heavy heart visits Rabbi Shimmel of Cracow. "God has given me an ugly daughter." "How ugly?" the Seer asked. "If she were lying on a plate with a herring, you wouldn't be able to tell the difference."

After the text in each book ends, a few paragraphs tell us about the author. We are reminded that Allen was expelled from both New York University and City College. These miniature profiles each end with "His one regret in life is that he is not someone else."

82 An Orphan in History

Paul Cowan

Prior to 1982, the name of Paul Cowan was associated exclusively with newspaper journalism. His supple style graced the pages of the *Village Voice* for many years. As a Peace Corps volunteer and civil rights and antiwar activist, his liberal approach to contemporary issues fit the paper's ideology. Then in 1982, Paul Cowan wrote *An Orphan in History*, which leaped to the top of the Jewish bestseller charts. Within its pages, Cowan recorded a personal odyssey of faith to Judaism and a past he never knew existed.

Cowan introduces himself in the following dramatic way: "I am Paul Cowan, the New York-bred son of Louis Cowan and Pauline Spiegel Cowan, Chicago-born, very American, very successful parents; and I am Saul Cohen, the descendant of rabbis in Germany and Lithuania. I am the grandson of Modie Spiegel, a mail-order magnate, who was born a Reform Jew, became a Christian Scientist, and died in his spacious house in the wealthy gentile suburb of Kenilworth, Illinois, with a picture of Jesus Christ in his breast pocket; and of Jacob Cohen, a used-cement-bag dealer from Chicago, an Orthodox Jew, who lost everything he had—his wife, his son, his business, his self-esteem—except for the superstition-tinged faith that gave moments of structure and meaning to his last, lonely years."

In a story that reads more like a novel than an autobiography, the author records his childhood growing up on Manhattan's East Side. He lived among people to whom he refers as Jewish WASPS. His father, an only child, had changed his name to Cowan from Cohen, and Paul had no idea of his rich Jewish ancestry. The family celebrated Christmas and Easter, and Paul attended Choate, a New England prep school under Episcopalian sponsorship.

Cowan never had a bar mitzvah and, falling in love with a New England Protestant woman, Rachel Brown, married her without the slightest concern about intermarriage. Rachel later converted to Judaism at a Manhattan synagogue, subsequently entered rabbinical school, and was ordained a rabbi at the Hebrew Union College–Jewish Institute of Religion in New York.

Cowan speaks of his father, onetime president of CBS-TV, and his mother, an ardent civil rights activist, who believed that Jews had a special responsibility to fight for civil rights because of the Holocaust, and encouraged Paul, when he went to Mississippi in 1964, to register black voters. As he grew older, he also learned more about his cruel and angry grandfather, Jake Cohen, and his grandmother, Hettie.

Cowan encountered a great deal of anti-Semitism at Choate prep school in spite of the fact that he became an important figure at the school and was accepted as "the exception who proves the rule"; the bigotry directed toward other Jewish class-mates led him to reflect increasingly on his Jewish roots. His father declined to tell him much about his grandfather, Jake Cohen, nor did his years at the University of Chicago enable him to garner any further information on the Cohens of Chicago.

Finally, when Cowan was in this thirties and already writing for the *Village Voice,* his father at last revealed to him some of the family's history. It turned out that Paul had an uncle living in Chicago, but his father asked Paul not to see him, lest he ask for money! It turned out to be a moot point, for within a year, both of Paul's parents died in a tragic fire at the Westbury Hotel in New York. At the funeral, a long-lost relative appeared, and revealed the news that Paul's great-grandfather had been a rabbi in Romania, and that the oldest Orthodox synagogue in Chicago was named after him. Shortly thereafter, the author met Rabbi Joseph Singer, a rabbi of Hasidic origin, who opened an entirely new world to him. In the process, he also gave Paul back his history.

Rabbi Jacob Cohen was not only a rabbi, but a *rav,* a term of honor reserved for a revered teacher and leader. His son, Moses Cohen, came to Chicago, a scrap-iron salesman who spoke seven languages and was equally at home with Tolstoy and the Talmud. He married and raised ten children, three daughters and seven sons, one of whom was Paul's grandfather Jake. Like his own father the rabbi, Moses was often sought out for his rulings on religious issues or for the elucidation of some difficult textual problem.

Jake, in turn, married, and Paul's father, Lou, was one of his sons. Lou valued education for young people, and prayed that Paul would gain recognition through his scholarship. That hope for his own child led to the creation of the television show *The Quiz Kids,* which transformed some of America's brightest children into national celebrities. Lou went on to create *The $64,000 Question,* then resigned his post at CBS in the wake of the quiz show scandals. He subsequently taught at Brandeis and Columbia University in the field of communications.

Cowan describes his first trip to Israel, his work on a kibbutz, and his temporary Israeli name, Saul Cohen. There he encountered a world in which Jews were proud of their Jewishness. He returned to the United States forever changed, and married Rachel, a fellow spiritual seeker. They served together in the Peace Corps in Ecuador, then moved to Washington in 1968, the year of the King and Kennedy assassinations. Together they witnessed the 1968 anti-Vietnam War rally at the Democratic National Convention in Chicago, and were present at the 1969 student takeover of buildings at the Massachusetts Institute of Technology.

Cowan takes us through the changes that finally made him a Jew: the birth of his children, their enrollment in a Jewish school, the introduction of Jewish ritual into his and Rachel's home, the influence of his teacher, Rabbi Joseph Singer, his decision to put on tefillin, and finally his decision to no longer to work on Shabbat. The book concludes with a moving description of Paul and Rachel's daughter Lisa celebrating her bat mitzvah. For the first time in two generations, a Cowan was called to the Torah. And Cowan writes: "Now, as I sat in our synagogue, I realized that I was no longer an orphan in time, but a wandering Jew who had come home."

83 Only in America

Harry Golden

In the early days of America, our heroes were rugged individualists. They confronted the wilderness, shaped the environment, and contributed to the industrial revolution. They built this country with determination, courage, creativity, and even audacious daring. From a culture valuing uniqueness, we became a culture of mass consumption. We were all urged to buy the same toothpaste, the same grocery products, the same cars, the same clothes. All our inner moods were worked on: our vanity, our desire for status, our wish to be people of distinction. Instead of being a nation of inwardly directed people who created our environment, we became an outwardly directed people influenced by our environment.

The consequence of outer directedness is a devaluation of individuality, a great danger to democracy, which ultimately depends on individuality as a balance to a mass consumption mentality. We want to be like others, but retain our individuality; we rebel against the notion of being thought of merely as a number or statistic.

One of the last bastions of unbridled individuality in America is the press, as epitomized by Harry Golden. Raised on New York City's Lower East Side, this chubby little Jewish man moved to Charlotte, North Carolina. And there, in the Tar Heel State, with all its southern traditions, he created a Jewish newspaper, the *Carolina Israelite*. He wrote and edited all the articles himself, published when he felt like it, expressed his opinions freely, often infuriating the subjects of his stories. His personal journalism made his paper famous throughout the United States.

Only in America, a book filled with columns selected by his son, became a bestseller. This charming individualist also charmed the American public.

251

The book is easy to read, clear, brief, vivid, and often humorous, containing thoughts on a myriad of subjects. One of the earliest essays is entitled: "Why I Never Bawl Out a Waitress." He begins as follows: "Our earth is part of the solar system, and the sun is ninety million miles away, and our solar system is a tiny fragment of a huge galaxy...and there are a hundred million island universes...so what difference does it make if she brings me lima beans instead of string beans?"

In another section, he reflects that at a certain convention he attended, there were call girls available for a hundred dollars, and people were astonished at the high cost. Not Harry Golden. He goes back into history to the time of Julius Caesar and the rise of Marc Antony. Then he points out how Marc Antony, after meeting Cleopatra, gave her Palestine and Syria and half of Asia Minor. Golden says: *"That's* a call girl!"

Golden also speaks lovingly about the Lower East Side and his mother, who had a sure sense of her personal relationship with God. She would give God orders to "take care of him" whenever Harry went out for the evening.

One of the most hilarious stories in the book appears in "The Methodist Guardians of Israel." Golden speaks of a group of Jews building a new temple in Charlotte. They were invited to use the local Methodist church for worship during the construction process. Many church members attended the Jewish services, embarrassing the Jewish members into being there too! Thus, says Golden, this little temple not only sped up the completion of its building program, but had a hundred percent attendance at services for an entire year because of their Methodist neighbors!

In a series of rapier-like attacks on segregation, he suggests three plans for its elimination. One among them holds that blacks (then called Negroes) were clearly allowed to pay their bills and shop in stores while standing up. Therefore, problems only arise when they *sit down*, at lunch counters and in classrooms. He proposes that all chairs be removed from classrooms and that all students stand during class, thus ending the need for segregation in schools!

Above all, Golden speaks of the promise of America. He recalls how the Jews, Italians, and Irish came to America in poverty. Each group had its gangsters and athletic heroes, but gradually ascended the social ladder with education and opportunity. The same, he says, will be true of Negroes, Puerto Ricans, and all immigrants. If they work hard, attain a solid education, and determine to succeed, they will also have their athletes, writers, judges, and great national leaders. As a case in point, Golden tells the story of a young singing waiter in a dingy saloon in China-town, who wrote a song called "Marie from Sunny Italy." He then changed jobs, working at a better saloon owned by an Irishman, where he wrote a second song, "Alexander's Ragtime Band." The scruffy waiter would later compose "White Christmas" and "God Bless America," songs loved and revered by Americans. That boy was Irving Berlin.

Harry Golden was an individualist, who in turn treasured individual men, women, and children. He believed in America and its opportunity, as well as the success to be claimed through hard work and determined dreams. With humor, with profundity, with social concern and charm, he spins out a vision of a nation in which gentleness, goodness, and greatness are attainable if only we recognize the power of the individual to change the world.

84 On Being a Jewish Feminist

Edited by Susannah Heschel

This classic collection of essays, originally published in 1987, includes such diverse female perspectives as a rabbi, a lesbian, and the tenth member—and only woman—of a minyan. Among the many important essays in *On Being a Jewish Feminist* are Sara Reguer's superb piece about saying "Kaddish From the 'Wrong' Side of the Mehitzah" to Mimi Scarf's depiction of battered Jewish women, "Marriages Made in Heaven?," and Thena Kendall's "Memories of an Orthodox Youth."

Rachel Adler's important essay, "The Jew Who Wasn't There," discusses halachic law and the Jewish woman. Paula Hyman talks about family life, and what communities need to do to make child rearing easier when both parents work outside the home. Lesley Hazleton investigates three myths about Israeli women.

In her essay, Mimi Scarf not only dispels the notion that Jewish men aren't batterers, but, in a general portrait of the battered wife syndrome, records the shame and guilt that the wives of such husbands feel because of this myth's perpetuation. When Scarf's typical victim finally seeks the parental help she needs, her mother asks what she did to cause her husband's anger. She is told to go home to her husband, where she belongs. Her husband is presented as a hard worker, faithful, a man who loves his family. All the traditional support systems for a woman—her parents, his parents, the community—perceive him as a fine man. The belief that Jewish men do not engage in physical abuse (it's what could have happened to her had she married out of the faith) is reinforced through denial.

How can abuse end? Generally, there are three ways out: she can take her own life (although she fantasizes about something deadly happening to him), divorce him, or, to keep her marriage intact, threaten to expose him publicly.

Thena Kendall reflects on her Orthodox upbringing in England and why she left Orthodox life. The rigorous demands of living by Jewish law seemed to dominate everything. Even holidays were more about drudgery than about celebrating life's miracles. It was her Sabbath that was dark—not the weekdays. Although her mother had a beautiful singing voice, she wasn't allowed to sing at temple (since her voice could arouse sexual feelings in men), so she stayed home with her daughter with the lights off; they were not allowed to switch them on.

Such restrictions seemed untenable; her girlfriends, from even stricter families, were forbidden to brush their hair on Shabbat. When her mother was dying, there was no talk about death or how her mother was feeling; Orthodox acquaintances sat at the foot of her bed with her father discussing the Talmud. Since Orthodox Jews are not supposed to use electricity on Shabbat: "I remember with particular poignancy one visitor who arrived on the Sabbath and spent his entire visit agonizing as to whether he had desecrated the Sabbath by coming into the hospital through the electronically-operated doors set in motion by his approach."

Kendall was able to attend her mother's funeral only because her father allowed her to do so. When her father died, she was not allowed to say Kaddish, for no Orthodox synagogue would include her in a minyan. Of her feelings at his burial, she writes: "But with every clod that was thrown onto my father's coffin, another link that connected me to the Orthodox tradition was broken." Now she is a member of a Reform temple, where she no longer has to hear endless hours of discussion about what is and what is not kosher, which "seemed a long way from religion." She is grateful to be in a place where her voice can be heard.

In Cynthia Ozick's essay, "Notes Toward Finding the Right Question," she writes, "When my rabbi says, 'A Jew is called to the Torah,' he never means me or any other living Jewish woman.... My own synagogue is the only place in the world where I am not named Jew." There isn't a commandment in the Torah which reads, "Thou shalt not lessen the humanity of women." However, the editor of *On Being a Jewish Feminist* responds by writing, "precisely because it stands for justice as an absolute requirement—even to the extent of opposing aspects of the natural and social order—the Torah provides its own basis for radical change of women's position within Judaism."

Ozick also talks about how the Holocaust affects us today.

"Having lost so much and so many...every Jew will be more a Jew than ever before—and not just superficially and generally, but in every path, taken or untaken, deliberate or haphazard, looked-for or come upon." Relating this to the women's movement, she explains, "The point is not that Jewish women want equality as women with men, but as Jews with Jews. The point is the necessity—having lost so much and so many—to share Jewish history to the hilt."

In Rita M. Gross's essay, "Steps Toward Feminine Imagery of Deity in Jewish Theology," she shows, merely through role reversal, how sexist and absurd the exclusion of women has been. Her narrative replaces men with women instead. "No one is wise enough to know why God made female reproductive organs compact and internal so that woman is physically free to move about unencumbered and take her natural place of leadership in the world of womankind. Or why she made male organs external and exposed so that man would demand sheltering and protection...."

Sara Reguer, an Orthodox feminist, wrote "Kaddish From the 'Wrong' Side of the Mehitzah," one of the finest essays in the book. She admits that saying kaddish after her mother died kept her sane. After her mother's body was buried, the mourners, all men, walked past two rows of people, signifying that they were amongst the living. Told by the head of the burial society that she was forbidden to walk there, she asked why. "Because it was not modest for women to go between two rows of men." Until that point she had not even noticed that the lines were male. She replied that this custom had nothing to do with men or women but with mourners, and if it bothered the burial society leader so much, he should have two rows of women for her. The logic of the statement, she later asserts, was rumored to have made the rounds of the ultra-Orthodox communities in Jerusalem.

This book should be read by anyone wanting to understand the concerns of Judaism from a feminist perspective.

85 The Best of Sholom Aleichem

Irving Howe and Ruth R. Wisse, Editors

When Sholom Aleichem arrived in New York in 1906, one of his first visitors was Mark Twain, who told him,"I wanted to meet you because I understand that I am the American Sholom Aleichem." Each of these gifted writers had his own unique talent, but they shared a wonderful sense of the absurd and a sensitive ear for the expressive colloquial phrases that authenticate the archetypal characters that they would write about.

Solomon Rabinovitch, who adopted the nom de plume of Sholom Aleichem ("peace be unto you"), was born in Pereyeslav, Ukraine, in 1859 and died in New York City in 1916. He was brought up in the shtetl. Later he lived in Kiev but had to leave because he did not have a residence permit. He moved from one area to another to escape the pogroms and finally joined the great migration to America. Writing in Yiddish, he published over three hundred stories, five novels, a number of plays, and innumerable articles. Most of his stories are based on actual experiences, his own or those related to him by others.

Sholom Aleichem's most famous character is Tevye, the dairy-man in *Fiddler on the Roof.* Understandably, this very successful and beloved musical depicts a sentimentalized and somewhat sanitized Tevye. The character was originally developed in eight short stories written over a twenty-year period and subsequently assembled into a book. Tevye emerges as a cheerful, sympathetic, philosophical, pious man who embodies the traditional culture of the small Ukrainian shtetl. The stories revolve around Tevye, his wife Golde, and their five daughters. Each daughter's choice of a husband initiates a conflict and ends in a succession of misfor-tunes, including poverty, conversion, and emigration. Each con-flict reflects the vicissitudes of Jewish life in Eastern Europe at the time that this traditional way of life was beginning to disappear.

Sholom Aleichem does not cast Tevye as a heroic figure beset by a series of undeserved trials, like Job, but rather as a sympathetic but comic schlimazel, a person who simply has no luck, a poor man with five daughters and a scolding wife. Tevye responds to most challenges with an ironical biblical quotation. When asked about his children, Tevye responds: "How does it say in the prayer book? 'Hamavdil beyn kodesh l'chol.' (He who separates between the holy and the secular.) There are people who have money and I have daughters."

When his peasant neighbors force him to move from his home and land, he says, "What portion of the Bible are you studying this week? Vayikrah? I am on a different portion, on Lech l'choh: 'Get thee out—out of thy country and from thy father's house— the village where you spent all of the years of your life, to the land that I will show thee,' that's the lesson that I am on now." Tevye compares his own expulsion from Kasrilevke to God's initial call to Abraham to leave his father's house and start the journey to the Promised Land.

These out-of-context quotations suggest the reaffirmation of faith that not only sustains Tevye through each difficulty, but also gives him the resilience to face the next problem. It is also Tevye's method of calling God to account for an imperfect world.

Jewish humor laughs at the human qualities of its hero-victims, their perversity, anxiety, and hopefulness. This ability to laugh at adversity permitted Jews to survive and transcend difficulties. In addition to Tevye, Sholom Aleichem developed a number of other memorable characters to tell his stories. They include Tevye's distant cousin Menachem-Mendel, the speculator; Mottel, the cantor's son; Shimon Eli-'Shma Koleinu', the tailor; Fishel, the Melamed; among others.

In "The Bubble Bursts," a short story, we meet Menachem-Mendel, who travels from one stock exchange to the next investing borrowed money in the frantic pursuit of instant wealth. He convinces Tevye to invest his hard-earned money in foolish speculation. The money is quickly lost and Menachem-Mendel moves on to continue his search. Sholom Aleichem himself went bankrupt at one point, an experience which probably influenced his development of the Menachem-Mendel stories.

Mottel, the cantor's son, sees the hardships of shtetl life through the eyes of an innocent and playful twelve-year-old child. He visits a neighbor's calf, steals an apple from a rich man's orchard, and tries to become a businessman after his father's death. The irrepressible Mottel's enjoyment of simple childhood pleasures in the face of the daily realities of life around him is one more version of Sholom Aleichem's basic theme of innocence confronting the world.

Another version of this theme in Sholom Aleichem's short stories is good intentions leading to disastrous results, exposing the disorder undermining the apparent order of the world. In "Eternal Life," a young inexperienced traveler agrees to perform the mitzvah of bringing a corpse to town for ritual burial in the midst of a snowstorm. On reaching the town he finds that the townspeople will not accept the corpse and will not bear the expense of burying it. As a reward for his good deed he ends up penniless and in jail and has to be rescued by his suspicious and unsympathetic mother-in-law.

In "Station Baranovich," a traveler on a train tells how the shtetl saved a bar owner from a court-ordered flogging by issuing a false death certificate and smuggling the man across the border in a casket. The former bar owner shows his gratitude by threatening to return unless the community pays him a substantial sum of money. The blackmail demands escalate until the community can no longer meet them. At this point the train arrives at Station Baranovich, and the narrator leaves without completing his story. During his many travels Sholom Aleichem himself once had to leave a train at Station Baranovich due to a serious illness.

One of Sholom Aleichem's classic tales of the breakdown of the social and cultural system of values in the shtetl is the "Yom Kippur Scandal." This story also includes one of Sholom Aleichem's classic O. Henry-like surprise endings. A guest in the synagogue on Yom Kippur claims that he has been robbed of eighteen hundred rubles. The rabbi, who is very upset, orders everyone searched. The search uncovers an even greater scandal than the theft of the money. One of the most learned and pious young men in the community is found to have freshly gnawed chicken bones in his pocket on the most holy fast day of the year.

These stories are close to the oral tradition of Jewish folklore.

Like the tales of the Hasidim, the stories are full of life, despite the fact that the people are always living in fear. Sholom Aleichem's innocents, unlike Voltaire's Candide, do not see their world as "the best of all possible worlds," but it is God's world and so must be accepted. Buoyed up by their faith, they manage to remain naive and hopeful, and they refuse to be defeated.

86 The Fixer

Bernard Malamud

Bernard Malamud, a novelist and short story writer, was born and raised in Brooklyn. He used the home of his childhood as the setting for much of his literary work. Malamud's first novel, *The Natural*, written in 1952, is an allegorical story about a baseball player, which was ultimately transformed into a film starring Robert Redford. In 1957, he wrote a second novel, *The Assistant*, about a poor New York shopkeeper and his aide. Just twelve months later, Malamud completed his first collection of short stories, *The Magic Barrel*, in which he brought Jewish Eastern European culture into the lives of his characters in America.

In his writings, Malamud is deeply concerned with the relationships between Jews and non-Jews, and portrays the Jew as a symbol of all human problems and tragedy. It was in that spirit that in 1966 Bernard Malamud wrote *The Fixer*, based on the real-life story of Mendel Beilis, a victim of the Kiev Blood Libel of 1913. Malamud wrote this novel in part because he saw the ordeal of Beilis as a universal possibility in a world of mindless hate, applicable to any society of that era.

The Fixer is the story of a poor handyman, Yakov Bok, who lived in Kiev during a virulent anti-Semitic period in Czarist Russia. The story opens with a commotion on the street which attracts Yakov's attention. After questioning a peasant woman, Yakov discovers that the body of a dead child has been found. It is not until the next day, however, that Yakov discovers the details of the tragedy from the newspaper. The child was a twelve-year-old boy who had been dead for longer than a week. His body, covered with stab wounds, was discovered in a cave near the brickyard where Yakov lived. Yakov was handed an anti-Semitic leaflet accusing the Jews of the murder. That night, as he read the article stating that the child's blood had been taken to the synagogue to make matzoh, Yakov became concerned. Although he knew that the accusation was absurd, he lived in area where Jews were forbidden, and the newspaper threatened a vicious pogrom.

This possibility evoked painful memories of Yakov's past. He had been orphaned as a young boy when the cossacks killed his father during a raid, and his mother died shortly after his birth. Already touched by pain in the most profound of ways, Yakov moved to Kiev after his wife, Raisl, ran off with another man without even a good-bye. Refusing to despair, Yakov placed his faith in the future, foreseeing better fortune in Kiev, Amsterdam, and then maybe even America.

Soon after arriving in Kiev, Yakov found himself lying about being Jewish. He had stopped to pick up an old man who had fallen in the snow. If he hoped to collect the reward, he knew that he could not admit to being a Jew. In addition to giving him a reward, the old man offered him employment and got him the room in which he lived overlooking the brickyard. Yakov began to live out his dreams. He was able to save some money to order fake papers and even to buy a few books to study. As a non-Jew, Yakov began to develop a new life in Kiev. Everything seemed to be going well, but still Yakov continued to live in fear.

The day after the young boy's murder, Yakov was arrested and confessed his Jewish identity. Although he pleaded innocent to the crime, he was dragged off to prison. Yakov's deceit had created a nightmare. There was no way out. He discovered that you can never escape who you really are. In the anti-Semitic climate of Russia, Yakov had become a victim. He was in the wrong place at the wrong time, and because he was Jewish in a restricted area, he was the most likely suspect.

While in jail, Yakov felt the hatred of the guards and that of the other prisoners. There was no one on the outside who even knew he had been arrested. Yakov ended up in a cell alone and longed for the companionship of a cellmate, even a bigot. Days, weeks, and months passed as Yakov waited in his prison cell. Even though it felt hopeless, he managed to cling to life. Yakov read and reread the writings from the biblical books of Exodus and Deuteronomy, taken from one of the phylacteries that had been left in his cell, but a guard took them from him and replaced them with a copy of the New Testament. Out of boredom, Yakov began to read the New Testament and found the teachings of Christianity interesting.

After more than a year in prison and hundreds of hallucinations, one night Shmuel, his father-in-law, came to visit him. He had paid off a guard for a ten-minute visit. But the visit was discovered by the prison warden. As a result, Yakov spent countless days bolted to a wall and nights shackled to his bed. He thought about dying all the time. He was depressed, and frequently fantasized about taking his own life, for it was the only way that he felt he could be in control of himself. The irony was that his terrible dreams were keeping Yakov alive.

After more than two years, Yakov finally received the long-awaited indictment, and shortly thereafter an attorney came to visit him in his cell. The long ordeal seemed to be coming to a conclusion. Yakov's wife had come to visit him, and tried to have him sign a confession, since it was the only way they would allow her to visit. But Yakov had learned to fear less and to hate more. He had grown to understand that no one can remain uninvolved politically, especially a Jew. Especially during the final years of his incarceration, Yakov developed a strength great enough to endure anything. As he rode off to face his trial (whose outcome is not revealed) at last, Yakov fully knew that in trying to be someone he wasn't he had come to know who he really was.

87 The Shawl

Cynthia Ozick

Cynthia Ozick's writing deserves many accolades; she observes things keenly, and in a Jewish way, by taking the ordinary and transforming it. What makes Ozick's writing unparalleled is that she also takes out-of-the-ordinary people and records them in extraordinary ways. *The Shawl* is as much about feelings as it is about the details of events themselves.

All this said, *The Shawl,* published in 1990, certainly serves as a graceful introduction to Ozick's work. "The Shawl" is a short story, followed by its sequel, "Rosa," a novella. Set in Poland, "The Shawl" opens with Rosa as a young woman both cradling and concealing her infant daughter, Magda, in a shawl, as she marches to a concentration camp alongside her fourteen-year-old niece, Stella. Rosa senses Stella's jealousy of her daughter early on, and the shawl's immense symbolism is seen right away; it not only protects Magda from the Nazis, who are unaware of her existence, but it also soothes her sucking mouth when Rosa's own nipples no longer give milk: "Magda took a corner of the shawl and milked it instead. She sucked and sucked, flooding the threads with wetness. The shawl's good flavor, milk of linen....It was a magic shawl, it could nourish an infant for three days and three nights."

And, later: "Still, Magda laughed at her shawl when the wind blew its corners, the bad wind with pieces of black in it, that made Stella's and Rosa's eyes tear...she guarded her shawl. No one could touch it; only Rosa could touch it. Stella was not allowed. The shawl was Magda's own baby, her pet, her little sister.... Then Stella took the shawl away and made Magda die. Afterward Stella said: "I was cold."

The ensuing scene, involving Magda "with her little pencil legs scribbling this way and that, in search of the shawl" climaxes with her being caught and murdered. Rosa, helpless, witnesses her daughter's death. It is one of the most riveting passages of Holocaust fiction.

And so *The Shawl* is not only about being Jewish in Poland during the war, but also about motherly love and loss. We are left to imagine Rosa in the ensuing years, surviving but riding on the brink of emotional destruction, her mind filled with Stella's unbearable passive-aggressive explanation for taking Magda's shawl. We meet Rosa again thirty years later in the novella that bears her name.

Finding more meaning in madness than in reality, Rosa has left Brooklyn, where she deliberately demolished her entire junk shop with a hammer and construction metal. Now fifty-eight years old, she lives in a seedy hotel room in Miami, surrounded by the elderly, dependent on Stella for long-distance financial support.

Plummeting to the depths of Rosa's mind, Ozick brings forth an unassailable, highly intelligent character, whose emotional undercurrent is always about her lost life, and mostly, her obsession with her dead daughter. Rosa is consumed with a void that nothing can fill, save her own mind and the shawl itself, which propels her into a fantasy life so rich in detail that she achieves ecstasy through her imaginings.

Through the events leading up to Magda's death and in the detailed letters she writes regularly to Magda, who is completely alive in her mind, we come to understand Rosa, and her erratic logic makes sense to us. We empathize. Her character is completely evoked. In one of these letters Rosa tells Magda about her father, about Stella's lies, and gives a tender account of her feeling of motherhood, "to have the power to create another human being, to be the instrument of such mystery."

In another letter we learn about the four-story house in which she was raised, with its fine architectural features, and her prominent, well-educated family; she speaks of her erudite father, a banker; her shy, refined mother, a poetess; and her brothers. She writes about the transition to life in the ghetto, cramped among "Jew peasants worn out from their rituals and superstitions." Her account of the tramcar that ran through the ghetto, and her description of the passengers in it, and how now she is like one of them, is absolutely fascinating.

Looking down on her peers in Florida, she sees their ignorance, and judges them as inferior for not having experienced the war firsthand. Yet she views herself as an old woman, aware that she appears poorly groomed and speaks in broken English. "It seemed to Rosa Lublin that the whole peninsula of Florida was weighted down with regret. Everyone had left behind a real life. Here they had nothing. They were all scarecrows, blown about under the murdering sunball with empty ribcages."

At the laundromat, she meets Simon Persky, a man who wears dentures and a toupee. His wife is crazy and institutionalized. Befriending Rosa, he becomes part of her external life, and it is through their interactions that more of Rosa's inner life is revealed.

She is disgusted by a doctor who writes to her explaining his research on survivors; he wants to include her in his study. Her relationships are minimal: Stella, Persky, and, of course, Magda, to whom she gives everything. Her daughter lives on vividly in her mind, the beneficiary of her deep maternal love.

She tells Persky about three lives: "The life before, the life during, the life after.... The life after is now. The life before is our real life, at home, where we was born." "And during?" he asks. "This was Hitler," she responds.

Rosa is called a scavenger, and her secondhand store serves as an apt metaphor for her life. The war itself took everything significant and tangible from her; first the people and the lives they led were discarded, then violently shattered. The intricate remnants come fully alive only in Rosa's memory, even though her family cannot ever return, and Rosa's own life itself will never come truly alive again.

88 My Name Is Asher Lev

Chaim Potok

One of the greatest achievements of the former Soviet Union was its marvelous growth in literacy. In the old Russia under the Czar, only ten percent of the people could read. Under communism the literacy rate ultimately rose to over 90 percent. Yet we confront a startling fact. Czarist Russia with its mass illiteracy produced geniuses in the realm of literature, while communism, with all its literate people, has produced few, if any, writers who can compare with Tolstoy, Turgenev, Dostoevsky, Gorky, and Chekhov. The reason may stem in part from the fact that communist dictatorships required that its most talented authors adhere to a party line, lest they be censured and silenced. Thus, their personality and creativity shriveled up. Democracy, on the other hand, stresses the uniqueness of every person, the right of individuals to strive for personal dreams, with the support of loved ones.

Families can reflect that same dichotomy. They can be either dictatorships or democracies. In a dictatorship family, the members are forced, emotionally bludgeoned, to follow the family line, to enter the family business or a parent's profession, whether or not they have the ability or desire. Alternatively, the family can be a democracy, where each person is encouraged to express his or her individuality and unique talents. That tension, that conflict, between dictatorship and democracy in a family, is the theme of Chaim Potok's novel *My Name Is Asher Lev*.

The story of Asher Lev begins in Brooklyn in 1943 when Asher is born, the only child of Rivkeh and Aryeh Lev. Asher's parents trace their ancestry to some of the great Hasidic rabbis of Eastern Europe. Aryeh came to America at the age of fourteen, graduated from a yeshiva, then received degrees from Brooklyn Col-

267

lege and New York University. Rivkeh was born in Crown Heights in Brooklyn. As a member of the Hasidic aristocracy, she attended the Ladover school for girls, married Aryeh one week after graduating from high school, and gave birth to Asher at the age of nineteen. This little boy was blessed with Jewish potentiality and burdened with Jewish responsibility from the moment of his birth, for it was his task to carry on the great and grand tradition of the rabbis who had proceeded him.

But Asher was born with an artistic gift. At the age of four, he started to draw, and it was obvious that he had great talent. His father, at first indifferent, then impatient, ultimately reprimands Asher for wasting time and energy on such "foolishness." Asher listens respectfully, but continues to draw secretly when his father is away on one of his highly confidential missions for the Ladover rebbe.

When Asher is six years old, his mother's brother is killed in a car accident in Detroit. Rivkeh has a nervous breakdown, recovers, and decides to continue her brother's work of rescuing Jews from the Soviet Union. She enrolls at Brooklyn College and attends classes while Asher is at yeshiva. All of his attention, however, is on drawing. He fails arithmetic and *chumash* (Bible), and endures harsh criticism by his father. In an effort to comfort him, Rivkeh buys him art supplies and takes him to the museum, where she is stunned to discover his astonishing talent.

Just before Asher's bar mitzvah, the Ladover rebbe arranges a meeting between Asher and the great sculptor and artist, Jacob Kahn. Kahn agrees to take Asher on as a student, recognizing his artistic genius. Over the ensuing years, Kahn secures an agent for Asher, who mounts two exhibitions that are extremely successful. In the second show, almost of his paintings are sold even before the show begins, including two purchased by a New York museum. After his parents come to the exhibit, they discover to their horror that those two paintings depict the crucifixion—with his mother on the cross!

At the rabbi's instruction, Asher, now in his twenties, moves to Paris. He is hurting too many people. It is time to leave his father's house and build a life of his own.

Potok's writing raises numerous issues of profound interest. First of all, he takes us inside the Hasidic psyche, a sense that living in an open society is a threat to tradition. Accordingly, if certain professions are taboo, the belief is that somehow a traditional way of life is made more secure.

In a ghetto world, that may have been so, but not in today's world. Potok shows us America as an open society, with museums, schools, and culture available to every citizen. In such a setting, any authoritarian behavior is doomed to failure. By implication, Potok demonstrates that modern ultra-Orthodoxy cannot be preserved simply through isolation from the world. There must now be twin foci for parental aspiration: strong rootedness in Jewish tradition and practice via education and a strong Jewish home, as well as the ability to encourage each child's full potential, wherever that path may lead. Aryeh and Rivkeh made gestures in that direction, but perhaps the denigration of Asher's ability as a youth cost them a son in adulthood.

A second insight emerges from the names of the characters. The father is named Aryeh, meaning "lion," a metaphor for a proud and stubborn personality. The son is named Asher, meaning "fortunate" or "blessed." And the mother is Rivkeh, the equivalent of the matriarch Rebecca. In the Torah, Rebecca gives birth to twins, Jacob and Esau, who vie with and betray one another. In *My Name Is Asher Lev,* Rivkeh is caught between two men, torn between loyalty to her husband and love for her son, a scenario seen often in our modern world. In this novel, she cannot resolve the dilemma, and the painting of her on the crucifix seems to symbolize the pain of her frustration.

Chaim Potok points to a decision that increasing numbers of Hasidic and ultra-Orthodox parents must make: the ghetto or the world. In Brooklyn and elsewhere, some Jews have opted for closed communities, the risk being that their children will leave them altogether. Others have moved into the larger society, hoping that their sons and daughters will embrace modernity without sacrificing their Jewish roots. Asher Lev's father insisted on dictatorship, and lost his son on many levels.

My Name Is Asher Lev will provoke substantive discussion in families with similar circumstances. It serves as a metaphor for any family in which the battle between authoritarian rule and democracy is still being waged.

89 The Chosen

Chaim Potok

In Hasidic culture, only a special few are fit to bear the mantle of tzadik. The word *tzadik* literally means "righteous," but to Hasidism it connotes extraordinary wisdom, vision, and divine insight. Though an honor, the designation of tzadik also imposes a terrible burden. For the tzadik alone carries the weight of his people's suffering, alone cries the tears of a million souls. It demands a journey few can walk—a journey which often is made in solitude and whose mystical language is heard only through silence. A tzadik is not born into life. A tzadik is born through life.

As the mantle of hardship is passed down through Hasidic dynasties from father to son, the former trains his son to assume not only the reins of leadership through study and observation, but trains him in the way of the tzadik—through words never spoken and affection devoid of emotion. Chaim Potok's novel *The Chosen* begins with this silent lonely world. Enter Danny Saunders, brilliant fifteen-year-old heir to his father's dynasty, participating in a baseball game against another religious school. The sense of rivalry is palpable as Danny smashes a line drive directly into the eye of an opponent. This boy—a stranger until that moment—will, in the world of mystical journeys, become the predetermined catalyst for Danny's ultimate destiny.

The story takes place near the end of World War II in the Williamsburg neighborhood of Brooklyn, New York. The Hasidic community consists of a loose confederation of different sects, each ruled by rabbinic dynasties generations old. The Hasidim struggled to maintain the image of Jewish life in eighteenth- and nineteenth-century Eastern Europe. Once an answer to a Judaism that had withdrawn from the experience happening around it, Hasidism at the turn of the century began itself to turn its back on the ever-advancing approach of modernity. A world of unquestioned authority, obedience, and faith, it stood defiantly against Zionism, science, and secular life, which threatened just outside the synagogue walls. The lines were drawn. Either you were Hasidic, a keeper, a guardian of the faith, or you weren't. For those who weren't, at least three different categories applied: merely Orthodox, or, just barely better than an infidel; infidel; and worse than infidel—the *apikoros,* the secular Jew—the offspring of the modern age.

The baseball game, therefore, was an extraordinary event. That a group of yeshiva students, from a Hasidic community, gathered to play baseball rather than further their Talmudic studies, was an attempt to put the non-Hasidic boys in their place. It was initiated by Danny Saunders as a fifteen-year-old religious war. Reb Saunders, spiritual leader of his Hasidic community, had sanctioned his son's request to play the game. One must wonder if he had understood Danny's ulterior motive and if, as a true tzadik, he understood the destiny his son was meant to fulfill: if somehow he perceived the line drive and the injury which would ensue, an accident that ultimately might take his son, his dream, his hope, from his side.

Onward from that accident, a fast, intense relationship forms between Danny Saunders and the boy hurt in the game—Reuven Malter—a modern Orthodox son of a gentle Orthodox scholar and teacher. The two boys' lives become inextricably intertwined, their souls bound together on a journey toward maturity.

With a deliberate, simple, literary style, Chaim Potok mimics the tzadik's use of silence, allowing the spaces between the words to paint pictures beyond the page. As the tale unfolds, the mystery of Danny's torment, of his upbringing, of the world of his father and his fathers before him, is slowly revealed. Through the window of the young boy's soul—a universe in which the worlds of faith and science, family and self, friendship and love, collide with cosmic force and sometimes with brutality—we share the journey. Our souls interlock, the tale becomes our tale, the time our time.

The mystics teach that appearance is almost always deceiving, that God works in ways that at best we only understand as coincidence. *The Chosen* affirms that to everything there is a purpose and a direction toward which we are meant to journey. If we fail to hear life calling us to fulfill our purpose, it is because we are trapped by the language of everyday words and actions. Those who succeed listen not only to the words, but to the silence between the words—where truth and spirituality reside. Thus the truly religious are never bound by their religion, but rather are freed by it. Their religion serves as the very launching field of their liberation. Thus freed, they pursue their innermost soul and set it upon the path it is meant to find.

Chaim Potok, in *The Chosen,* presents us with much more than a moving, compelling story of friendship and love, of honor and pain, of loyalty and triumph. He provides a window on the soul—our soul—where potential and purpose await.

90 Ishmael

Daniel Quinn

Ishmael, by Daniel Quinn, is the story of a desperate young man in search of a teacher. While looking through the newspaper, he sees a classified ad that provokes his interest:

> TEACHER seeks pupil. Must have an earnest desire to save the world. Apply in person.

While the man attempts to rationalize why he is so infuriated by the blatantly shallow ad, he suddenly realizes that a teacher is indeed what he seeks.

He arrives at the location listed in the ad, and looks around. "I was surprised to find it to be a very ordinary kind of office building....I'd expected something a little more atmospheric." He finds his way to room 105 and opens the door to discover near emptiness. As he gazes at the nearly opaque plate glass window separating an office from the rest of the room, he feels two eyes staring back at him. He stands back, a bit surprised. After taking a closer look, he moves back further, now frightened, gazing behind the plate glass at a full-grown gorilla!

"*Full grown* says nothing of course. He was terrifyingly enormous, a boulder, a Stonehenge."

He gawks at the huge beast, still in shock—not only at his size, and his mere presence behind plate glass in an office building, but at his perfection. He looks up at the wall—at the poster above the gorilla's head.

WITH MAN GONE,

WILL THERE

BE HOPE

FOR GORILLA?

As if by some divine suggestion, he takes a seat in the large chair in front of the gorilla, and looks further into his eyes. He wonders how it would be here, and suddenly the answer to his question finds a way into his mind, almost as if by telepathy. The gorilla can talk!

The gorilla speaks and begins to tell the story of his life, first describing his capture by animal collectors in the 1930s, then being moved into a zoo. Shortly thereafter, the zoo closed; he was sold to a circus, and people began to speak to him while in his cage, as if he could understand. After a number of years, he actually began to comprehend most of the discussions that took place around him, not necessarily the substance of exactly what was being said, but the speech itself.

Before long, a private owner—a wealthy Jewish man—a survivor of the Holocaust, purchased the gorilla. The man named the gorilla Ishmael, and nurtured its need to acquire knowledge about the world around it. When the man died, Ishmael was left to his daughter, who in turn moved him to a retreat, from which he quickly fled. At that point, Ishmael decided that he needed to pass on the knowledge that he had acquired throughout his life, and his unique perspective as a nonmember of the human race. So he began to teach.

> "And you've had many pupils?" asked the man.
> "I've had four, and failed with all four."
> "Oh. Why did you fail?"
> "I failed because I underestimated the difficulty of what I was trying to teach—and because I don't understand the minds of my pupils well enough."
> "And what do you teach?"
> "....My subject is: *captivity*."

The book won the Turner Tomorrow Fellowship in 1991 for a work of fiction offering positive solutions to global problems. It was selected from more than 2,500 entries from around the world by a panel of judges that included Nadine Gordimer and Ray Bradbury. Since its initial publication in English in 1992, it has been published in German, Italian, Hungarian, Japanese, Korean, Portuguese, Spanish, and Dutch.

The worldwide popularity of *Ishmael* owes largely to its global appeal. Explaining the way the world works, and letting readers find their own solutions to world problems, the book is being used in middle school, high school, university, and graduate school classes the world over.

The name *Ishmael* for both the gorilla and the book is particularly appropriate. Daniel Quinn has said, "According to our cultural mythology, God lost interest in all other creatures on this planet when human beings came along. According to Genesis, this is exactly what happened to Ishmael when Isaac came along; his father Abraham sent him out into the wilderness. In other words, what Genesis says happened to Ishmael is exactly what our mythology says happened to the non-human community on this planet." This makes *Ishmael* an appropriate name for someone who speaks for a community wandering and searching for meaning.

Ishmael raises many questions. Why does the narrator have no name? How did Ishmael get into an office building? Why is Ishmael seated behind a pane of glass at the beginning? What exactly is Ishmael suggesting we do?

Just as the pupil in the book learns how to find solutions in the book through questioning Ishmael and himself or herself, the reader is left with endless unanswered questions. What *Ishmael* does do, however, is raise issues and questions that will lead to a reevaluation of our everyday acts, and hopefully to a change in direction of our "taker" society.

At the very end of the novel, the pupil takes Ishmael's poster to get it framed and keep for his own use after Ishmael dies. It isn't until he gets the poster to the framing shop that he finds that it has messages on both sides. The message on one side, the side that Ishmael displayed, read:

> WITH MAN GONE,
> WILL THERE
> BE HOPE
> FOR GORILLA?

The other side reads:

> WITH GORILLA GONE
> WILL THERE
> BE HOPE
> FOR MAN?

91 Jephte's Daughter

Naomi Ragen

Hasidism was started in the 1700s in Eastern Europe by a man called the Baal Shem Tov. He was an orphan, not too learned in the Talmud, but he achieved a reputation as a charismatic leader and healer. He expelled demons; he performed miracle cures. Naomi Ragan's novel, *Jephte's Daughter,* takes us into the world of Hasidism and its modern manifestation.

Who was the biblical Jephtha? In the book of Judges we are told that Jephtha was a great fighter. When the Children of Israel are attacked by the Ammonites, he is asked to lead the Israelites in battle. He accepts, but before he marches out to war, he promises God that if he is victorious, he will sacrifice the first living thing that comes to meet him when he returns home, thinking that it would be a cow or a lamb. Instead, his daughter, his only child, comes out to meet him, so he sacrifices her to keep his word.

Jephte's Daughter begins with a description of Ben-Gurion Airport in Israel. Hundreds of Hasidim, as well as a large group of newspaper reporters, are gathered to greet a wealthy visitor from California by the name of Abraham Halevi. No one know why he is there, but it is obvious that he must be wealthy, as he steps into a silver Rolls Royce that he had brought with him on a cargo plane headed for Jerusalem.

We are now given the background of Abraham Halevi. In 1780, one of his ancestors, Israel Halevi, a distinguished student of the Baal Shem Tov, established himself as a Hasidic rebbe and lived in opulent splendor. The Halevi family was known for its scholarship for generations. Then came Hitler, and Abraham's father and brothers were all murdered; Abraham Halevi was the sole survivor. Unfortunately, he was the least scholarly of the family—but had a talent for making money—and he amassed a tremendous fortune. When his mother was on her way to Auschwitz, she made him promise to preserve the chain of scholarship in the Halevi family.

In Israel, his chauffeur brings him to the greatest yeshiva in Jerusalem, where he is ushered into the office of the scholarly Rabbi Magnes.

Abraham says to the rabbi: "I am looking for a son-in-law, a man who will continue the Halevi dynasty. Money is no object, and I am prepared to make a sizable gift to the yeshiva as a token of my gratitude."

The rabbi replies in a rather unfriendly tone: "You've come to the wrong place. The shuk—the marketplace—is a block away. Go there, if you want to make a purchase."

Abraham disregards the insult, and finally prevails upon the rabbi to find a husband for his teenage daughter, Batsheva, the only requisite being that the young man must be a great scholar.

The rabbi promises that he will try to fulfill his request. On the flight back to California, Abraham reflects on his life, his marriage to Fruma—a simple woman who adores him, who loved him when he was only a bricklayer and they lived in poverty. He remembers how he saved up enough money to buy a burned-out apartment house in New York, and rebuilt it, then gradually climbed the ladder of affluence, buying property in Texas and California.

Then he smiles, recalling how overjoyed he was when Batsheva was born. Father and daughter had a special relationship. Every Saturday morning she went to the synagogue with him. On Sundays, while other children would spend the day at the Bronx Zoo, he would take Batsheva to the Metropolitan Museum or the Museum of Modern Art. He saw to it that his daughter attended the finest Jewish parochial schools, where she studied the Bible and Talmud. He even hired a young Protestant girl, Elizabeth, to tutor his daughter in English literature. And now, on his return to California, he is thinking what he will say to his beautiful daughter regarding this mission.

As she greets him lovingly, he says: "Batsheva, I have just returned from Jerusalem where I went to find the finest scholar in the Jewish world. When he is found, he will come here to meet you, and will then marry you." She begins to cry. She tells him that she is not ready for marriage. Just turned eighteen, she wants to travel, to go to a university.

In the meantime, twenty-three-year-old Isaac Mayer Harshen has been chosen for Batsheva. Reputed to be a great scholar with a remarkable memory, he has lived a secluded life, never left Israel, or even listened to radio or watched television because it was treif, unkosher, unfit. He has certain preconceived ideas of what a Jewish wife should be. Her role is to bear children and make it possible for her husband to study and learn. That should be her ultimate ambition.

Isaac and his chaperon come to Los Angeles. When Batsheva sees him, she is impressed with his physical appearance—tall and thin. They have a little trouble communicating, since he speaks Yiddish and very little English. But that is only the beginning. Soon she begins to realize that he has other deficiencies that are much more serious. When she tells him that she studied Talmud, he criticizes her and says: "It is not the custom to teach Talmud to women." She tries to brush aside all the little irritations that come up.

But one day, when he is alone near the pool, reading, she sees him punish a little dog, and she witnesses his face contorted with anger and hatred. It dawns on her that this is a very cruel man. She goes to her mother, Fruma, and tells her she will not marry Isaac, explaining why. Fruma pleads with her husband not to force Batsheva into a loveless marriage. Abraham attacks her, and denounces her until she is silenced. Then he takes Batsheva for a ride and persuades her that Isaac will be a wonderful husband, and that together they will produce children who will preserve the Halevi heritage of scholarship.

It soon becomes apparent that the marriage is headed for disaster. Isaac disapproves of everything she does. He tells her: "I own you. I am the final authority over what you can read, how you dress, and what you do."

Batsheva bears a son named Akiva. Her parents come to Israel for the bris, and her father gives her a magnificent diamond necklace as a gift. By now, the marriage has deteriorated. Although Isaac hasn't beat her anymore since the baby was born, he remains cruel to her and the baby. She goes to a marriage counselor who advises her to obey her husband's wishes: "That's the secret of a good marriage, to acknowledge your husband as the head of the household, and God will help you."

God doesn't help her. When Akiva is three years old, Isaac informs her that the child is to be enrolled in a school reputed to have cruel discipline. Batsheva decides that she will not expose her child to such treatment. She takes Akiva to a shorefront hotel in Tel Aviv and rents a boat. The next day, police find the missing boat, along with some clothing washed up on the beach. In her hotel room, there is a suicide note addressed to Abraham Halevi of Los Angeles.

Then follows a description of the shiva—as her father reads and rereads the last letter that she had written to him in which she tells him that she forgives him, just as Jephte's daughter had forgiven her father for making the vow that ended her life. At the same time, in Jerusalem, Isaac is sitting shiva, and his mother is doing a good job of circulating stories, that Batsheva was really insane, that she was immoral, that on their wedding night her son discovered that she was not a virgin.

In the next chapter we learn that Batsheva and her son are really alive. Somehow, she managed to get to Cyprus and then to London. She sold the jewelry that her father had given her for forty thousand dollars, and is preparing to start a new life together with her little boy.

Batsheva falls in love with a young man named David Hope. When she finds out that he is a candidate for the priesthood, she tells him they must separate. David then discovers that his mother was Jewish and died when he was born; no one told him of his ancestry. He goes to Jerusalem, where he studies Talmud with one of the rabbis. In the meantime, Batsheva decides to call her mother and let her know she is alive and living in London. Her mother is overjoyed, but when she tells her husband, he angrily denounces her and says: "I have no daughter. My daughter died two years ago."

Batsheva goes to Jerusalem to obtain a divorce in order to marry David. There is a trial in which Isaac tries to retain custody of his son. His plea is rejected. David and Batsheva marry in the presence of her parents. The book concludes on that happy note, teaching that maintaining both one's Jewish heritage and happiness are truly compatible.

92 The Joys of Yiddish

Leo Rosten

Though the conversational use of Yiddish is waning, its influence on English vocabulary remains. Yiddish is an amazing language of a different time, but what makes it so remarkable is its sentimentality and passion, shaped out of many languages and emotions, out of love, loss, and disappointment. It has inimitable charm, due in large part to its sarcasm and humor.

Leo Rosten's *Joys of Yiddish,* first published in 1968, has become a classic. Even the preface is a delight to read. We learn about language, how English has been influenced by Yiddish, and also delve into folklore, history, humor, and Judaism. Rosten must have continually smiled while writing this "Lexicon of Yiddish-in-English." The book feels like a love affair with Judaism.

Technically, Yiddish isn't Jewish. There is no such language as "Jewish." Yiddish is written using the Hebrew alphabet, and read from right to left. Yiddish began to emerge in the thirteenth century, in the ghettos of Spain, a blend of Hebrew, Old German, Old Italian, and Old French. After the fifteenth century, when Jews migrated to Eastern Europe, the language grew, and fully blossomed in the mid-nineteenth century, "building a literature of its own." Yiddish, Isaac Bashevis Singer said, is possibly the only language that has never been spoken by men in power.

There are many words and phrases which originated in Yiddish that enrich the English language. Some include "blithe dismissal via repetition with an *sh* play on the first sound: 'Fat-shmat, as long as she's happy,'" and "mordant syntax: 'Smart, he isn't'" and "sarcasm via innocuous diction: 'He only tried to shoot himself.'"

Much has to do with emphasis on certain words.

"Or consider the growing effect on English of those exquisite shades of meaning, and those priceless nuances of contempt, that are achieved in Yiddish simply by shifting the stress in a sentence from one word to another. 'Him you *trust?*' is entirely different, and worlds removed from '*Him* you trust?' The first merely questions your judgment; the second vilifies the character of the scoundrel anyone must be an idiot to repose faith in."

This book isn't just a lexicon of Yiddish words. Each entry is filled with historical information and jokes relating to the word. To quote Rosten, "In nothing is Jewish psychology so vividly revealed as in Jewish jokes. The style and stance of its humor reflect a culture, I think, not less than its patterns of shame, guilt, hostility, and approval."

Since words are arranged alphabetically, *The Joys of Yiddish* is not necessarily read from cover to cover at one sitting. Instead, the book becomes a trustworthy friend one turns to again and again. The history of Jewish life and lore unfolds, beginning with Adonai to *no-goodnik, shlemiel, shlep,* and *tsatske.*

Rosten's compilation of information and anecdotes make this book marvelously rich. The definition of *bordekeh,* for example, is a "female boarder." After its definition and an explanation about the monetary necessity of taking in boarders, Rosten offers the following:

Scene: *Classroom, Lower East Side, 1926*
Teacher: "Who can tell us where the Roumanian border is?"
Student: "In the park with my aunt, and my mother doesn't trust him!"

We use many Yiddish words in English, Jews and non-Jews alike, such as maven and klutz. There are also certain obscene Yiddish words which are slang in colloquial English, and people frequently use them without knowing their original definition.

The word *mensh* literally means "person," but implies much more than that. Rosten gives three definitions, but his explanation sums it up. "To be a mensh has nothing to do with success, wealth, status. A judge can be a zhlob; a millionaire can be a momzer; a professor can be a shlemiel, a doctor a klutz, a lawyer a bulvon. The key to being 'a real mensh' is nothing less than— character: rectitude, dignity, a sense of what is right, responsible, decorous. Many a poor man, many an ignorant man, is a mensh."

Bubkes is another word whose meaning far exceeds its literal definition. Technically, bubkes means "beans," but that is not how Jews use it. Bubkes indicates something trivial: "I worked on it three hours—and what did he give me? Bubkes!" or "something absurd, foolish, nonsensical. 'I'll sum up his idea in one word: bubkes!'"

The appendixes include information about a number of topics, including "Naming and Names Among Jews." Traditionally, Sephardic Jews name their children after a living relative, while the Ashkenazim name their children after a deceased family member. Rosten also lists many names Anglicized by first-generation immigrants, including Avrum which became Alan, Albert, Alvin, or Arnold.

Rosten's book will inform, entertain, and, most of all, help deepen your love of Judaism. Ann Landers so aptly put it, "I chuckled, I roared, I wept. This is more than just a book, it is an experience."

93 Call It Sleep

Henry Roth

Henry Roth's *Call It Sleep* is considered one of the finest novels ever written by an American author. But broad public recognition of its greatness did not come for three decades. Originally published in 1934, during the Great Depression, the novel was largely ignored by a readership seeking answers and solutions to a world in economic chaos.

Roth, only twenty-eight years old when the book was issued, tells the story of a Yiddish-speaking immigrant family, the Schearls, arriving in "The Golden Land" to live on New York's Lower East Side at a time when the American dream lay in shambles. Albert Schearl, the head of the family, is a bitter, ugly-tempered man. A printer by trade, he cannot hold a job because of his constant outbursts of anger and violence against coworkers and supervisors. As the novel begins in May 1907, Albert stands at New York harbor, awaiting the arrival of his wife, Genya, and his two-year-old son, David, from Austrian Galicia. What might have been a warm family reunion is transformed instead into an ugly confrontation between Albert and Genya, setting the tone for the progressive revelation of their tortured relationship.

In the course of the story, we learn that Genya, a gentle and loving woman, had a torrid love affair in Galicia with a gentile named Ludwig. The shame and disgrace of the public disclosure of the relationship led her father to issue Genya an ultimatum: marry a Jew or live with the contempt of her family forever. Six months later, Genya met Albert and married him, as much for forgiveness as for a fresh start in life.

Albert, however, learned of the affair, and harbored great bitterness about it. In addition, he could not rid himself of the obsessive thought that David was the illegitimate child of Genya's former lover. Thus, he despised his wife and hated his son, ruling the household with an iron hand, and driving Genya and David together into the only warm and loving relationship possible in this dysfunctional family.

Albert's only friend is a fellow countryman named Joe Luter, who welcomed into his home as a guest and quasi-tenant. Throughout the book, Luter is clearly attracted to Genya, but remains respectful of her marital status. And finally, there is Genya's sister, David's Aunt Bertha, who moves in and further disrupts the family with her irascible personality and dogged search for a husband who will take care of her.

The author plays out his tale in two settings. In the home, where Yiddish is the sole language employed, the dialogue is often graceful and elegant. But the family also lives on the Lower East Side, where they employ broken English to make themselves understood.

David, the central character of the book, must find his own way in this strange new world. Tied to his mother for love and protection, he reluctantly ventures out on the streets of New York alone, experiencing the cruelty and kindness of playmates and strangers, often living in his imagination and suppressing anger and frustration at his treatment at the hands of this father.

At the age of five David goes with his father to a factory to pick up clothes and a severance check resulting from Albert's most recent dismissal from work. He hears the workers refer to his father as crazy as they describe his attack with a hammer on the shop's owner, a fearsome image that remains in David's mind, though he says nothing to his father.

David makes a friend, a boy named Yussie, whose sister, Annie, wears a brace on her leg. It is Annie who first introduces David to sex, in the language of the street:

> "Yuh know w'ea babies comm from?"
> "N-no"
> "From de knish. Between de legs. Who puts id in is de poppa. De poppa's god de petzel."
> "Put yuh hand in my knish," she coaxed. "Jus' once."
> "No!"
> "I'll hol' yoh petzel."

He is rescued from the encounter by his mother calling him, relieved but ashamed.

As the story continues, the tension in the Schearl house grows more palpable. Albert refers to David, not by name, but as "the prayer," an allusion to David's responsibility to say the Kaddish prayer for his father when he dies. Thus objectified, David draws further inward, verbally and physically abused by his father, protected by his mother, fearful that the most inadvertent action on his part will cause a family explosion.

Even David's enrolling in a Jewish school cannot insulate him from his father's viciousness. Having secured a new job as a milkman, Albert takes David on the route with him before dropping him off at the cheder (school). While Albert makes a delivery, two men steal some milk from the wagon and the defenseless David. Returning to the wagon, Albert flies into a rage, calls David a "cursed fool," then runs down and beats the thieves before turning to David again.

> "False son! You, the cause! Say anything to your mother and I'll beat you to death!"

Shortly thereafter, David makes a new friend, Leo, a Polish Catholic boy who wears a rosary. David sees them as "lucky beads" and covets them.

So loyal is he to Leo that he stands guard as Leo "plays bad" with David's cousin Esther. They are discovered by Esther's sister, Polly, who threatens to "Call my modder."

David runs away to the cheder, where he invents the incredible story that he is half-Christian, the son of a church organist. The rabbi rushes to David's home and repeats the story to David's father, Albert. Albert, already haunted by his obsession with David's possible illegitimacy, beats him severely, whereupon Leo's rosary beads fall out of David's hands. Albert explodes again, whereupon David rushes out of the house to the subway line, where he appears to attempt suicide by touching the highly charged third rail with a metal milk ladle.

Burned severely, David survives, alternating in his dazed condition between the Yiddish of his house and the English of his future. His father, Albert, chastened by almost losing his son, resolves to work with Genya at rebuilding their marriage. His mother urges him to rest and forget. And David reflects: "One might as well call it sleep."

This superb novel was finally published in paperback in 1964.

Irving Howe described it as "one of the few genuinely distinguished novels written by a twentieth-century American." With millions of copies in print, Roth's novel has become a classic.

Soon after completing *Call It Sleep*, Roth had contracted for a second novel with the editor Maxwell Perkins, of Charles Scribner and Sons. But his growing ideological frustration and personal confusion created a profound writer's block, which lasted until 1979, when he began the first drafts of *Mercy of a Rude Stream*, a four-volume work, published by St. Martin's Press.

Roth died at the age of eighty-nine in Albuquerque, New Mexico. He had one of the most extraordinary careers of any American novelist who lived in this century.

94 Portnoy's Complaint

Philip Roth

Philip Roth's 1967 novel *Portnoy's Complaint* broke new ground, when it was first published, with the hilarious, lewd voice of its thirty-three-year-old narrator, Alexander Portnoy, as he speaks about his life to his psychiatrist, Dr. Spielvogel.

Whiny, neurotic Portnoy is bright enough to have graduated at the top of his law school class, and now works as the assistant commissioner of human opportunity for the City of New York. Through his monologue, which has an underlying, pathetic sadness, we return to his childhood and adolescence in New Jersey and learn about his college years and life up to the present.

His liberal, Jewish middle-class upbringing consists of a cloying, smothering mother, a pitiful shadow of a father, and his older sister, Hannah, whose dirty underwear he takes out of the hamper to use as visual aids while he masturbates.

Portnoy cannot get enough sex because he is so guilt-ridden, due to his overprotective, equally neurotic (although not sexually obsessed) mother. When the book first came out, its sexual explicitness shocked and delighted Jews; Alexander Portnoy also happens to capture the essence of the Jewish-American experience. Roth wrote what every adolescent boy thought. Today the book is regarded as a classic, and is far less likely to shock its audience.

The portrayals of Jewish family members are also memorable. Portnoy's mother, Sophie, is the ultimate stereotype of an overbearing Jewish mother. One can't help but visualize her as a caricature to be laughed at as she worries or kvetches. (She must have been the prototype for a multitude of annoying mothers; George's mother on *Seinfeld* comes to mind).

A chapter entitled "Wacking Off" shows that a huge portion of

Portnoy's adolescence is spent masturbating. His emerging sexuality is accompanied by furtiveness and shame in the bathroom, where he spends an enormous amount of time, later explaining to his family that his stomach is upset. The scenes are funny, but Sophie keeps questioning him about his stomach, and, in her typically invasive manner, even wants to take a peek at what's in the bowl before he flushes. She expects him to fess up that he's really been eating junk food after school.

Meanwhile, Jack Portnoy, an insurance salesman, is a pathetic example of the Jewish father, with the worst case of constipation imaginable. This is symbolic of his entire condition—being bottled up and dominated by his wife. Sophie is a castrating female who shuts her man down.

Portnoy also shows how Jewish parents, particularly mothers, can convince their sons that they are inadequate while paradoxically putting them on a pedestal, then helping them turn into hard-driving achievers. Nowhere does it seem more prevalent than in Jewish society that external, public accolades matter. We see here parental obsession with meritocracy. If the children, sons especially, are accomplished, the parents have succeeded.

The book, for all its anguish, is very funny. Here's this "nice Jewish lawyer" struggling to do well and be good, in an unfulfilling (and one suspects not very lucrative) government job where he is supposed to help people. He is completely unsatisfied in both his personal and work life, and his only relief comes from sexual encounters which are then tempered with massive doses of guilt.

Of all the women with whom Alexander Portnoy has ever had sex—and some were very bright and likable—the most memorable and significant is Mary Jane, "the Monkey." Read the book for the origin of the well-deserved nickname. They pick each other up on the street one night. At first, she's every Jewish man's fantasy: she has blond hair, a tiny nose, and a great body; she is a fashion model. Mary Jane is also sexually accomplished and completely uninhibited; she quickly whets his appetite in new ways, with a drive that nearly surpasses his own. She performs on him almost anywhere, and thinks, conversely, that by doing whatever he wishes, regardless of how base, she'll be able to keep him.

Later he learns her history. This glamorous blond is near-illiterate white trash. She arrived in New York missing all her back teeth, came from an impoverished family in West Virginia, and wound up marrying a wealthy Frenchman who had a penchant for bizarre, truly disgusting sexual encounters. She finally has the sense to leave him but keeps searching for a man to save her.

In one of the book's funniest scenes, Portnoy discovers a note in Mary Jane's apartment to the maid, which he first thinks the maid wrote because of the incredibly bad, phonetic spelling: "Dear" is spelled "dir." Portnoy really wonders what he's doing. Their first sexual encounter, he recalled, happened before she even knew his name. He thinks back to all he's done for her, and how mismatched they are. He took her desire for self-improvement seriously and bought her James Agee's *Let Us Now Praise Famous Men,* the Pulitzer Prize–winning documentary, with photographs by Walker Evans, about poverty-stricken migrant workers in Appalachia. He thought she'd have a better understanding of where she came from, and she toted the book around, as if to impress any onlooker, but never read it.

Initially, she represented the allure of assimilation. Then Portnoy tries to teach her qualities important to him—qualities embedded in him through traditional Jewish values, like a love of learning and political justice—but she's already been pushed to her limits.

What Portnoy does best, next to having sex and feeling guilty, is never to forget that he's a Jew.

95 The Brothers Ashkenzai

I. J. Singer

96 The War Goes On

Sholem Asch

Novels by Jewish authors have frequently aroused mixed feelings among Jewish readers, especially when the writer teaches history through biography. Since Jewish authors tend to write in vivid language, bringing the Jews of different eras to life with all their strengths and all their failings, readers concerned about the image of Jews portrayed therein peruse the text with special attention.

Although American Jews feel more secure today, there was a time when they worried about the negative portrayal of Jews in literature—even when the author was Jewish. One example was *Mottke the Thief* by Sholem Asch, which portrayed the slums of Warsaw, the Jewish underworld, Jewish prostitutes, and white slave traffic. Brilliantly written, it nevertheless occasioned a sense of danger in the Jewish community. How could it be used against us? In what way would it reinforce anti-Semitic feelings?

Two other books by Jewish authors also engendered such concern. One such book is *The Brothers Ashkenazi* by I. J. Singer. It takes place in the Polish city of Lodz, a center of textile production, where a Christian, Heinz Huntze, is the chief manufacturer. Abraham Ashkenazi, an old pious scholar, succeeds in helping Huntze merge with his chief competitor, and becomes the business agent for the united entity.

Abraham has twin sons, Meyer and Jacob. Meyer is small and thin, intense and studious; Jacob is tall and strong, healthy and happy. At the age of twelve, Meyer is betrothed and subsequently married to the daughter of a prosperous Jewish weaver, Chaim Alter. A few years later, facing business disaster, Alter borrows the dowry he gave to Meyer in exchange for a first mortgage on the business. Meyer ends his Talmudic studies, enters the business, runs it efficiently, but cruelly ousts his father-in-law from the firm, while he personally becomes wealthy.

Meyer, however, is most unhappy. His brother, Jacob, married the daughter of a rich Warsaw merchant, and has become wealthy without any effort. Driven by a desire to outdo his brother, Meyer increases the factory workload, resulting in a strike and police intervention. But his ambition remains unchecked. He takes over the Huntze factory and fires his own father, increasing his wealth immensely, only to find that Jacob has outstripped him once again in stature and wealth with a prestigious promotion.

Meyer moves to Petrograd, where he once again establishes a great factory, only to be a victim of the Russian Revolution, imprisoned and broken by his incarceration. Jacob secures Meyer's release, but then is killed by Polish soldiers before Meyer's eyes. Meyer, in deep mourning for his brother, returns to Poland, rebuilds his business without the jealousy of Jacob that once plagued him so, but dies suddenly of a heart attack and never gets to enjoy his victory over adversity.

The Brothers Ashkenazi is clearly an allegory for the biblical story of Jacob and Esau; twin brothers, one strong and healthy, one weak and cunning. But there is a deeper social significance, made crystal clear through a second novel.

The War Goes On, by Sholem Asch, begins in almost the same way as *The Brothers Ashkenazi,* in a Ukrainian village near the Polish border at the close of the war. An old rabbi and merchant, Shlomo Judkewitch, is murdered by the Bolsheviks, but one of his two sons, Aron, escapes to Germany with a vast quantity of diamonds and coins. In Danzig, he speculates in real estate and currency and becomes enormously wealthy. But Aron has a darker side. Lusting for the wife of another speculator, he forces the man into semi-bankruptcy, then bails him out on the condition that he divorce his wife. Aron marries the woman, who begins to lead a wildly extravagant life.

In the midst of his speculation, Aron establishes a bank, and in turn takes over a larger bank. His speculation and resulting wealth, however, attract the attention of Germany's largest speculator, Hugo Stinnes. Stinnes leads Aron like a lamb to the slaughter, flattering him while slowly forcing him into bankruptcy. He does to Aron what Aron had done to others, and Aron ultimately leaves Germany a pauper.

Both *The Brothers Ashkenazi* and *The War Goes On* have common themes. Both begin with a description of people rising remarkably toward wealth, then dropping catastrophically toward poverty. And personal catastrophes in both novels go hand in hand with world economic dislocation. A second theme common to both novels is the heroism of the working class. Workingmen are idealized. A third parallel is the portrayal of the capitalist bosses as rapacious, without scruples, willing to destroy even their own families in pursuit of wealth, willing to take the wife of another man as part of a business transaction.

These ideas, common to both novels, are not coincidental. Both I. J. Singer and Sholem Asch, though Europeans, were regular contributors to the American-Yiddish socialist newspaper, *The Forward,* and socialist by conviction. The views which they express are the classic socialist principles: capitalism dying, corruption of the middle class, and a hope for salvation through the masses.

When Singer and Asch wrote their books, they touched a responsive chord among many workers. But the average Jew in America felt a sense of uneasiness regarding these sentiments. American growth and stability—and therefore Jewish security—rested on the healthy growth of capitalism. The average Jew wanted to work, to place himself in better circumstances, to save money, to educate his children, and to see them exceed his accomplishments.

Furthermore, the average Jew perceived the middle class in a far more sympathetic manner than either Singer or Asch. They had their vices, to be sure, but the Jew fortunate enough to be upwardly mobile in a land of freedom treated that privilege with respect. In some ways American Jews resented the tone of these two novels, particularly since they would be read by masses of non-Jewish Americans as a reflection of how all Jews felt about a capitalist society.

One thing is certain. Both authors portray the Jews as resilient and determined in the face of any hardship. Meyer Ashkenazi, beaten a dozen times, nevertheless begins to rebuild over and over again. Aron Judkewitch, living in Paris, and having lost several fortunes, will clearly try once again.

97 All-of-a-Kind Family

Sydney Taylor

When Sydney Taylor's daughter was growing up, she loved to hear her mother reminisce about her childhood on New York's Lower East Side. There were stories about a large family that was not well off, but always had more than enough love to go around. It was a happy, busy childhood, in a different time and place. Thus began the wonderful, classic *All-of-a-Kind Family* stories, which have delighted children for over forty years. Particularly geared for girls eight and up, these are lovely books to read aloud to younger children. There are four sequels, so readers can follow the girls as they grow.

The first book, *All-of-a-Kind Family*, sets the stage. The year is 1912, the place New York City. A family of five girls, their mother—a kind, wise woman—and their father—a hardworking peddler—live in a tenement on Manhattan's Lower East Side. They are fortunate enough to share four rooms—a whole floor of a house. The five children have only one bedroom, two youngsters to a bed (one likes to sleep alone). But they experience the joys of a close-knit family, where siblings share their lives together.

Taylor is a splendid storyteller, enriching her stories with detailed descriptions, and she also imbues her past with a rich Jewish heritage. Jewish holidays are remembered with great happiness and enthusiasm, as are American celebrations such as the Fourth of July. Helen John's charming black-and-white illustrations help readers visualize different settings.

Just as in *Little Women*, we come to know and care about each of the girls. There is little Gertie, who is four; six-year-old Charlotte; eight-year-old Sarah; Henny, who is ten; and twelve-year-old Ella. There is a constant reminder that true family values emerge through actions rather than mere talk, and people—not accomplishments or possessions—take center stage. The children are thrilled when dressing up in Purim costumes and visiting their friends and relatives, sometimes giving out Purim baskets. They are equally excited when Charlie, a handsome, kind Christian man who works with their father, brings Fourth of July surprises.

Celebrating Shabbat together is a very special time, since Papa blesses them individually. When Mama takes the girls shopping for Shabbat on the Lower East Side, Taylor's lively descriptions of the vendors and various foods evoke smells, sights, and sounds. Each merchant promises a bargain, whether he is selling notions, shoelaces, fruits and vegetables, or soap powders. Stands in front of the shops display pickles, sauerkraut, and watermelon rind, while others have open sacks of cereal products. There are stores for fish, others for dairy, and delicatessens with frankfurters hanging on wall hooks. There is the pretzel lady, the garlic man, the mushroom man—always, the streets are crowded with people.

Taylor also describes the joys of sharing a bed with a sibling and the closeness of family life, where sisters are each other's dearest friends, each watching out for the other. Mamma lets them talk in bed at night. They sneak candy and crackers into bed, playing games with how they have to eat it, and two of the sisters regularly talk late into the night about how to decorate an imaginary home.

Mama, an attractive, resourceful woman, infuses her home with warmth, taking constant pleasure in family life. She always does the right thing; even when disciplining her daughters, she remains stern but is ever loving. When the children have to dust the house (they take turns doing household chores), no one looks forward to the task. Mama is inventive, though, and figures out a way to make the chore fun. She hides twelve buttons in the parlor—these will be discovered one by one when cleaning. Suddenly everyone wants to dust. Mama knows that the game's delight will wear off with repetition, so she hides buttons only occasionally to keep the surprise alive, and unpredictably changes the number of buttons.

Whether the girls save their money for a birthday present for Papa, or band together to pay for Sarah's lost library book, they solve problems as a group. When scarlet fever strikes two sisters, the family works together to ease the pain, even though the sickness spreads. Christian friends, including Charlie and Miss Allen, the kind librarian, enrich their lives. There is a surprising love story reuniting this man and woman, who, unbeknownst to the girls, are separated sweethearts.

Taylor's descriptions of everyday life also deal with physical hardships, but they are filled with much more joy than sorrow because she is able to elevate the ordinary into the holy, an intrinsically Jewish way of looking at the world.

Toward the end of the book, another surprise occurs. Mama is pregnant again, and Papa is wishful that he will at last have the son he has longed for. Tante, Mama's widowed sister who works in a factory, is there to help with the delivery. Doctor Fuchs, who had treated the girls when scarlet fever struck, is resting on a cot, waiting. The sisters are all excited, except little Gertie, who has been feeling strange about this all along. Suddenly she spills out to her sisters that she doesn't want Mama to have another child: she's the baby! Her sisters try to console her.

When the baby arrives, however, the girls are thrilled to meet their little brother. Papa is overcome with joy, and begins to sob. Everyone admires the soft sweet boy, even Gertie. That's how a new Charlie, named after Papa's grandfather, Chaim, becomes part of the family.

98 Jewish Humor

Joseph Telushkin

Often subjected to denigration, anti-Semitism, persecution, stereotyping, and ridicule, Jews created their own unique brand of humor. We learned to laugh and make fun of ourselves before the cruelty of others could hurt us. And, especially in recent times, the comeback has been raised to an art form by Jewish comedians, who in many ways are spiritual descendants of the Yiddish-speaking Eastern European Jews, whose sharp tongues could cut you off at the knees with a smile.

Rabbi Joseph Telushkin proposes to address humor that emerges from anxiety and fear, from life's dilemmas and family relationships, and from world history, exemplified in the classic Jewish telegram: "Start worrying. Details to follow!"

In a chapter on the family, the author shares a number of stories which illustrate the close, intense bond that Jewish families feel, starting almost at birth; the dreams for children, for example: "Mr. and Mrs. Marvin Rosenbloom are pleased to announce the birth of their son, *Doctor* Jonathan Rosenbloom."

Jewish humor finds redemptive value even in circumstances that seem disastrous:

> Two Jewish women...run into each other...
> "How's your daughter, Deborah?" the first woman asks, "the one who married that lawyer?"
> "They were divorced," the second woman answers.
> "Oh, I'm so sorry."
> "But she got married to a surgeon."
> "Mazel Tov!"
> "They were also divorced....But now everything is all right, she's married to a very successful architect!"

The first woman shakes her head from side to side.
"Mmm. Mmm. So much Nachas [joy] from one daughter!"

The reader will delight in jokes about the Jewish mother-son
relationship, parental worry about unmarried children, and
parental sacrifice for children. Each of these complex relationships are part of the Jewish psyche. In treating them with humor,
Jews recognize their reality and centrality, and at the same time,
make light of the consternation they often provoke.

So pervasive is the perception of the Jewish love of education
that a *New York Times* article shares the following tips for real
estate brokers: "If they're rich, tell them about the country club
and the high quality of people they'll meet there. If they're a
young couple buying their first home, emphasize the low
property taxes. If they're Jews, tell them how good the school
system is."

Telushkin shares a plethora of jokes illustrating Talmudic
logic, the Jewish love of food, and Jewish quick-wittedness, and
along with them stories that poke fun at the stereotypical rich
Jew: "In the 1950s, when General Motors announced, coinciden-
tally on the eve of Yom Kippur, that it was recalling 72,000
Cadillacs, comedian Jack Benny commented: 'I've never seen so
many Jews walking to the synagogue in my life.'"

Ostentatious social affairs also come in for ridicule as Henny
Youngman commented: "A few years ago...at a bar mitzvah on
Long island...on the table was a life-sized sculpture of the bar
mitzvah boy rendered in ice....I heard the women behind me
commenting on the sculpture: 'It's beautiful,' said the first
woman. 'It's a perfect likeness,' agreed the second woman. 'Who
did it? Epstein?' 'Don't be silly. Epstein only works in chopped
liver.'"

The fact that Jews love to celebrate happy occasions is never
mocked. Indeed, life is too short to refrain from relishing joyous
moments. It is in the excess that is the stuff of Jewish humor.

The humor of self-deprecation, quite rare in modern times,
filled Judaism in countries where powerlessness left Jews helpless
to defend themselves. Their very survival often depended on
obsequiousness: "Two Jews are dragged by anti-Semites before a
firing squad. The first one cries out: 'Stop! Stop! You're murdering an innocent man.' 'Sh...Sh...,' says the second. 'Don't make
trouble.'"

This genre of humor was quite common until 1967, when Israel's victory in the Six-Day War revolutionized the Jewish self-image. No longer were we powerless. Israel was there.

Contemporary comedians have taken self-deprecation and transformed it from self-mocking to absurd hilarity. Woody Allen is a classic example: "I'm not the heroic type, really. I was beaten up by the Quakers."

Or Rodney Dangerfield: "I got lost. A cop helped me look for my parents. I said: 'Do you think we'll find them?' He said, 'I don't know, kid. There's so many places they could hide.'"

Jewish Humor is not merely a collection of wonderful jokes, though it certainly does contain them. Rather, Rabbi Telushkin utilizes Jewish humor as a means of teaching the Jewish gestalt of life.

99 The Drama
of Albert Einstein

Antonina Vallentin

Antonina Vallentin's *The Drama of Albert Einstein* is a warm, often tender biography. Vallentin, who knew Einstein for many years, writes of Einstein the man, as well as Einstein the scientist.

Einstein was born on March 14, 1879, in Ulm, Germany. He was somewhat of a backward boy and learned to speak at a much later age than other children did. His parents sent him to a Catholic primary school, where he was the only Jewish pupil. Due to his father's business reversals, the family moved to Munich in 1889, and then, in 1894, to Milan. The teenaged Einstein went away to school in Zurich, where he failed mathematics and was turned down for an assistantship at the university.

Einstein could not hold a job. His interviews were disastrous, and he was even fired from a part-time job tutoring children. Finally, in 1902, after becoming a Swiss citizen, he was engaged as a clerk by the government patent office in Berne. He married a Serbian woman, a teacher of physics, and the couple had two sons. Thereafter, Einstein's career took an upward turn. In 1905, he wrote five articles developing the theory of relativity and a theoretical formula for atomic energy. Four years later, at the age of thirty, he was appointed to a chair at the University of Zurich, and one year later as a professor at the German University in Prague. In 1914, he accepted an appointment as a professor at the Kaiser Wilhelm Institute in Berlin.

After divorcing his first wife, Einstein married a cousin who lived in Berlin. She was no scientist, but tolerated his eccentricities, among them his refusal to wear socks, anywhere, any time. They were already married when, in 1914, World War I was declared.

Einstein, a pacifist, condemned German involvement in the war, but was tolerated by his fellow Germans because they considered him an eccentric. By 1919, however, he had become world famous. With no laboratory, with only a pencil and paper, he calculated formulas that keen scientific instruments only later confirmed. But Einstein, who could have become a wealthy man, declined to do so, for he was absorbed in his work and the opportunities it gave him to serve humanity: "Only a life lived for others is worthwhile.... Never forget that among your diagrams and equations." He was awarded the Nobel Prize in physics in 1922.

Soon after World War I, Einstein became a champion of Zionism. Sensing the latent anti-Semitism in Germany, abhorring the assimilationist snobbery of German Jewry, and drawn to the religious fervor of their Zionist Eastern European counterparts, Einstein accompanied Chaim Weizmann to America in 1921 to speak of the Zionist dream. During this visit, Einstein received an honorary doctorate from Princeton University.

But dark clouds were already on the horizon in Germany. A distinguished German Jew, Walter Rathenau, was assassinated. When it was discovered that Einstein was also on the assassins' hit list, his wife, Elsa, spirited her husband away to Holland. When Hitler rose to power, he and Elsa went to Belgium, where he openly criticized the Nazis and was verbally attacked by German Jews, who accused him of feeding anti-Semitism. Appalled at his fellow Jews' lack of awareness of their danger, the Einsteins renounced their German citizenship and moved to the United States in 1933, where Albert became a professor at Princeton University.

As World War II began, Einstein's theory of relativity, $E = mc^2$, first jotted down in 1903, made possible the creation of the atomic bomb. He reported his conclusions to President Roosevelt in 1939, findings that helped to produce a weapon that would transform the world.

When the bomb was ready, several years later, Einstein pleaded with Pres. Harry Truman to drop it in a neutral area rather than on Hiroshima, certain that the Japanese would capitulate in the face of such an awesome display of power. The military leadership prevailed in their urging that the bomb be dropped on a populated area, however, and sixty thousand people died.

Albert Einstein was a remarkable man, who never lost his sense of compassion for others. He was concerned about the use of his discoveries, and treated them as a sacred trust. He believed in religion as well as science. And finally, he remained a proud Jew. He once said: "I am sorry that I was born a Jew, for that prevented me from choosing to be one."

Antonina Vallentin has written a fascinating biography about one of the great figures of the twentieth century.

100 This Is My God

Herman Wouk

Herman Wouk, author of the bestseller *The Caine Mutiny,* then wrote *This Is My God,* in which he describes the Jewish religion with deep scholarship and tender affection. In the prologue he explains how he came to write the book. An irreligious friend approached him and asked him to recommend some Chanukah reading material for his son—"not for religion but purely for culture." As a result of that innocent request, this book came into being.

The author recalls that twenty years earlier, when he was twenty-four, he had already achieved financial success as a staff writer for Fred Allen. He had a penthouse in New York, frequent trips to Hollywood, the companionship of beautiful women, everything that many people dream about. Then he realized that pleasure and money and hits and bestsellers were not the foundation upon which to build a worthwhile life. He decided that he was going to become an Orthodox Jew.

His childhood environment had prepared him for this kind of life. When he was thirteen years of age, his grandfather came to America from Minsk. His grandfather was a learned rabbi, and for twenty-three years made his home with Herman Wouk's parents. Throughout the book, the author emphasizes the role that his grandfather played in his life. Virtually every day the learned rabbi would sit down with the young boy and teach him, so that before long the youngster became adept in the intricacies of the Talmud. The book is steeped in Jewish knowledge, filled with a passion for Jewish ideals.

This is his description of the Sabbath: "My wife and my boys, whose existence I had almost forgotten...are waiting for me, gay, dressed in holiday clothes, and marvelously attractive. We have sat down to a splendid dinner, at a table graced with flowers and the old Sabbath symbols: the burning candles, the twisted loaves, stuffed fish, and my grandfather's silver goblet brimming with wine. I have blessed my boys with the ancient blessings; we have sung the pleasantly syncopated Sabbath table hymns. My wife and I have caught up with our week's conversation. The boys, knowing that the Sabbath is the occasion for asking questions, have asked them. The Bible, the Encyclopedia, the Atlas, have piled up on the table. We talk of Judaism, and there are the usual impossible boy's queries about God, which my wife and I field clumsily but as well as we can.

"Saturday has passed in much the same manner. The boys are at home in the synagogue, and they like it. They like even more the assured presence of their parents. In the weekday press of schooling, household chores and work—and especially in a play-producing time [when Wouk was busy in rehearsals]—it often happens that they see little of us. On the Sabbath we are always there, and they know it. They know too that I am not working, and that my wife is at her ease. It is their day.

"It is my day, too. The telephone is silent. I can think, read, study, walk, or do nothing. It is an oasis of quiet. When night falls, I go back to the wonderful nerve-racking Broadway game.... My producer one Saturday night said to me: 'I don't envy you your religion, but I envy you your Sabbath.'"

Wouk brilliantly describes the holidays, the dietary laws, bar mitzvah, and marriage. He compares his reaction to his first Israel visit to someone who falls in love for the first time, or a young woman who has her first child. From the perspective of an American Jew prior to the rise of P.L.O., terrorism, and genuine hardball Israeli politics, he speaks of the disagreements in the Israeli government and says that most people in Israel do not take them seriously because after all, it is only Uncle David or Cousin Moshe who wants to make a speech.

Wouk emphasizes that the uniqueness of the Jewish people lies in the Torah: "But for the Torah we are the most insignificant of the nations. What else can we show against the wisdom and the genius God has given to the world? Did we produce Socrates or Aristotle, Shakespeare or Cervantes, Newton or Galileo, Bach or Beethoven, Michelangelo or Rembrandt, Dickens or Tolstoy, Gandhi or Lincoln?...

"Our place in the world, I believe, depends on what we

contribute to mankind. We have contributed the Torah, the Mosaic vision of right conduct and of first and last things. It is our life, and the length of our days. As we keep that flame burning, it seems to me we earn our right to survive as a people before God and men."

There is much in the book with which the biblical Jewish reader may disagree. There are problems in modern Orthodoxy which he blithely skips over, such as the *agunah*. In Orthodox life, if a woman's husband disappears, and is presumed dead, that is not enough for her to remarry in Jewish law. Two witnesses must testify that he died. If no such witnesses come forward, this woman becomes chained, and can never remarry.

The beauty of the book lies in the gentle manner in which Wouk describes his own religious convictions without denouncing those who differ with him.

This Is My God is like a visit with grandfather. It is reminiscent of the biblical account of the children of Israel wandering in the desert. And finally God says to them, "Return unto Me," and there echoes the answer: "This is my God, and I will exalt Him."

Titles, Authors, and Publishers of the 100 Essential Books for Jewish Readers

All-of-a-Kind Family, Sidney Taylor; Dell Books

Antisemitism in America Today: Outspoken Experts Explode the Myths, Jerome H. Chanes, ed.; Birch Lane Press

The Apostle, Sholem Asch; Carroll & Graf

Basic Judaism, Milton Steinberg; Harcourt Brace

The Best of Sholom Aleichem, Irving Howe and Ruth R. Wisse, eds.; Walker & Co.

A Bintel Brief, Isaac Metzker, ed., Diana Shalet Levy, trans.; Schocken Books

The Book of Legends, William G. Braude, trans.; Schocken Books

The Book of Miracles, Lawrence J. Kushner; UAHC Press

The Brothers Ashkenazi, I. J. Singer; Viking Press

Bubby, Me, and Memories, Barbara Pomerantz; UAHC Press

Call It Sleep, Henry Roth; Farrar, Straus & Giroux

A Candle for Grandpa, David Techner and Judith Hirt-Mannheimer; UAHC Press

The Chosen, Chaim Potok; Fawcett Book Group

Complete Dictionary of English and Hebrew First Names, Alfred J. Kolatch; Jonathan David

Contemporary American Reform Responsa, Walter Jacob; CCAR

The Crucifixion of the Jews, Franklin Littel; Mercer University Press

Diary of a Young Girl, Anne Frank; Doubleday

Does God Have a Big Toe? Marc Gellman; HarperCollins

The Drama of Albert Einstein, Antonia Vallentin; Doubleday

Exodus, Leon Uris; Bantam Books

The First Jewish Catalog, Richard Siegel, Michael Strassfeld, and Sharon Strassfeld; Jewish Publication Society

The Fixer, Bernard Malamud; Pocket Books

Forty Things You Can Do to Save the Jewish People, Joel Lurie Grishaver; Alef Design Group

The Gates of the Forest, Elie Wiesel; Schocken Books

Getting Even/Side Effects/Without Feathers, Woody Allen; Ballantine

God in Search of Man, Abraham Joshua Heschel; Farrar, Straus & Giroux

Good People, Danny Siegel; Townhouse Press

The Grandees, Stephen Birmingham; Syracuse University Press

Great Jews in Music, Darryl Lyman; Jonathan David

Great Jews in Sports, Robert Slater; Jonathan David

Guess Who's Jewish in American History, Bernard Postal and Lionel Koppman; Fleet Press

The Hebrew Bible; Artscroll

Heroes and Hustlers, Hard Hats and Holy Men, Ze'ev Chafets; William Morrow

Hitler's Willing Executioners, Daniel Jonah Goldhagen; Alfred A. Knopf

Holy Days, Lis Harris; Simon & Schuster

Honey From the Rock, Lawrence J. Kushner; Jewish Lights

I and Thou, Martin Buber; Peter Smith

The Invisible Thread: A Portrait of Jewish-American Women Interviews, Diana Bletter; Jewish Publication Society

Ishmael, Daniel Quinn; Bantam Books

J.B., Archibald MacLeish; Houghton Mifflin

The Janowska Road, Leon Wells; United States Holocaust Memorial Museum

Jephte's Daughter, Naomi Ragen; Warner Books

Jewish Cooking in America, Joan Nathan; Alfred A. Knopf

The Jewish Home: A Guide for Living, Daniel B. Syme; UAHC Press

Jewish Humor, Joseph Telushkin; William Morrow

Jewish Music, Abraham Idelsohn; Temecula Reprint Services

The Jewish Way in Death and Mourning, Maurice Lamm; Jonathan David

The Jewish You Wouldn't Believe It Book, M. Hirsch Goldberg; Shapolsky

Jews, God, and History, Max I. Dimont; Dutton

The Joys of Yiddish, Leo Rosten; Pocket Books

The Last of the Just, André Schwarz-Bart; Simon & Schuster

Man's Search for Meaning, Victor E. Frankl; Pocket Books

Maus I, Art Spiegelman; Pantheon Books

Maus II, Art Spiegelman; Pantheon Books

Max and Helen, Simon Wiesenthal; Granada

The Merchant of Venice, William Shakespeare; Dutton

My Father, His Daughter, Yael Dayan; Farrar, Straus & Giroux

My Generations, Arthur Kurzweil; Behrman House

My Name Is Asher Lev, Chaim Potok; Alfred A. Knopf

The New Jewish Wedding, Anita Diamant; Simon & Schuster

New Reform Responsa, Solomon B. Freehof; HUC Press

Night, Elie Wiesel; Avon Books

9¹/₂ Mystics, Herbert Wiener; Collier Books

The Nine Questions People Ask About Judaism, Dennis Prager and Joseph Telushkin; Simon & Schuster

Number Our Days, Barbara Meyerhoff; Simon & Schuster

On Being a Jewish Feminist, Susannah Heschel, ed.; Schocken Books

On Women and Judaism, Blu Greenberg; Jewish Publication Society

Only in America, Harry Golden; Greenwood Press

An Orphan in History, Paul Cowan; William Morrow

Our Crowd, Steven Birmingham; Syracuse University Press

Out of the Shadows: A Photographic Portrait of Jewish Life in Central Europe Since the Holocaust, Edward Serotta; Birch Lane Press

Peace of Mind, Joshua Loth Liebman; Citadel Press

The Pledge, Leonard Slater; Amitter Meyer

Portnoy's Complaint, Philip Roth; Random House

Putting God on the Guest List: How to Reclaim the Spiritual Meaning of Your Child's Bar or Bat Mitzvah, Jeffrey K. Salkin; Jewish Lights

Response to Modernity, Michael M. Meyer; Wayne State University Press

Schindler's List, Thomas Keneally; Simon & Schuster

The Second Jewish Catalog, Richard Siegel, Michael Strassfeld, and Sharon Strassfeld; Jewish Publication Society

The Shawl, Cynthia Ozick; Random House

Ship of Fools, Katherine Anne Porter; Little, Brown and Company

Sophie's Choice, William Styron; Random House

The Source, James Michener; Random House

The Sunflower, Simon Wiesenthal; Schocken Books

Talking About Death, Earl A. Grollman; Beacon Press

The Teachings of Contempt: Christian Roots of Anti-Semitism, Jules Isaac; Anti-Defamation League of B'nai B'rith

The Third Jewish Catalog, Richard Siegel, Michael Strassfeld, and Sharon Strassfeld; Jewish Publication Society

This Is My God, Herman Wouk; Walker & Co.

To Life! Harold S. Kushner; Warner Books

To Touch a Dream, Aviva Hellman; Windsor New York

Voices of Wisdom, Francine Klagsbrun; Jonathan David

Voices Within the Ark: The Modern Jewish Poets, Howard Schwartz and Anthony Rudolph, eds.; Avon Books

The Wall, John Hersey; Random House

The War Goes On, Sholem Asch; Putnam

What Happens After I Die? Rifat Sonsino and Daniel B. Syme; UAHC Press

What They Say Behind Our Backs, William B. Helmreich; Transaction Books

When Bad Things Happen to Good People, Harold S. Kushner; Avon Books

When Living Hurts, Sol Gordon; UAHC Press

While Six Million Died, Arthur Morse; Overlook Press

World of Our Fathers, Irving Howe; Harcourt Brace

Index